JUDGE FOR YOURSELF

JOHN PATRICK JUDGE

EDITOR'S NOTE

I am very happy to have been involved in getting this material out in print again where it belongs. It's also gratifying to know that the proceeds from the sales of the book will help the Hidden History Center, which was a great dream of his. Thank you for purchasing this book and if you want to help the HHC further, please check out the website. Thanks.

This book is dedicated to Marilyn Tenenoff, who has worked tirelessly to preserve the legacy of John Judge.

-Joseph E. Green

FOREWORD

It has been many months since John Judge passed away and, as expected the parapolitical research community – the "conspiracy theorists" – have not been the same. One pillar of that group, the JFK researchers, only recently had observed its 50th anniversary. A new evolution was upon it even before the passing of its most articulate spokesman.

Judge helped lead that community to many victories, including the 1976 House investigation. That made the official government conclusion one of conspiracy in the JFK case. Judge's work went beyond that, of course, and wrought many revelations over a lifetime of research and activism, demonstrating more the ubiquity of conspiratorial phenomena. The group he founded, the Coalition on Political Assassinations, became the national nexus of study about JFK, RFK, Martin Luther King, Malcolm X, as well as JJ's many other research tributaries, including Jonestown, the secret Nazi space program and 9/11. In his lifetime, JJ illuminated the process and the people involved in these high crimes and became the model of the activist/researcher.

I met John Judge somewhere in the mid-1980s at a UFO conference in Los Angeles. He was selling an early, *samizdat* version of the present volume, *Judge For Yourself,* and was loosely associated with Prevailing Winds, a catalog/magazine that specialized in alternative press that often dipped from New Age crystal philosophizing to hardcore parapolitics. It was an age of zine. My own, *Steamshovel Press*, was fledgling at the time; Jim Keith's *Dharma Combat* was well-known and we both reprinted Judge material wherever we could fit it in. JJ's writing then also often appeared in *Critique*, the most well-known conspiracy zine, actually a square-bounded, respectable looking journal at the time.

Judge famously had a falling out with another faction of the Brussels

Sprouts, students of the great parapolitics teacher Mae Brussell. It was a great source of humor in the alternative press that such infighting had beset the folks who ostensibly found conspiratorial infighting everywhere. Two camps emerged from that. One became the angry white guy camp, best typified currently by broadcasters like Alex Jones and his many imitators in the mainstream (like Bill O'Reilly). Judge's camp became COPA, a true coalition of the diversified effort to not only study and learn from the crimes and corruption of conspiracy, but to organize against it, with some intelligence and humor and not just dour frustration.

"Judge For Yourself"—that's a step above Tim Leary's admonition to think for yourself. Judge compiled data and ferreted out information that made possible an intelligent judgment about the oft covered-up facts of history. Another scholar, Acharya S, who did much the same for religious culture as Judge did for parapolitics, passed away shortly after him. They didn't know each other but they both knew Keith, who died in 1999. Their passing may represent the end of an era; but surely, they rest confidently in the light of the new era into which they brought a grateful audience.

      -Kenn Thomas
      June 23, 2016

TABLE OF CONTENTS

INTRODUCTION

John Judge, a Remembrance
by David Ratcliffe
Remarks delivered at the Celebration of the
Life of John Patrick Judge
National Press Club, Washington DC
31 May 2014

It is good to be here. I am grateful for the honor of sharing this remembrance with all of you and to Marilyn for putting all this together. I teach piano in Boston.

I am going to speak about a significant period in John's life[1] that involved his efforts to carry on the work of his dear friend Mae Brussell. For more than 25 years Mae Brussell was America's foremost researcher into the hidden history of war, political assassinations, covert operations and espionage, terrorism and mind control, secret societies, banking and organized crime, and the origins and rise of international fascism. She held the George Seldes Award for 1987 from the Society of Journalists, and was listed in The International Who's Who of Intellectuals in 1983.

Mae authored many articles including "Why Was Martha Mitchell Kidnapped?" and "Why Is the Senate Watergate Committee Functioning As Part of the Cover Up?," "Why Was Patty Hearst Kidnapped?" (about the SLA and the CIA) in The Realist, and "The Nazi Connection to the John F. Kennedy Assassination" in Rebel. Mae's weekly radio show, World Watchers International ran for 851 weeks on California stations KLRB-FM, Carmel, and KAZU-FM, Pacific Grove for a total of 17 years of newscasting.

Mae lectured at various universities on the subject of political assassinations, their inter-locking links, the causes, and the people behind the murders. She was among the first researchers to connect the murders of John and Robert Kennedy, Martin Luther King,

Malcolm X and others, relying on her exhaustive cross-reference index of the Warren Commission evidence, and a steady diet of 15 daily newspapers, 150 monthly periodicals, and some 1,000 books a year.

I met John in 1987 through Tom Davis. I was living in Santa Cruz and for some years had been listening to World Watchers. Tom was another first-generation assassination researcher and a friend of Mae's who ran Tom Davis Books (PDF),[2] and provided Mae with all her book purchases. After first ordering books from Tom through the mail, in time I was able to visit him at his office-warehouse in Capitola.

Tom told me about the work John had been doing and gave me printed copy of some of his writings and his address. I corresponded with John and saw him in Santa Cruz when he was in the area speaking.

In June 1988 Mae Brussell was diagnosed with cancer which became terminal. John wrote a proposal[3] dated September 3 and submitted an outline for a Mae Brussell Library and Research Center that included four sections: "Purpose", "Functions and Services", "Income Generation", and "Basic Structure, Requirements".

Mae accepted John's proposal and asked him to "make it so." John moved to Santa Cruz from D.C. with the help of Bill Kelly and threw himself into this endeavor with all his passion, drive, and saavy. Although the challenges were immense, John intended to leverage what Mae had studied and amassed over 25 years and create a self-supporting research center. It is noteworthy that in John's proposal, three of the four similar libraries in other topic areas he cited still exist: Data Center in Oakland, Edgar Cayce Association for Research and Enlightenment in Newport News, and Highlander Center in Tennessee.

Initially John set up the Center under the umbrella of Downwinders, Preston Truman's established non-profit. There were many processes John was endeavoring to establish in parallel as well as lay the ground work for. One was a flyer (PDF)[4] mailed out to many introducing the center and its goals. Another was creating and publishing a Newsletter to further help raise income. An outline[5] for the first newsletter lists a super-set of content from what was later published.

In a February 1992 letter (PDF)[6] to both the MBRC and his own CONSPIRACY! mailing lists, John wrote that "Mae Brussell designated me to set up the research center in her name in Santa Cruz ... because we had worked together as researchers for close to 16 years, and she trusted my judgment and knowledge.... Unfortunately, Mae made no provisions in her will, or any financial planning for this continued work."

With publication of the first 20-page Newsletter in late summer, 1989 (PDF),[7] John believed that the organization had turned the corner financially. Tragically, it was at this point that the rug began to be pulled out from under him by individuals who did not want him to run the center. One of Mae's daughters felt the collection should have been put in her care and moved to force John from the organization. A fellow researcher gave in to personal jealousy and professional envy at John's being chosen by Mae to be the director of promoting and furthering her life's work, and began making baseless public attacks on John's integrity, agent-baiting, and claims that he had stolen money, as well as ridiculous charges including supposed links to the Charles Manson family, the Aryan Brotherhood, and Western Goals, all of them fascist intelligence operations that John helped Mae expose.

Since the fall of 1988 I had volunteered in various capacities to help John get the center established. The work was demanding and as time passed I was more and more aware of how John was not receiving essential support and help from a number of Mae's friends and followers who did not agree with Mae's decision to entrust her work to John.

In a February 1990 letter of resignation, I wrote,

> John alone took on the fundamental financial responsibility of launching this project, and without his own initial seed-money/non-interest loans, it would not have come this far. Mae trusted John's judgment enough to leave her work in his care with the goal of establishing a research organization and

directing its course. John's experience and background in studying and chronicling the story of how fascism came to America made him a viable and credible choice for Mae to entrust her life's work to. However lack of support for John, including theft of center materials which were never returned as they were promised to be, unjustified rejection of Wendy Govier who offered a tremendous array of news media resources and MBRC access to such media as well as a prior history of substantial support for the center's goals, and a desire by board members to have control of the center's charter and direction without an accompanying acceptance of the responsibilities and duties inherent with such authority, all demonstrate a violation of Mae's trust in John to continue and further her own work.

John eventually resigned, as he wrote in 1992, "unable in good conscience to bring anyone into such an organization, or continue working with any sense of integrity." The way this period in John's life came to a close was one of the most painful and heartbreaking phases of his journey here. He had the highest hopes for what he envisioned was possible to increase awareness of what Mae had put together for an ever widening audience of people in America and the world.

Earlier this week my dear friend Marty Schotz wrote Marilyn the following:

> Though I am unable to attend the event commemorating John's life, I wanted to share a quote from a recent issue of The Monthly Review, which I think is very relevant to John. John's hope for a museum of hidden history, was really a hope for a museum of true history. In this connection, consider the following from W.E.B. DuBois:

> I remember once offering to an editor an article which began with a reference to the experience of the last century. "Oh," he said, "leave out the history and come to the present." I felt like going to him over a

thousand miles and taking him by the lapels and say, "Dear, dear jackass! Don't you understand that the past is the present; that without what was, nothing is? That, of the infinite dead, the living are but unimportant bits?" W.E.B. DuBois, The World and Africa, (1947) p.80.

In this present moment it is vital to appreciate how similar John's goal of creating the Museum of Hidden History is to what he sought to manifest in the late eighties. Each of these projects expresses a recurring desire and purpose of his life: the Museum of Hidden and True History is now ever more vital to pursue manifesting. Marilyn urges all of you who understand this to explore with her the multitude of ways you can contribute to making it so.

Since 1987 I have treasured John's friendship through the years. Among other gifts, it was John who introduced me to Fletcher Prouty at the end of 1988 while work at the MBRC was ramping up. In the end, this introduction resulted in my self-publishing Understanding Special Operations,[8] the interview I conducted with Fletcher in May 1989.

Twenty-five years later, in a May 2013 e-mail[9] to a few friends including John, I posed the question "who are the David Phillipses, the Richard Helmses, the James Angletons, Ted Shackleys, David Sanchez Moraleses, and William Harveys of today, who execute the imperatives of this era's Terror Warriors? It seems that people who physically or psychologically murder other people are, in some elemental respects, walking dead themselves."

John replied to me alone with the following:

> In an old and vivid dream I want to write into a story, I was with a group of people trying to confront and catch a killer who had traveled over time, a sort of Jekyll/Hyde/Jack the Ripper character. In the dream we were in the Victorian era London streets of fogs, carriages and gas lamps in a brick factory district, hiding in an alcove to see him go by in his hat and cape.

Then we began to pursue him until he became aware of us and some lit torches and the chase was on. It led down an alley, brick wall building backs on one side, backyard fences and gates on the other. He stopped just as we were gaining on him and tried to insert a key in one of the wooden gates, but fumbled and cursed as he dropped the key, realizing we were then too close to escape. He then turned towards us, his face a grinning skull of evil but also wide eyed with fear of what our retribution would be.

The others had only torchlight and no weapons. I stepped forward and looked directly into his face and eyes, and removed something from a pouch on my belt. I unfolded it and held it up to his eyes. It was the skin of his human face and I offered it back to him. This I think is symbolically how we nonviolently love those who do us evil, by not returning the violence and evil we give them back their humanity, if they are willing to take it. JJ

John's devotion to honoring and serving Life's needs was an extraordinary boon to our single, fragile, and miraculously gifted human family. His understanding, sensitivity, brilliance, vulnerability, ironic and farcical sense of humor was a tonic to all who knew him. The light from the fire in his heart continues to light Life's love and all who serve it – and the glow from that fire can truly light the world.

References

1. "John Judge, 66; alternate historian, renowned researcher, educator, investigator, advocate for real democracy," by Marilyn Tenenoff, April 20, 2014

2. PDF copy of: Political Conspiracy Books Catalog from Tom Davis Books, circa 1989

3. Proposal for Mae Brussell Library and Research Center, by John Judge, September 3, 1988

ABOUT THE AUTHOR

When John Patrick Judge died on Tax Day 2014, the Washington Post gave him an obituary taking up three-quarters of the page. It was filled with the nicest words the Post had ever written about him.

That the CIA paper of record would belatedly recognize his importance to the community – which is to say, in his case, the world – is par for the course. John grew up in the shadow of the Pentagon, which he discusses in some of the interviews included in this book. He grew up without naïveté about how the world actually works, and when President Kennedy was murdered by domestic forces on November 22, 1963, he went to work. A few years later, he was in the library, studying the Warren Commission volumes to try and uncover the facts that Allen Dulles and friends had buried in irrelevant facts and deliberate diversions.

In 1972, John began working with Mae Brussell on her radio program World Watchers International. In the course of researching he made other friends: Sherman Skolnick, Fletcher Prouty, R. B. Cutler, and Penn Jones, among others. Following Oliver Stone's film *JFK*, in the explosion of interest in the assassination, he co-founded the Coalition on Political Assassinations (COPA). The aim of COPA was to present the best material by the most important researchers in the field of study Professor Peter Dale Scott calls Deep Politics. Deep Politics doesn't stop at the Kennedy assassination, but treats all the activities of the Deep State as a proper field of study – assassinations foreign and domestic, international finance, drug policies, the surveillance state, the search for alternative historical points of view, and the means and motives of war. The fact that recent events have suddenly thrust the Deep State into popular parlance in newspaper around the U.S. would have filled him with a mix of good humor and irritation.

John used to tell a story about COPA having an event at the same venue where Hillary Clinton was giving a speech. Her protection raised eyebrows at the name of his organization. "We don't do assassinations," he told them dryly. "We study 'em."

He was also fond of repeating an anecdote in which he was with Mae Brussell when a fan began effusively praising Mae: "You're wonderful, Mae, you do so many things…" And she thanked her fan politely and said. "Yes. And what do *you* do?" The intent was not to insult but to inspire. *You can do this too. We all can.*

And indeed, we can.

John has passed from this plane but is forever remembered. Inside this book are some of his words. Hopefully they'll inspire you like they did all of us when he was alive. Because you can do this, too.

"UNIDENTIFIED FASCIST OBSERVATORIES" (1989)

John Judge interviewed on KPFK radio, Los Angeles, August 12 1989

Roy: *It's a nice surprise to be able to get in contact with you and get some things down on tape. We had a program a couple weeks ago about unidentified flying objects, which has had a huge response of interest, so we're collecting information about them. This was an excerpt from the MUFON conference that took place in Las Vegas and we heard from John Lear, M.W. "Bill" Cooper, and Bill English. I think Don Ecker was on. We heard an amazing story about aliens, many different types of aliens, maybe up to a hundred dead and some alive, being held by the U.S. government, U.S.-Soviet space stations on the Moon and Mars, a deal between the government and aliens to allow them to take and mutilate bodies in exchange for high technology information, even (I don't remember the exact connections here, there's so much material), but also dipping into the Kennedy assassination and the reasons, the motivation behind the drug-running by the U.S. government in Southeast Asia and Central*

America. So that's quite a mouthful. The interest is high. Do you know anything about UFOs and this kind of stuff?

John: I started studying UFO phenomenon when I was about twelve or thirteen. My parents were civilian employees of the Pentagon and I was often brought into the Pentagon during the workday and left off in the library. In the Pentagon library I had access to such things as Project Bluebook and Grudge and Twinkle, the formal reports that were given from these U.S. Air Force studies in the 1950's of UFO phenomena, as well as international publications like UFO World Report which gave every sighting around the world. In those years I was also getting many of the independent small magazines by investigators that were looking into the phenomena. My conclusion in that period, and it's been nothing but bolstered since, by anything that I've seen, is that these sightings, most of which took place right around U.S. military bases, some of which went into and out of water, were actually sightings of an advanced but hidden technology controlled by the United States government and developed under the auspices of the advanced aerospace and munitions rocket work done in Nazi Germany at the end of the war as part of Hitler's push to develop ultimate weapons.

The existence of these weapons, I found later, was known to the U.S. occupying forces and I believe that part of the motivation in bringing the top Nazi scientists here under Project Paperclip was to determine what they knew about these advanced technologies (because, for instance, in the early 40's the Nazis had already developed jet engines). I have reports in several publications from American GI's who went into these caves outside of Berlin and in some other areas of Germany which were being used to conceal aerospace and munitions work and in these caves were functional saucers or "flying discs," both manned and unmanned, that could travel at tremendous speeds.

I have articles that I picked up in the 1970's, one by a member of the Royal Astronomical Society in England, where he admits that upwards of 10,000 remotely piloted vehicles (RPV's) were under the control of British intelligence and known also the U.S. Forces at the time being used basically as reconnaissance or low-level spy craft. He admits that these were hidden technology that could go at tremendous speeds, could make the equivalent of right-angle turns in certain circumstances, and had a technology beyond what was generally admitted at the time.

I think we know what they were; I think we were testing them in 1947 and 1948 in the early years over civilian populations. I think they served as low-level cloud cover and also served additional purposes like to go below cloud cover for satellite spying and did other kinds of reconnaissance. They were either remotely piloted or could be manned and looked like the discs that people describe. But the official position of the government was either what Jacques Vallee in his book *Messengers of Deception* says is the Republican and Democratic view on UFOs: either they're swamp gas and you didn't see it at all, or you did see it and it's extra-terrestrial. The truth of the matter is that they are real but they're terrestrial craft. They're spy craft and they're controlled by the U.S. government.

I think it's telling that many of the people who came here in the 1950's to take over these fields and started some of the national agencies that grew into MUFON and the group that you heard from, were themselves military intelligence agents. Donald Kehoe from Air Force Intelligence, Allen Heinek, who worked with the secretive Blue Book projects and these others who were supposedly trying to determine what the UFOs were but, in fact, were really just trying to find out what people were seeing and what effect they were having and to cover up what really was going on. These people became the experts and the independent investigators and the small magazines folded in '58 and '59 to be replaced with either government denial, these phony scientific committees, or people like George Adamski, who I heard speak when I was 13 years old and knew that he was lying at that time. He claimed he'd been to Mars and the Moon and had traveled in the ships of the aliens. It came out years later that Adamski was being financed in these lectures worldwide by the Central Intelligence Agency. But I knew that he protested too much about government cover-up when I heard him when I was 13. I could tell he wasn't straightforward and that he was making up stories.

I believe this is yet another flap and it doesn't surprise me that people like John Lear admit to CIA backgrounds. Others in this MUFON group, for example this guy [William] Cooper, are pushing this idea that certain deals were cut with the aliens and, like you say, they were given bodies to mutilate in exchange for high technology. All of this is smoke screen and cover for the reality, which is that the U.S. government has an advanced technology and they get psychological manipulation points by pushing the UFO line, they're able to manipulate people in different ways.

Jacques Vallee, in his work, discovered that the main people in the contactee cults are themselves long-time military intelligence agents. This is true in a number of the cults, including this one, I don't know if you've heard of the one out in Arizona desert that involves one of the NASA astronauts, but the guy who runs that cult is not only military intelligence but he's also a close friend of John Singlaub. They do the preparatory work and then a UFO appears which proves to people that they've been in touch with the aliens. And then, as their psychic spiritual exercise, what the aliens tell them to do is concentrate all their mental and psychic powers with the purpose of killing the Soviet premier and getting rid of Gorbachev. So we're supposed to believe that's the kind of things the aliens want us to do but I think it's much more likely that NASA and Navy Intelligence and John Singlaub, who heads the World Anti-Communist League, would like us to do those kinds of things. They want us to think it's little green men instead of the U.S. Government that's telling us to do it.

I find it interesting that they would mention the stuff about Mars and the Moon. There's a big push on right now from the [Lyndon] Larouche faction to reinstate the Nazi rocket scientists that have been kicked out of the country like Rudolf, to have a Manhattan style project like we did on the nuclear weapons to colonize outer space. George Bush recently came out and was talking about colonies on Mars and the Moon. There's a book that Mae Brussell mentioned in her shows years ago in England, it's not printed in the United States, called *Alternative 3*, which suggested that bases already existed on Mars and the Moon back in the late 70's, that people were being brought up there from the earth with our technology, not with any alien technology, and that this was part of trying to find out if they could colonize worlds in the future and live on other planets within enclosed shells.

It sounds fairly wild but they had quite a bit of evidence. It was this guy Davies who'd done a British documentary on what nuclear war would look like put the book out and he said that scientists involved with it who tried to defect were being killed with what he called "burn jobs" which would be an ability to concentrate microwaves from satellites. I think it's interesting with regard to Star Wars technology we're told the satellite's going to have a beam that can hit an ICBM travelling at 5,000 miles an hour. Well, if it can do that and if it can see a golf ball on the ground, don't you think it can hit you walking five miles an hour along the road or traveling in your car? A number of these people appear to have spontaneously combusted from inside out in the situations that Alternative 3 suggests and he was positing that microwave or other kinds of wave energy could be beamed down enough to kill a person and/or to start fires in large cities, both part of the original planning for SDI.

The Star Wars defense really dates back to 1964 or '65. Time magazine had one of those "where are they now" columns about General Walter Dornberger, who was one of the top Nazi scientists brought here. He helped do the rocket work with Von Braun at Thor at the slave camp there and he was brought to the United States and he was living in Buffalo and he wanted satellites to go around the planet once every 90 minutes carrying nuclear warheads. This was back in 1963-64 he had this kind of plans. We talk now about the shuttle going up and down, well, the Nazi rocket scientists were working on craft that would go out into space and then return back through the atmosphere so that they wouldn't be radar detected and they would carry a bomb payload.

So I don't call them unidentified flying objects, I call them unidentified fascist observatories and I think that what we've got in the air are these technological advancements that the government doesn't want us to know about and when we get close to it we're told that it's little green men from Mars or some other distant galaxy and that they manipulate the consciousness around it and use it as a programming device.

I do believe aliens in the 1940s, thousands of aliens, invaded us: they were German nationals, Russian and Eastern European revanchists, and other Nazis and fascist sympathizers. The "little green men" people see in those saucers are just good old American GI's in their green uniforms.

I talked to somebody in one of the cults and one of the people running that cult; they used the drug ecstasy, bragged to them about having programmed Mark David Chapman and there's a link-in between a number of the key Kennedy assassination figures, I'd be interested to know what they said on the show about the Kennedy assassination because there's a link between some of the Kennedy assassination figures and the early UFO incidents that were reported to the government in 1947.

Kenneth Arnold, who reported the first of what were called "flying saucers" in Spokane, Washington in 1947, was a co-pilot with Jack Parsons. Parsons was a member of Navy Intelligence, he has working in Navy Intelligence with L. Ron Hubbard who later founded Scientology, and the two of them were busy infiltrating the Ordo Templi Orientis, the O.T.O., one of the Satanic cults, for Navy intelligence. It's very much in the interest of intelligence agencies to have a handle into any of the existing cults and to study psychic phenomena because (1) they want to see if any of it is powerful enough to be used as a weapon or some sort of precognition device, they look at it that way, and (2) even if they know it's phony, it's a good programming device and so they will put up phony psychics.

Navy intelligence, for instance, provided the alloy that's hard at room temperature but melts with a little bit of rubbing from the fingers so that when it gets to body temperature it becomes flexible. It's a special metal alloy that Naval intelligence developed. They gave it to Uri Geller and ran Uri Geller around supposedly using Martian energy to bend the spoons. The space brothers would come through him and bend these spoons and forks. Well, the reason they were bending with him just touching them was that, they were a different alloy than stainless steel or the things normal spoons are made of. He used legerdemain and sleight of hand stuff in order to make people believe he was some kind of a psychic.

Geller's dentist was the person who developed the patents on six different of the earliest mind-control devices for the CIA and military intelligence, which were actually radio transmitter implants into the jaw and teeth so that instructions could be heard through the teeth. So, this guy Uri Geller uses him as a dentist, and maybe was programmed by himself, holds patents on six of these early mind-control devices dating back to the time when Nelson Rockefeller, General Edwin Lansdale and the U.S. military was developing the Manchurian candidate capability.

They didn't wait 30 years to get that capability like John Mark's cover-up book (*The Search for the Manchurian Candidate*) suggested. They had programming ability for assassins back in the late 1940s. What we've got today is a situation where they will use these cults as the programming matrix, and create somebody like "Son of Sam" who thinks the devil talks to him through a black dog and goes out and does these mass murders. I have an article about Berkowitz's best friend, which appeared in the Philadelphia Inquirer. This guy was with Berkowitz in his military unit in Korea when he was a supply clerk in the Anny. The guy says that Son of Sam, then David Berkowitz, applied for conscientious objector status. He's quoted in the paper as saying that when he applied for CO the brass "gave him acid."

Well, the brass doesn't supply acid to the troops, but they may have given him some acid drug or derivative that was part of the study called MKULTRA, the study by military intelligence and CIA to control the mind with drugs, which made him acceptable for programming. Mae Brussell used to call him "Son of Uncle Sam." Berkowitz can think the devil told him to do it or little green men tell the current assassins to do it, but the reality is that it's only the U.S. government and military intelligence forces issuing the orders. People need to look beyond all this hype to see what is actually going on. It isn't anything any more alien than the alienation that people should feel from fascism and from people who try to manipulate our consciousness and control it. So that's my hit on the so-called UFO phenomena.

Roy: *Well, if this is the case, that the U.S. government has access to this high technology since the 40's, what are the entire space program and the giant rockets taking off and occasionally exploding in Florida?*

John: I think, as Mae thought, that some of these explosions are for political purposes- they're actually sabotage situations. She certainly thought that about the shuttle Challenger that, along with the other shuttles had been used consistently for military missions. It came out at the time that if the next shuttle had gone up as scheduled and it had been the one to blow up, it would have been carrying a huge payload of radioactive plutonium because many of these outer space vehicles are using nuclear reactors or have nuclear payloads on them. Had that been the one to blow up, it would have spread plutonium across the state of Florida and could have killed millions of people.

Mae felt that the explosion of the Challenger served several purposes, one of which was the death of a lot of the key non-traditional astronauts that had come in the 1970's, the only women, the only Jews, the only blacks, the only Vietnam vets. She called it the "Rainbow Coalition" that died in the shuttle Challenger explosion. Then we come back in with the right stuff with the Aryan boys and the, you know, all male, all white, blond haired and athletic again, just the stuff the NASA Nazis were looking for.

You have to understand that NASA was really developed right from the beginning by Werner Von Braun; the Nazis who worked on the rockets for Hitler were the ones that developed the Saturn V and got us to the Moon. Maybe we think that getting two men to the Moon was worth the death of 6 million Jews, the 13 million altogether that died in the war under the Holocaust, but I hardly think it was worth it. But that's the energy, that's the people who are doing the outer space technology from the beginning and of course it would be in their interest to hide this kind of thing from us and to manipulate it.

Mae felt that the additional bonus on the Challenger was that it got rid of all of the civilian input, the civilian programming. That was the last one where they were going to suggest putting up somebody like this teacher, Christie McAuliffe, who was a peace and labor rights activist and was the one chosen to go up, then blows up in the situation. They're not saying now that they want teachers to go up on the new shuttle. I just saw in the paper yesterday that the public is going to be kept away from the landing of the shuttle when it comes back down.

Roy: '*We're going to be allowed to pay for it though.*

John: Well, yeah, we're allowed to pay for it; we're allowed to pay for all the secret stuff in the whole national security state. They take it out of our pocket but now it's all secret military missions. They're bringing the Star Wars satellites up or whatever they're doing; we 're not allowed to know about it. It has no civilian purpose; it's all military purpose and military run and total security so Mae really felt that was the advantage of some of these explosions.

Of course, things do happen and they make mistakes Even with the best technology things can go wrong. I don't want to suggest that nothing could happen just because it's advanced. But what I'm saying is that it's to their interest, if you think about it, if they discover a technology that's really going to boost them forward, it's better for them to keep that secret and use it as a weapon or do things that they figure that the other side or us (who are really their enemies), don't know about, then bring it in over time in a way that they can market or manipulate it to their best advantage. So I think that what we got from the Nazis was a great deal more than we've admitted.

We know now, for instance that the Japanese war criminals that were testing chemical and biological warfare on American and other prisoners, Chinese prisoners, were (through the intervention of Douglas MacArthur and the intelligence people on his staff), and kept from being charged with any crimes. In exchange they gave us the actual scientific results of their studies so we could use those results in future chemical and biological warfare. People who had done these gruesomely anti-human experiments put us in the position of protecting them so we could get the hidden dirt on how they were best being able to kill people with chemical and biological agents.

All these things interrelate. They interrelate to the secrecy. I was talking to somebody today about how the whole mind-control and MK-ULTRA really started in the 1950's and what it had to do with was the U.S. use of chemical and biological warfare agents in Korea. But rather than admit that we did use them in Korea when our pilots were downed and signed confessions to the Koreans, when they were presented with the direct evidence of unopened and unexploded canisters of the chemical and biological agents, they admitted in signed confessions that they were doing chemical and biological warfare.

Roy: *That was called brainwashing.*

John: That's right. They sent in psychiatrists who said that these people had been brainwashed. But the point of saying that they were brainwashed was to discredit the confessions so that the truth would never come out. There were three American journalists who began to write about the information the Koreans had, proving that we were doing chemical and biological warfare. Eisenhower, on grounds of national security, had the three of them arrested and thrown into jail and the book was suppressed. So it never got out to the American public. What the public heard, instead, was that these psychiatrists went in and they talked to these people, these pilots, and came out and to report that the Koreans had started this brain-washing.

Not only does that cover up the chemical and biological warfare that we were really doing, it then gives us the excuse in return to say that well, if the enemy is doing that, then we have to learn to do it. Then it becomes the rationale for all of our own experiments in mind control and the whole thing is fabricated and the two psychiatrists who were used, one by the Army and one by the Air Force, go one into the top positions in that MK-ULTRA work.

One of them is currently at the UCLA Neuropsychiatric Institute, an infamous psychiatrist by the name of Dr. Jolly West, who was part of the plans here in California to build a Center for the Reduction of Violence that would have used an abandoned Nike missile base and tested on prisoners and other populations. He continues testing with LSD and other derivatives of mind control stuff under government contract out at the Neuropsychiatric Institute to this day. He's involved in a number of manipulations, including being president (I believe) of the Board of the American Family Foundation, which is an attempt by families to stop some of the cult activity. Much of the cult activity is instituted and run in the United States through government means and this guy pretends to be anti-cult! I mean, he's an infiltrator into that group, he's on the board and pretending he's anti-cult when, in fact, he's developing techniques the Moonies and the other cults ultimately use in their operations.

The other scientist for the Army, the psychiatrist who went to prove the brainwashing and wrote a book about it back in the 1950's, is a well-respected, supposedly "liberal" psychiatrist named Robert J. Lifton. He talks about the psychic numbing after Hiroshima and Nagasaki. He's well liked in the anti-nuclear community. He's written a recent book, which is basically a cover-up, called *Nazi Doctors*, where he interviewed a number of the Nazi psychiatrists who were part of the mass killings. The first killings in Nazi Germany, 300,000 psychiatric inmates, 78% of the population of the institutions was wiped out in killing centers by these experts who developed the gas for the chambers and all of the techniques of death that would be used later. This was '37-'38 they started this killing.

Roy: *We just had some Malathion sprayed on the city again last week.*

John: I hear your LAPD choppers going over the house right now. This is more of the escalation of the poisons. But these psychiatrists were then used as the experts at Bergen-Belsen and Auschwitz. And so, he goes in, he gets permission to talk to these people, he says it's a study on stress which I think it was because he's an expert on war stress, and he interviews these guys and he does the book Nazi Doctors, but he doesn't name a single Nazi criminal even though he admits in there that some of them might have been hurt by the situation

He knows them, he interviews them, and then he very cutely says that he's going to follow the Nuremburg principles, that actually had to be set up because of the crimes of these very people, he's going to follow the principle that doctors should maintain confidentiality with patients. Well, he's not a doctor going in, presumably, to give these guys therapy; he says that he's an investigator going in to find out the history of what happened. So which is it? Or is he a therapist and is he going in to study their stress levels in order to write a handbook basically of how to get past the stress of carrying out genocide for the next holocaust? If he's an investigator, then he owes us the names. But he plays cute and he says, "I'm going to be more decent than these Nazis, I'm going to give them the advantage of the Nuremburg principles that had to be set up because of their crimes and I'm going to protect their privacy by not naming them." One of them says to him "if anybody knew about this stuff I'm telling you, l could go to jail," and they could. The laws are still open, the books are still open in Germany on the war crimes and these people can and should be tried from the crimes that they committed.

Instead, Lifton plays this cute little game and comes out with this book, no names mentioned, and then in the book develops this nonsense thesis where he gives each one of these Nazi killers, these psychiatrists, and the vast benefit of the doubt. He says they were really very decent human beings who suddenly got pushed out of shape by the Nazi government and forced to kill. The way they were able to do it, he says, is that they "doubled themselves" they created second "doubled personalities." They had the killer personality and a decent personality and that was the way they operated.

So this is the work of Robert J. Lifton and Jolly West, the two psychiatrists who were quoted, one in the New York Times and the other out here in the Los Angeles papers on November 19 1978, the day after the Jonestown massacre, these are the two that came forward to tell the press and the public that there's "nothing unusual" about a mass suicide and that what happened in Guyana is "typical psychological behavior" for masses of humans.

I suggest you go through history and try to find real documentable examples. Right after that the television played this Masada thing about the supposed self-suicide of the Jews at Masada under Roman attack, but the Roman historian who wrote about the period and what happened there said that only a few committed suicide and the rest were massacred by the Romans.

If you push an old Nazi far enough about the camps, they 'll say that the Jews died of *lebensmude*. They became sick of life and they formed suicide pacts and they killed themselves.

Roy: *We'll let you go in a minute. I just wanted to mention that the story they had on the JFK assassination is that on the original Zapruder film the whole car or most of the car is shown. In the original film as he's going through it step-by-step, I imagine by slides, he says that the driver is one of the assassins and the driver is seen on the film turning around and shooting Kennedy with a revolver and that Jackie is running, when she jumped out of the car, she's running from the driver.*

John: Another guy down here in Los Angeles was pushing this thesis actually. I got wind of it briefly. He claimed to have had footage. I don't know what you're meaning by the original film,

Zapruder was one of a number of people who filmed there. Most of the films were confiscated. Zapruder filmed from one side of the street, Mary Moorman filmed from another. The claim of this person, I don't know what you saw was that they had frames from the Zapruder film showing this guy turning around and shooting Kennedy. He does, in fact, turn around. He lied to the Commission about watching Kennedy. There is a little glint of sun on the car's windshield that somebody might have thought was a shot coming out of his hand

But in doing hard work on Kennedy and on the ballistics and on the direction of the shot, we know that somebody in the driver's seat shooting Kennedy would have driven him back and to his right, which is not the direction that he goes. He's lifted upwards and thrown back and to the left at over 100 mph. All of his brain matter travels out of the left. It hits the motorcycle cop at the left rear of the motorcade hard enough through his jacket that he stops and gets off the motorcycle thinking he's been shot. Brain matter shows up 30 yards to the left rear of the motorcycle, so everything is in the opposite direction of a shot from the driver. The driver would have pushed him back and to the right and the debris and the brain matter would have come off to the right of the motorcade.

I think Jackie was responding in crisis. She was in shock. She said in her testimony, which wasn't revealed for eight years, that she'd climbed out in order to get a piece of the brain matter and skull off the top of the motorcade and she does grab it, tries to put his head back together. She held on to the piece of brain until she was actually in Parkland hospital and one of the aides gets her to release it. I think she was basically in trauma. She might have been frightened, there were shells going everywhere, Connally said, "My God, they're going to kill us all!" when he got hit, and Kellerman, one of the Secret

Service guys up front, described a "flurry of shots" which is exactly what there were.

I had evidence in my work of upwards of six different shots from different directions. But the fatal headshot, by my work, comes from the right front of the motorcade, not actually up on the grassy knoll; there are too many people in the way for a shot from there, but from a sewer from the right front. A storm sewer, I've been in it. It's a clear shot. It's a good military concealed location. I believe it was a .45 pistol slug. There was a .45 slug found on the other side of the street in line with the shot and there's photographs of an FBI agent and Bill Decker from the Sheriff's department, looking at it.

The FBI agent picks it up and pockets it and that bullet disappears from any official evidence or testimony but we do know that they picked a .45 slug up over there. I think that's the one that blew Kennedy's head apart. I think that's why he's lifted up and out of the seat, not just thrown back, but also lifted upwards. I've watched the film hundreds of times. But did their exposition on the Kennedy assassination have some connection with the alien matter?

Roy: *Well, Kennedy was murdered ostensibly because he was going to expose and release all these UFO and alien information, which had been put in secret...*

John: Well, he may have been interested in releasing the alien information I'm talking about, which is the infiltration by Nazis of the CIA. He said that he was going to scatter the CIA to the four winds. Presumably that might have included scattering NASA, at least in terms of who was in charge of it. He favored the space programs while he was in, but if he was concerned about the Gehlen network and the Nazi spies and the CIA, he might also have been planning to spill the beans on some of the other stuff. I don't know. I never found any evidence of extraterrestrial contact. I found loads of evidence of hidden technology, terrestrial spy craft and technology that was developed by the Nazis and covered up by the U.S. for all those years.

For instance, in Torbitt's document *The Nomenclature of an Assassination Cabal*, he mentions one of the five groups responsible for the death of Kennedy; this was the book that Mae Brussell felt was the closest and I feel also was the closest to describing by name and by organization who arranged the operation level of the hit. One of the groups he names was the security at NASA and the people around Werner Von Braun and the Nazis at NASA and Defense Industrial Security Command, which would have included NASA security in those days.

I have no question that some of the top Nazi rocket scientists were intimately involved in the planning and execution of the murder of John F. Kennedy, but I think that was more because he was threatening to blow open the CIA which would, in turn, have blown open NASA – [not] that had anything to do with special deals cut with little green men with wiggly ears.

REAGAN – BITBURG – NAZI SS
(THE GERMANS MADE ME DO IT)

(10/1/1984)

President Reagan's planned visit to the Bitburg Cemetery in Germany, on May 5, surprised and angered many Americans. Most have felt the decision was a combination of ignorance, bad planning, diplomatic necessity and refusal to change on the part of both German chancellor Kohl and President Reagan. However, a full history of U.S./Nazi relations, Ronald Reagan's political career, and current White House appointments suggests it may be more than 'unfortunate coincidences' that have led Reagan to the insupportable position of honoring the Nazi SS so openly.

The U.S. Fascist Connection

1943 Well before World War II drew to a close, U.S. Office of Special Services (OSS) agents **Allen**

Dulles, **William Casey** and **'Wild Bill' Donovan** began planning for post-war cooperation with Nazi military and intelligence networks for future U.S. hegemony. Deals were cut with top Nazi SS agents **Karl Wolff** and **Walter Schellenberg,**

Hitler's spymaster **Reinhardt Gehlen, 'Butcher' Klaus Barbie** and other Nazi war criminals. Code name: Operation Sunrise.

The Nazi defeat at Stalingrad by Soviet forces marked the turning point in a war designed to take control of Russia and to destroy communism. It left 20 million Soviets dead, and caused a total of 80 million deaths worldwide. It was at this point that allied and Axis agents agreed that communism was the 'real enemy.'

1944 U.S. intelligence agents contacted SS Sturmbahnfuehrer **Werner von Braun**, General **Walter Dornberger**, and the Nazi 'Rocket Team' scientists who developed the deadly V-2 rockets used against England, and built by slave labor at Camp Dora, to invite them into the U.S. after the war *Code name*: Operation Overcast.

Hitler's ambassador to the Vatican and personal advisor, SS Baron **Ernst von Weizsacker**, proposed a final Nazi offensive at the Battle of the Bulge, a delaying action that would allow Nazi gold, spies, documents, scientists and SS criminals to escape Germany as pre-arranged with the OSS agents. General **Reinhardt Gehlen** arranged his 'surrender' to American troops at this point.

On December 17, the First Panzer Division, led by **Waffen SS Otto Skorzeny**, Sepp Dietrich and

General **Fritz Gustav Anton Kraemer**, illegally disguised by wearing U.S. uniforms, captured and massacred American GI's at Malmedy.

1944-45 The Second and Tenth Panzer units waged battle at Bitburg, led by General **Pavlo**

Shandruk and **Gerd von Runstead**, Waffen SS commanders of the infamous SS Galician Division (who collected Ukrainian victims for Auschwitz concentration camp).

1945-46 Only a tiny percentage of the 70,000 known Nazi war criminals faced prosecution and trial at Nuremberg and Dachau, only 8 were executed. John J. McCloy of the Allied Command served as 'High Commissioner' of Germany, following the temporary military rule of American

General Lucius Clay. During this period of promised 'Denazification,' McCloy eventually pardoned almost every Nazi war criminal imprisoned; most had served only a few years of their sentences. Many of them, especially top industrialists and militarists, assumed key positions in the post-war economic and political structure of Germany.

1946 General **Lucius Clay, John J. McCloy,** SS Generals **Burckhardt and Franz Six**, SS criminal

Klaus Barbie and **Henry Kissinger** formed and trained 5,000 German Nazis, U.S. troops and Eastern European fascists as 'Special Forces Against Communism' in Oberarnmergau, Germany. Some of these same trainers later established our 'Special Forces' in the U.S., the 'Green Berets.'

1945-47 U.S. Generals **George Patton** and **Douglas MacArthur** surrounded themselves with top Nazi SS and Axis criminals to gather military intelligence, and write the official history of World

War II, covering up critical information. MacArthur's intelligence chief, Colonel **Charles** Willoughby (actually Nazi **Kurt Weidenbach**) covered up criminal Japanese germ warfare tests done on U.S. prisoners in order to gain secrets for future use. The Nazi and U.S. intelligence network created in 1943 began plans for Cold War propaganda, and World War III to destroy the Soviet Union. **Winston Churchill**, England's Prime Minister at the time, promoted one German officer's phrase, 'The Iron Curtain' to describe the Soviet Union.

1945-48 Key Nazi war criminals, scientists and intelligence agents began moving worldwide under false passports, to be employed in the emerging Cold War. The U.S. Army 970th Counter Intelligence Corps (which employed Henry Kissinger), the OSS (later the CIA), the U.S. Office of Naval Intelligence, and top Vatican figures (the Knights of Malta), set up the 'Rat Line' to hide and aid the escape of fugitive Nazi war criminals like **Klaus Barbie, Martin Bormann** and others.

The Nazi treasuries and gold were transported to Switzerland and South America, and forged international currency was printed to finance the 'Fourth Reich.' *Code name*: Operation Bernhard.

SS **Otto Skorzeny**, acquitted at Dachau for the Malmedy Massacre through the efforts of American attorney **Robert Durst**, set up Die Spinne (the web) and Odessa (SS, the spider) to place Nazi criminals around the globe. Another network *Kameradenwerk,* helped to create new identities for Nazis hiding inside Germany, though many culpable Nazi agents were never indicted, and were openly re-employed.

Werner von Braun and his 'Rocket Team' were 'captured' in Switzerland by U.S. General **Thurston** and his aide-de-camp **Clay Shaw**. They were brought to the U.S. and placed in top positions in aerospace and munitions industries and NASA 'with hundreds of other Nazi scientists. *Code name*: Project Paperclip. At the same time, European revanchists and White Russian fascists were brought into the U.S. along with other Nazi collaborators, including the entire Nazi puppet government of Byelorussia. *Code name*: Project Belarus.

1946-51 Hundreds of Nazi intelligence agents (the Gehlen Organization) helped to form the CIA operations division, the German BND (state security). Radio Liberty, Voice of America, NASA, the U.S. Army Historical Division, aerospace and munitions industries and top Pentagon posts. These SS criminals were not only immune from prosecution; they were and are well paid.

1945-85 A newly emerging fascist network was formed internationally. In Italy, a vast post-war intelligence structure was built up using former agents of Mussolini's fascist rule. A secret fascist cell was formed in Italy called **P-2**, involving key Vatican and government members. The aristocracy of, the Roman Catholic church, the secretive **Knights of Malta**, awarded knighthood and special status to '**Wild Bill' Donovan**, General **Reinhardt Gehlen**, **William Casey** and others during the reign of Pope Pius XII. **The World Anti-Communist League** (WACL) was formed, including members of the Waffen SS, neo-Nazis, the Solidarists (White Russians), the World Union of National Socialists, mercenaries and death squads.

1979-1985 The truth begins to emerge. The Justice Department sets up the Office of Special Investigations to locate a few fascists here. Forty years too late, 'Six cases to date'.

The Secret History of Ronald Reagan

1940's Ronald Reagan, an actor, makes films in Hollywood with actor **Errol Flynn**. Flynn, working as an agent of the Gestapo at the time, was under the direction of an SS agent Dr. Hermann Erban. Both Flynn and Reagan made regular visits to Erban, and Nazi sympathizers like the **Duke and Duchess of Windsor** in the Bahamas. During World War II, the U.S. Army and the OSS used Reagan in training films, stateside of course.

These same OSS units were responsible for the movement of the Odessa networks. One figure intimately involved was **Richard Nixon**, working for Navy Intelligence after the war to house and assist in the immigration of Nazi war criminals, in Long Island, New York. Nixon was one of the principal organizers for Project Belarus as well.

1950's Reagan gains national prominence from TV appearances, working for General Electric. **Charles Wilson**, president of GE at the time, promoted the idea of a 'permanent war economy' for the on-going Cold War. This period marked the beginnings of the vast military-industrial complex that was to dominate the American economy from then on. This complex was run and established in large part by the Nazi technicians and scientists imported after the war. GE, for example, relied heavily on military contracts and employed **Robert Schmitz**, whose uncle Herman Schmitz headed the Nazi drug and spy cartel, I.G. Farben in Germany. Schmitz worked closely with SS **Otto Skorzeny**, Hitler's Commando. Reagan joined the Free Europe Committee, headed by revanchists and Nazis.

1953 Adolph Eichmann's superior in the Einsatzgruppen (Nazi death squad for the Final Solution) was **Otto Albrecht von Bolschwing**. Eichmann was later hanged for 'following orders' from von Bolschwing. Otto von Bolschwing came to the United States, followed later by an Austrian, Helene von Damm, who worked as his personal translator. Together, they formed a CIA-front corporation in California, TCI. This front included, partners **Edwin Wilson** and **Frank Terpil**, later indicted as major international gun dealers connected with the CIA. When the Gehlen Organization was established inside the CIA, Gehlen returned to Germany to set up their state security network, the

BND, using other Nazi agents. In the interim, Gehlen appointed von Bolschwing to head up the Gehlen Organization in the U.S.

1960's Helene von Damm left the employ of von Bolschwing to become the personal secretary to

<u>Governor Ronald Reagan in California.</u>

1970's Reagan sat on the **Rockefeller Commission** studying the CIA, and aided the cover-up of past Nazi links and current crimes of the intelligence agencies. Reagan was also asked to attend meetings of the **Bilderberg Group**, an international financial cartel, by its administration, Prince **Bernhard** of the Netherlands (Operation Bernhard).

Governor Reagan carried out fascistic policies in California, including domestic repression and spying, social welfare cuts, and racist policies. Assisted by **Edwin Meese**, infamous for the secret police takeover plans code named **Garden Plot**, and aide **Lynn Nofziger** (Nazi Party, California), Reagan began his anti-communist campaigns for the presidency, pushing for World War III with the USSR.

1980's 'The presidential election relied on the theft of Jimmy Carter's 'briefing books' for his debate with Reagan, an act carried out by Reagan advisor **Sven Kraemer**, son of Fritz A.G. Kraemer. Reagan's close political connections to fascism began to be visible. Reagan appointees are closely linked to P-2 Italian fascists inside NA TO. Reagan worked to expand the role of U.S. Special Forces abroad.

When Reagan ordered American GI's to invade Grenada, they were dressed in 1943 Nazi Wehrmacht uniforms and helmets (in camouflage colors).

Reagan lied to foreign leaders about having made 'films' of Nazi concentration camps during the American liberation period. He was in the United States all through World War II. He bragged to several people about showing these films to his 'Jewish friends who don't believe there was a Holocaust.'

Reagan's administration works against the deportation of Nazi criminals from the U.S., blocking attempts to bring them to justice and trial. At the start of the Justice Department search for Nazi war criminals in the United States, president Reagan moved to return files including the names of 10.7 million Nazi Party members from World War II (660,000 SS, 40,000 Storm troopers and Special Police), documents captured by U.S. troops during the fall of the Third Reich. West Germany, where these records were sent, has effectively ended all prosecution of Nazi criminals. This act put the files outside Freedom of Information Act reach for Nazi hunters here. Nazi war criminals discovered here are treated with 'kid gloves.'

- **Otto von Bolschwing.** Deportation delayed from 1970's until his death in the U.S. in the 80's.
- **Valerian Trifa** Rumanian Iron Guard, mass murderer, was extradited to Portugal, not the Rumanian courts.
- **Andrija Artukovic** Croatian Ustachl, killings left 750,000 dead, extradition was delayed since 1953, current personal care costs the U.S. $30,000 daily.
- **Arthur Rudolph** 'Rocket Team,' Dora concentration camp administrator, later top NASA official, allowed to leave for West Germany, renounces U.S. citizenship and disappear before his case was made public here. Other NASA scientists are demanding citizenship be restored for Arthur Rudolph, citing the 'Spirit of Bitburg,' reconciliation with fascism.

Reagan's Appointments and Invitations

Friends and Advisers

Licio Gelli, considered the 'Puppetmaster' behind the Italian P-2, and a Vatican confidant, was invited to attend Reagan's inauguration in 1981. Gelli was later indicted for numerous crimes, and the 'exposure of P-2 nearly toppled the Italian government, yet he escaped from prison. He and his partner **Michele Sindona** were major figures in the recent Vatican bank scandals as well. He worked with Hitler.

Sven Kraemer, a key figure in Cartergate, and related to Fritz Kraemer, was appointed to the National Security Council.

Henry Kissinger, who has played such a central role in government policy since the Nixon era, was part of the Rat Line operations and CIA collaboration to move Nazi war criminals around the world. He has remained a close friend of **Fritz Kraemer** since World War II. Kraemer is considered a 'mentor' to Kissinger and **Alexander Haig**, former Secretary of State. Following his intimate involvement in the overthrow of democratic rule in Chile, Kissinger assisted in the rise to power of fascist ruler Pinochet and his appointment of Walter Rauff to train the deadly secret police forces, the DINA. SS

Walter Rauffhad operated the 'mobile oven' groups throughout Eastern Europe as part of the 'Einsatzgruppen's final Solution, Kissinger knew him well. Reagan has recently appointed Kissinger to head his Special Commission on Central America, forming future policy there.

J. Peter Grace, the American head of the Knights of Malta, has had extensive financial investment arrangements with Nazi war criminal **Friedrich Flick**, who owns a large percentage of the Grace Corporation in the United States. For years, Grace has employed Nazi chemist **Otto Ambros**, who invented the cyanide gas Zyklon-B, used in the gas chambers at concentration camps. Ambros was employed by the infamous I.G. Farben cartel. Reagan appointed Grace to head the Private Sector Survey on Cost Control in the Federal Government, a thinly disguised plan to further reduce corporate taxes. Grace was also instrumental in the formation of the American Institute for Free Labor Development, (AIFLD), a CIA affiliated effort that helped overthrow Allende in Chile.

John J. McCloy, the Rockefeller banker who is 'Godfather' to U.S. multinationals, was central to the pardoning of key Nazi criminals. Working under the Secretary of War, he had blocked Allied bombing of concentration camps in Germany, and helped Earl Warren set up Japanese internment camps in America. He was a central figure in the political career of Henry Kissinger. Reagan arranged for a recent White House ceremony for McCloy, where he accepted honors from the Kohl government in West Germany for his post-war accomplishments.

Robert Keith Gray, who heads a large public relations firm in Washington, DC, was linked with the SS in Argentina, and with CIA operations. Reagan appointed him to head his inauguration committee.

General John Singlaub, president of the World Anti-Communist League, worked with Colonel Charles Willoughby at the end of World War II. He is currently involved with the contra death squads in Central America, financing mercenary operations. Reagan relies on him as a top Pentagon advisor for foreign policy matters.

Harry Slatterman, a member of the Kissinger Commission, is really Nazi Schlaudeman, who worked for the CIA in Chile and Guatemala.

Leon Jaworski, once called 'the most trusted man in America' following his role in Watergate and Koreagate, was instrumental in protecting Nazi war criminals facing prosecution at Nuremberg, where he worked as a prosecutor.

As a director of the International Rescue Division of the Red Cross, he was pan of the Rat Line, providing passports and cover for Nazi killers. He later worked for CIA connected financial fronts. He agreed to head Democrats for Reagan in the last elections.

General **Albert Wedemeyer**, another Reagan advisor, worked with Fritz Kraemer at the Pentagon Plans Division, and was a member of the Nazi General Staff in World War II. SS General Fritz Kraemer, Kissinger's mentor, moved from Malmedy to Dachau, then to the Pentagon Plans Division for 30 years. He now works with General **Daniel Graham**, promoting Star Wars. Reagan appointed him to his Strategic Defense Initiative (Star Wars) advisory panel.

General Heine Arnholdt, another Pentagon advisor to Reagan, is pan of the Knights of Malta. He works closely with General Singlaub in funding assassinations and mercenary attacks in Central America.

Government *Posts & Ambassadors:*

William Casey, pan of Operation Sunrise, and a top figure in the Knights of Malta aided SS Karl Wolff and others escape Germany on the Rat Line. He is currently Reagan's appointed director of the CIA. His major investment firm, Capitol Cities now owns national TV network, ABC.

William Clark, Reagan's National Security Council Secretary was brought to the United States by Helene von Damm. Helene, a close associate of Nazi criminals, became Reagan's White House Appointments Secretary, choosing most of the cabinet level officials. She was later made U.S. Ambassador to Austria, living in Vienna. She recently left the post amid scandals.

William A. Wilson, who was linked in the past to the CIA, acted as personal financial advisor to Reagan for years. He was appointed as the first U.S. Ambassador to the Vatican, to the delight of the Knights of Malta. Numerous cabinet level appointments by Reagan have been long-time members of the Knights. The Vatican provided passports and key assistance to the fugitive Nazis.

Waffen SS officer Jacob Tiefenthaler involved in the recent Hitler Diary scandal, a scam that provided $5 million to the living SS members through the HIAG and the Odessa networks. The U.S. Army in West Germany employs him.

General Vernon Walters, a man whose intelligence involvements span many decades, is a top member of the Knights of Malta and a CIA operative responsible for many covert operations. Reagan appointed him as a 'roving ambassador' in Central America, then to the key post of U.N. representative, replacing Jeanne Kirkpatrick. Even Nancy Reagan's stepfather, Dr. **Loyal Davis**, once worked with General MacArthur and Colonel Charles Willoughby, the Nazi intelligence agent whose real name was Weidenbach.

The Bitburg Visit - Is Reagan a 'Good German'?

Reagan's White House staff was pictured as blundering blindly into arrangements to visit Bitburg. Actually, a thorough check was made to determine if any of the SS involved in the Malmedy massacre were buried there. The director, a member of the SS himself, shared cemetery records. A Jewish war veteran, present at the Malmedy site a few hours after the killings, told me, 'I'm so mad at Reagan I could spit! Mark my words, by December this year they won't be telling us to remember Pearl Harbor, but to forget it!'

To the media, Reagan claimed helplessness, and shifted diplomatic blame to German Chancellor Helmut Kohl. Kohl's administration had just weathered a major scandal involving illegal campaign funding from the **Nazi Flick Group**, also heavy financial investors in W.R. Grace Corporation.

Current West German President, **Richard von Weizsacker**, was a lawyer during the Nazi period, and defended his father, SS Baron **Ernst von Weizsacker** at the Nuremberg trials. Baron von Weizsacker, personal envoy from Hitler to the Vatican (and the Rat Line), had his defense costs paid from a special $46 million fund set up by Nazi criminal **Friedrich Flick**. Neither Kohl nor von Weizsacker did anything to interfere with plans for a reunion of 500 Waffen SS members during Reagan's visit. In fact, Kohl has recently appointed former Waffen SS member **Walther Florian** to the Ministry of Food and Agriculture, a cabinet post in West Germany. These are the Germans Reagan can't refuse.

To complete the cycle, Reagan's Ambassador to the Bahamas, scene of his earliest meetings with the SS, was until recently **Lev Dobriansky**, a member of WACL and editor of the neo-Nazi Ukrainian Quarterly, which recently eulogized SS General **Pavlo Shandruk**. Shandruk, the creator of the dreaded Waffen SS Galician Division attached to Auschwitz, was the commander of the SS Panzer Division that fought against U.S. forces at Bitburg.

Perhaps this historical entwinement explains why even the president of the United States is reduced to 'just following orders.' Astute political observers and students of recent U.S. history will also recognize here figures key to the assassination of President John F. Kennedy and its cover-up, an event central to the rise to presidential power of both Richard Nixon and Ronald Reagan. But that's another story in the secret history of American fascism.

(This information is based on my work as well as that of researcher Mae Brussell. Suggested readings include: *American Swastika* and *Trading With the Enemy* by Charles Higham, *The Secret History of Ronald Reagan* by Don Freed, *From Hitler to Uncle Sam* by Charles Allen, Jr., and *In God's Name* by David Yallop.)

TIED UP IN NAZIS

An Interview with John Judge by Corey Dubin (Other America Radio) (conducted in Santa Barbara, December 1 1989)

Corey Dubin: *John, let's start as a benchmark with Operation Sunrise, something I know you 're well versed in, the deal cut between the then OSS, the precursor to the CIA, and General Wolff in the SS. I think that's a good place for us to begin.*

John Judge: Operation Sunrise, as it was called, involved the secret surrender of the Nazi intelligence structure to the OSS American and British structure represented by Allen Dulles, William Casey, Sir William Stephenson from British Intelligence on one side and General Reinhardt Gehlen, head of Armies East for Hitler's intelligence SS commander Karl Wolff and others on the Nazi side. The context for that is the failure of the drive to destroy the Bolshevik gains of 1918 and reverse the Russian Revolution which was part of the long-term plan by European and American industrialists, monarchists, revanchists, and incipient fascists from Europe at the time the

Soviet czar's monarchy fell. Other monarchists felt threatened, so funds were collected and used to secretly refinance and re-arm Germany in order to make the drive again in the 1930's under Hitler's and under fascist rule- to take back the mother country, Russia, to take it away and put it back in the hands of the monarchists. And they had similar goals with regard to the rest of the other countries eventually in Eastern Europe.

But that drive failed at Stalingrad in 1943. It became clear to everyone except the most fanatical in the Nazi order that it was time for an international regrouping for the Nazis; in other words, to do as they had done at the end of World War I - go back underground, regroup, and get their finances out. So stalling procedures were begun that led to, among other things, the Battle of the Bulge which was basically only a holding pattern militarily to permit time to get the wealth out, to evacuate the key people. The planning for that stall and the movement of the Nazi gold, the Nazi spies, was done starting in 1943 with Operation Overcast, the search for the Nazi scientists. Sunrise ended it, with a meeting between the key figures in Nazi intelligence with American and British intelligence and the deals were cut there, the surrender was cut there. The Nazis would come into the western camp and be instrumental in giving us information we didn't have and couldn't have on the Soviet Union. Reinhardt Gehlen 's meticulous and well-established infiltration of Soviet intelligence and the Soviet system gave him a card to play in terms of what they needed for the post-war/cold war scenario- the division between East and West and what would rise from that. There was also Operation Overcast which ran from '43 to '45 - a searching out of key Nazi aerospace and munitions scientists to obtain agreements with the ilk of General Walter Dornberger and Werner von Braun and others to surrender to the Americans and bring the hidden technology here to the

United States in the postwar years. There were other similar operations starting in 1945 with Project Paperclip, Bloodstone and the Belerus Project. All of which had to do with the actual movement of these key Nazis out of Germany, Eastern Europe, and the Soviet Union, and into the infrastructure of the emerging National Security state here in the United States.

Corey Dubin: *Now, General Gehlen...? General Gehlen was chief of intelligence for Armies East for Hitler and he became essentially Chief of Intelligence for the East for NATO and the United States, isn't that true?*

John Judge: Yes, eventually he came here to the United States in 1945 dressed in an army general's uniform. They brought him over to the Army Historical Division. Many of the key Nazis, including the Nazi historians were drop-pointed at the Army Historical Division and given cover there. In fact, I found it interesting when I went through the records of the Warren Commission minutes that the actual author of the Warren Commission Report stirred quite a bit of controversy within the investigative teams of the Warren Commission and there are memos, line by line critiques of the report by almost every one of the investigating team saying, 'What's the basis for this?' 'Where does he get this conclusion?' But the actual author of the report didn't work with any of the investigative teams, all of which were interlinked with CIA anyway, and set up. He was brought in on a TDY (Technical Duty Roster) from the Pentagon and the Army Historical Division. His name was Otto Winnaker and he had been one of twenty-six official historians for Hitler. That Historical Division became a drop-point for Gehlen 's spies who were brought here in the hundreds to form the basis of the whole Operation Division of the emerging CIA - $200 million of Rockefeller and Mellon money was put up to help this project. Federal funds were pumped into it and a

Central Directorate of Intelligence was formed, which became the Central Intelligence Agency. But Gehlen' s operation was so powerful and what he knew was so powerful that he basically would answer questions but not explain how he was getting the answers.

Consequently, he maintained an actual army of spies, continuing to operate behind the lines in the Soviet Union after the war and with agents throughout the displaced persons camps in the post-war French and German situation. The beginnings of French and German intelligence really start at the Paris Ritz, right at the end of the war when Hemingway and David Bruce, working for the OSS.

Bruce was in charge of the whole Western European Division then for OSS arrived along with the partisans as part of the first people under the Arch de Triomphe. They set up at the Ritz and they met with Russell d'Oench, who was a scion of the W.R. Grace family that has many ties to the fascists. They started what became the German BND and the post-war SDC and French intelligence networks and it's those networks that inter-relate to Gehlen.

When Gehlen comes here, his sponsor is Peter Drucker, a major spokesman and writer for the capitalist regime in the current period and the person who debriefs him is Harry Pleasants, working at the Philadelphia Bulletin who, according to our analysis, is really the model for Felix Rider, the name Ian Fleming uses in the Bond novels for the American CIA agent, the friend of Bond. Many of the Bond stories are based on real intelligence operations with key independent figures like Howard Hughes and others are playing roles. Bond himself is a real historical figure, and part of the British intelligence structure that lived in Philadelphia. There's a real James Bond.

These people inter-relate to the networks of spies and agents who worked for the OSS, who worked under the North American Newspaper Alliance as one of their fronts, and various different agencies.

There were networks in place to enfold the Gehlen net, but after American intelligence was set up by Gehlen, he left the United States in the early 50's and went back into Germany and France where he set up the NATO intelligence structure you talk about where, again, he would head up all of their information about the Soviet Union.

His information is really the building block for the whole cold war lie that the Dulles brothers told so effectively and that has been the basis for American policy for that whole period. Whatever we knew about the Soviet Union we knew because Gehlen told us.

Corey Dubin: *Some have proposed that Gehlen may have really in this role he played, and given the impact the intelligence he generated had on the cold war, that Gehlen was in fact really playing his part in the overall Bormann strategy for the next edition of the Reich. Would you agree with that, John?*

John Judge: I think absolutely that these deals were cut with emerging proto-fascists in the United States. I think the Dulles brothers had no qualms about Hitler and the pogroms against the Jews. In fact, it was only the junior partners in Sullivan & Cromwell that forced the Dulles's to withdraw the financial investments in Germany even after the Cristalnacht and the Jewish attacks began. I think that these people were in league in an international fascist agenda and I think that, like you call it the 'Bormann Strategy,' the plan to move the monies and key figures of the Reich into a position where they would basically use the United States as their next jumping ground, their technological facility, a place where they could implement many of the ideas of the fourth Reich without the trappings of Hitler and the party fanatics.

These were the bright boys of the Reich, I mean these were the people who understood beyond the party ideology and knew what fascism was and what it could bring. Dohrnberger, for instance, Von Braun's mentor, was brought here in the 1950's because Von Braun wouldn't do any rocket work British prosecutor Shawcross said he should have been hanged for what he did at Auschwitz, he worked with 'the Butcher' Mengele there. John J. McCloy the Rockefeller banker from Sullivan & Cromwell, later to sit on the Warren Commission, intervened on his behalf with General Lucius Clay's office, the military prosecution, and got Dohrnberger here to the United States. He worked at Bell Helicopter Systems, ending up in Buffalo, New York. I have an article in 1963 in Time magazine, a 'Where Are They Now' about him. It says he continued to work at Bell Helicopter for many years and he also trained helicopter pilots for the Shah in Iran, noting that he had long-ranging interests in these areas. The article talked about how he's still a rocket scientist and still thinking about the plans he had back when he was at the Dorz concentration camp with Von Braun. In 1963 he was proposing satellites that would circle the earth with nuclear weapons and go round every 90 minutes - an early proponent of Star Wars. In fact, the shuttle itself, that design is from an early Dornberger idea to have a missile warhead that would go into outer space and therefore not be tracked easily by radar and then come back down. So they'd send it in Germany. It would orbit the earth, and come back down into New York and suddenly attack the United States from space too quickly for a response, unlike tracking something coming in all the way from Germany.

These ideas of shuttling the things into space really date back to the early conceptions of the German rocket scientists and much of the technology they brought with them is hidden technology that they continue to use. I think that both in terms of implementing their technology and social control they really were given free rein. I think that the cold war was almost the perfect paradigm for them to operate in. I mean, anti-communism is almost always fascism's best excuse that and domestic repression of what are considered 'problems' or 'terrorism' on a domestic level.

The kind of language that Bush and the others use now, if you go back and read the statements of the ilk of Klaus Barbie and the other 'administrators' of the European Reich in the occupied countries, there's really no difference. They talk about the terrorists when they refer to the anti-fascist partisans and, in fact, they've successfully confused anti-fascism to the point that if you say you're anti-fascist it must mean that you are a communist. There's no understanding of what the term means or what you're talking about when you say fascism. They've got it reduced, unfortunately I think, in the American Jewish community to fascism is solely anti-Semitism and not a political reality and under that rubric we end up with segments of the Jewish community here literally in bed with the most fascistic elements because anti-communism becomes a paradigm for them to operate under instead.

What would Goebbels have given for television at the scale that it came in in 1948? He would have cut off his saluting arm. I think they've implemented a friendly and covert fascism here in the United States that is finally openly showing its ugly face now under the regime of Bush and the open CIA control of the government.

Corey Dubin: *John, I want to return to some of the Nazi elements and where they end up, but I want to shift gears and move myself to another branch of the European movement and that's the Italian fascist movement because I think there are some figures to come out of the post-war period who have carried through, who have fathered a whole new generation, like Stefano del Chiaie. But I want to go into Prince Borghese and his work, moving into Spain following the war, and the moving of some of the key Nazis. It seems like while the Nazis were being infiltrated through the church, a number of them into Latin America - Barbie and others - there was this movement to Franco Spain of Borghese, Skorzeny... and how do you see that fitting into the whole Fascist International, if you will?*

John Judge: The Nazis not only moved through the United States by literally the thousands, but also all around the world. Wherever they could hide the money and have political sanctuary and establish themselves they went. I mean, it was common knowledge, for instance, that Stroessner in Paraguay protected many of them during his long regime and in many of the worst countries they held sway and were part and parcel of the rise of fascism in a more open way later. Within hours of the death of Allende, for example, there were swastika flags in the streets of Chile and signs saying to turn in the Jews and Blacks and the opening of the stadiums under Pinochet, so they operated to create much of the Death Squads in Latin and Central America, to maintain the rabidly anticommunist strains in Italy and Spain after the war.

This was part and parcel of the Dulles cold war strategy, which in actuality was designed to get rid of any progressive, pro-socialist and anti-fascist elements and replace them instead with reactionary anti-communist elements. While not all of these reactionary groups sided with Hitler due to nationalistic reasons, at the same time they were proto-fascists themselves. The Americans and British didn't have much confusion about this. I think they knew who was who and who threatened a progressive or open regime and whom they could manipulate. For most historians and people in the United States it seemed that the fascists fell, Hitler's regime ended, the war was over, Nazism was no longer a threat and what came in were what our political leaders liked to call 'democracies,' but democracy within the cold war rubric only means a system that protects privilege.

I think that these people like Skorzeny moved to many countries. They operated in Saudi Arabia through Aloise Breunner, one of the worst of the criminals, and in Egypt. They went wherever they could - Belgium, in Antwerp they had factions - even in Ireland there were Nazis during the war and in the post-war period. So there's hardly an area of the world they didn't infiltrate to and have some position or move in and out of. The bulk of the monies went, I think as you say, to Spain and eventually to Latin America for investment under the Peron family, that kind of thing, and what they were doing in those countries was setting up new pro-fascist and proto-fascist death squads, kill teams, the underpinnings of what now we see as the contras or the AAA, the groups that operate in Central America.

Really, the roots of that and their funding have to do with the Nazi gold and their printing of fake money. Prince Bernhardt and the Bernhardt operation at the end of the war printed fake currency for almost every major European country and the U.S. so the Nazis would have money to spend. Then, eventually their hand in the drug traffic became the financial underpinning for the movement. But there were many key

Americans involved in all this, into the Warren Commission cover-up and the death of John F. Kennedy.

Just to give you one: you mentioned using the church to move these people. One of the other major organizations that gave out the glossenspiel, the little plastic ID cards to the Germans that helped them get through the displaced camps and get out of the country- one of those organizations was the International Rescue Division of the International Red Cross which had long functioned as an anti-communist arm of the OSS. Even as early as World War I there was use of the Rescue Division going into the post-Bolshevik period. Ostensibly they raised money to help feed people, but their funds went instead to the White Russian commanders through Herbert Hoover and the food that was supposed to get to people starving in the Ukraine and instead went directly to the troops that were attacking the Bolshevik regime.

Someone else who moves in that period stepped out of his role in the army at the Nuremberg trials (where he undermined the prosecution of key figures in those trials) to the International Rescue Division to help move the Nazis. From there he went to a CIA firm, the J.M. Kaplan Fund, a CIA conduit in Texas for many years. Eventually he became the liaison between the Dallas, state, and local police investigation of the Kennedy assassination and the Warren Commission and he later shows up as 'the most trusted man in America,' as well as the boss of Mr. Nields, the Contragate questioner in the investigation of Koreagate. His name is Leon Jaworski.

So these people figure into the period, the Dulles brothers moved from the Operation Sunrise and the Bay of Pigs onto the Warren Commission. John J. McCloy, directly responsible as the post-war commissioner of Germany for pardoning these key Nazis, later shows up in the Warren commission too.

Dornberger whom I mentioned earlier, had as his right hand man for many years, a military intelligence agent named Michael Paine. Michael and Ruth Paine housed Marina Oswald, set Oswald up, 'lied about his ownership of the rifle, got him the job at the Book Depository, and other things, and these were people who worked directly with the fascists. They do show up and they are part of the implementation for Fascist International and the rise of the Reich again in different trappings that we're seeing come to bear now in the modern period.

Corey Dubin: *John, I want to go to Latin America because you say a lot, you pack it in there, and I want to split some of that down because I think for so many people who listen to our style of programs, Latin America is a key issue and I think you've got the roots of what's happening now. But I just want to just digress. I have to ask you a question that I think is important about 'The Kennedy Assassination'. Some view the Kennedy assassination as a coup d'état. Now, in America we never think of coups d'états. That's Chile, that's Salvador, that's Greece after the war. But we don't have of coups d'états the military stays in the Pentagon... How do you see that assassination?*

John Judge: I see it as exactly that, a coven military coup d'état on November 22nd, 1963, orchestrated at the top levels by the Joint Chiefs of Staff. I know from several sources that I've followed over the years that the events of that day fit directly into how a coup d'état is handled and operated. One good book to look at in light of that is by a former Reagan adviser and right-wing commentator, Edward Luttwak, who wrote Handbook/or Coup d'état. This book outlines how a coup d'état is done. For instance, the federal phone lines for federal offices, the separate phone lines, failed for a period of over an hour at the time of the Kennedy assassination on November 22nd, so federal offices could not communicate. Almost all of Kennedy's cabinet was out of the country on a flight from a meeting in the Philippine about the situation in Vietnam. He had just authored a National Security Memorandum to withdraw all U.S. troops by the end of 1964 and was reversing U.S. policy in Vietnam and that particular decision was completely reversed by the Monday following the Kennedy assassination on Friday

Corey Dubin: *As I understand it, that directive included pulling the CIA out. Is that true?*

John Judge: Yes. I think it would have included both military and intelligence troops. We have basically only reconstructions of that memorandum that Peter Dale Scott in the Gravel edition of the Pentagon Papers, and others have worked on. I think Fletcher Prouty saw the memorandum and reconstructed it. Kennedy had said, earlier in October, about the 10th of October, that he was going to scatter the CIA to the four winds and he had talked about putting his brother Bobby in charge of the CIA and getting rid of the Nazi network in the operation division. He was threatening the whole Gehlen net. He had fired key figures like Bissell and Cabell. Charles Cabell's brother, Earl Cabell, was mayor of Dallas the day of the Kennedy assassination. His wife is the one who gave Jackie the inappropriate red roses, everyone gets yellow roses in Texas - that she had in the car with her at the time and Charles Cabell went on to work for the Pacific Corporation, a major CIA subsidiary. But these people were tossed out due to Kennedy's realization that they had 'lied to him about the Bay of Pigs and so he had a whole faction there in the CIA that was quite upset with him.

My 'mother was five levels above top security in the Pentagon; She was a manpower analyst for the Joint Chiefs of Staff and Deputy Chief of Staff for Personnel. Her job was to project five years in advance, -: Within a hundred people either way, the annual national draft call. She would figure out from a current force level, a projected force level, a combat death level given to her by the Joint Chiefs, how many would die, how many would retire, how many would re-up, how many would discharge under each category. In this way, she'd determine how many you needed to draft and how many would enlist. She had to have that figure right within 100 people either way. In years when the draft might be 50,000 people in a given per annum she had to get that close and she had to do it five years ahead.

I asked her after she retired when they told her they would escalate in Vietnam because she had to be among the first to know. She said, 'Late November of 1963.' I said, 'The last week?' She said 'The Monday following the assassination.' I said, 'was this a few more troops or advisers?' She said, 'I couldn't believe the figures. I took them to the Joint Chiefs and I said 'these can't be right. Probably the first civilian protest of the war in Vietnam, They said, 'Those are the figures you'll use.' They told her, and remember this is November 25, 1963. As soon as Johnson is in office under a National Security Memorandum #1 drafted that weekend, the Joint Chiefs told her that the war would last ten years and that 57,000 Americans would die in it. They were exactly on target they knew where they were going and what they were going to do and what it took and told her to project the draft figures for that war as soon as Kennedy was dead.

Now that's a complete reversal of his policy, and further evidence, I believe, of the Joint Chiefs' involvement. He was threatening detente with the Soviet Union, normalization of relations with Cuba, arms limitation talks, all the things that the military industrial complex can't abide because they thrive on the continuation of the cold war mentality and the profits that they were going to reap from Vietnam and from the continuation of that era.

I also talked to SAC bomber pilots, Strategic Air Command pilots from Wright Patterson Air Force Base in the air that hour who told me that when they heard news that Kennedy was killed they ran for the lockers that contained the nuclear emergency response code books that allow them to respond immediately to nuclear commands from the White House or elsewhere and are basically the nuclear alert communication at a time of crisis. And, all of the SAC pilot bombers in the air at that hour; these pilots said that the codebooks were missing from the lockers.

There was no possibility of a nuclear response should someone outside the 'need to know' chain in the Joint Chiefs, getting wind of the 'Oswald did it' story, 'Oswald the red,' 'Oswald the defector,' come up with the conclusion that the Soviets had killed him and go inappropriately to a nuclear response to the Soviets. They had blocked that response and there's also a report in Pierre Salinger's account of Air Force II that the codebook there was missing too.

These code books couldn't be touched by some Mafia goon from New Orleans, they couldn't be messed with by the CIA-they go through a 16-man handling position, they are changed on a regular basis so that the encoding is different and can't be cracked. The only people who could have arranged that are the top levels of the Joint Chiefs of Staff.

Corey Dubin: *John, a couple of things we've got to stick in here for a minute I think. It seems to me that the Kennedy situation with regard to intelligence was anger over the Bay of Pigs, had nothing to do with the morality or the ethics because Bobby and*

John were, it seemed to me, always ready to pull that covert button against Fidel early on. I mean they didn't seem to be acting out of some higher morality. It seems to me that so far as the CIA goes, they were angry and John felt betrayed by the organization and that's why he wanted to go after the old boy network. Would you agree with that?

John Judge: I think there may be a combination of the two. I think the Kennedys, I don't want to paint them as saints, were pushed by the wave of change that was in progress in the early 60's and moving almost everyone in the country in terms of how we were looking at international relations and foreign affairs.

I think that the Kennedys did come from a background of feeling that intervention was the proper way to go. I mean there's the John F. Kennedy School of Counterinsurgency that trained the early Green Berets. Unfortunately, the trainers were almost entirely Eastern European revanchists and Nazis who came out to Fort Bragg during that period.

If you get into the real history of the Green Berets you'll see that's how they started it. There was a training camp in 1946 at Oberammergau that involved General Six and General Burckhardt from the SS and also Henry Kissinger and Lucius Clay were there. This camp held 5,000 anti communist elements who were trained there and called 'themselves 'Special Forces.' Then that concept was moved into Bragg, that was an OSS operation, but that was moved into Bragg and became the beginning of the Green Berets. The Green Berets functioned for a long time as a sort of private army of the Kennedy family. If you'll remember they put one black ribbon on the back of the beret at the time of the assassination of John F. Kennedy, a second when Robert was gone, and then after that they basically became errand boys for the international racketeers and the CIA. They were used, for instance, to traffic the dope out of Southeast Asia, the heroin, you know. They used the Green Berets. Every year you'll see the Green Berets from the old network go to the gravesite for Kennedy and have some remembrance.

So Kennedy came out of that school, the Organization of American States was certainly controlling the Monroe Doctrine ideas. I don't want to paint them as saints. On the other hand, they inherited many of these covert operations. They came to understand that the reality of the politics was not what they were being told and that there was no indigenous revolt against Castro, that the only way this was going to happen was basically by U.S. military intervention and at that point, not backing up an indigenous revolt, they felt that they should withdraw.

I think they came to similar conclusions about Vietnam, that there wasn't really a popular struggle that they were backing up Diem, introduced to them out of the U.S. seminaries by Cardinal Spellman and the worst elements, and put into power. Diem was a reactionary and causing strife trying to remake all the Buddhists into Catholics. I think the Kennedys were realists and came to understand that something else had to happen, causing them to move away from interventionist politics.

On the other hand, they were angry that they were being lied to. I remember one story I was told about Kennedy feeling that errand boys were giving him orders from the Pentagon who were sent over by the Joint Chiefs and telling him what to do. The story goes that he was fed up with it and wanted to do something different, make his own decisions. I think that when he began to do that he became too much of a liability. I think that he already was a liability as a result of taking the 1960 election away from Nixon, who had been chosen and handled by these elements. Let's not overlook the fact that Nixon worked at Jay Gould's castle on Long Island and actively helped bring the Nazis in and was part and parcel of their strategy. Had it not been for Mayor Daley and his intervention with the voting machines in Chicago to carry Cook County and thus the popular vote, Kennedy probably would have lost the 1960 election. The Kennedy family owed favors to the wrong people-they were close friends to Joe McCarthy through the father, the father who'd been basically a Nazi sympathizer during his ambassadorship to the Court of St. James and was relieved of that ambassadorship because of his open admiration of Hitler. They came from bad money and bad politics, but I think that they changed as the influence of the father ebbed, when he was ill. They began to move on their own and began to see that a continuing cold war was not going to solve the problems.

At the end, Kennedy was blocking interventions against Castro and this idea that Castro would have had him killed is ridiculous. First of all, how could Castro have survived had it come out? I mean, that small of a country? And whom was Castro putting in? Was LBJ to be a greater friend than Kennedy was?

In fact, Kennedy had sent people down to explore normalization of relations with Cuba at the time and was making approaches to Fidel. He had blocked use of the REX, a boat down in the Florida Keys, and other continuing plans for the intervention and invasion of Cuba by the anti-Castro armies and the Cusanos who wanted to go back in and take the regime. These groups had different funding, Prio-Socarras and the Trafficante mob had one element and the CIA had another. In short, there were different groups who wanted to go in and take Cuba. But Kennedy began to oppose them. There's a famous scene with George Smathers, the old family friend at a dinner down in Florida, where he leans over to Kennedy and says, 'Let's kill that S.O.B. Castro,' and Kennedy breaks a plate on the table and says, 'We're not going to have any more of that talk.' So he had begun, really, to actively oppose them and talk about changing the CIA in a way that would give him real intelligence information.

Whether he was completely out of that mold in a given instance, who knows? I mean he went to brinksmanship over the missile crisis. I always found it interesting, in this regard, that the Navy satellite pictures of the missiles in Cuba came from were contracted out for their photo reduction, analysis and enlargement to a firm in Dallas, Texas, called Jagger Chiles Stovall. The main photographic analyst for that firm was Lee Harvey Oswald who was working there in the weeks that the Cuban missile pictures appeared. So, I think even that crisis was engineered by Navy intelligence and the intelligence structure. But Kennedy was willing to go to a brinksmanship position on that issue. I talked to bomber pilots at Wright Patterson who told me that they put engineers on board the SAC bombers that day and they don't put the engineer on unless they're going to load the nuclear weapon. I was told that they came within 30 seconds of fail-safe from going into Cuba with nuclear attack. So they got very close, so as I say, he's a ruling class element, came from bad money, but he began to make decisions in late 1963 that endeared him to no part of the standing intelligence structure and the covert government so they took him out, replacing him with someone more reliable like Lyndon Johnson who had done their dirty work through Brown & Root company and other major military contractors for years.

Corey Dubin: *We've talked a lot about the Nazi network, the construction of the U.S. national security state with the Gehlen* *organization, Barbie, Schwend, Bormann himself, Walter Rauff in Chile, the mobile gas chamber nut, all these people went to Latin America thanks to Dulles, the Catholic church, and they set up these networks...*

John Judge: And Henry Kissinger, of course.

Corey Dubin*: Right. Now, how did they relate to two things: the development of these fascist national security states in Latin America, the death squad states of Argentina before Chile, El Salvador, Guatemala, and how do they relate to the Medellin cartel in Colombia and the cocaine trade?*

John Judge: The real basis of the modern cocaine trade is a setup in Bolivia by Klaus Barbie using a group of native fascist killers called the 'Handmaidens of Death,' and headed up at the period by Joachim Fieblekorn, a German national who came there and helped set it up under Barbie. But Mengele also traveled in and out of Bolivia and Colombia and Paraguay and had his hands into this cocaine traffic that formed the basis of funding for the future fascist states. I don't think there's any separation. I think that everywhere these Nazis were helped, like you mention Walter Rauff, he came as a technical expert to Pinochet and he's the guy who, as you say, ran the mobile ovens. They knew the technology, they knew how to do a coup d'état, they knew how to undermine a society, they knew how to kill the opposition off effectively and they had all the old techniques as well as 40 years of new technology. They put into power in those countries people who would support both the U.S. cold war policies and manipulation and corporate expansion, cheap labor, theft of resources, the whole agenda of the concentration of wealth and the genocide continued in those countries, experimentation with chemicals and other kinds of things on the population, expendable populations basically, a bloodbath that increased to the current period now when it's obvious to everyone the level of deaths that are going on there.

The Nazis control the financing and the model for whole sectors of the world, especially those areas containing key resources. These areas were known in, large pan by the end of World War II by the Natural Resources Defense Board and then that knowledge was implemented greatly by satellite photography so that they know now almost everywhere in the world where there's any significant deposit of a mineral or material they need. One of the most mineral-rich areas of the world is the interior of Guyana, especially in the gold rich and uranium rich sector around Matthews Ridge where populations have attempted to move into those areas since the 1900's for development. In fact, that was the sixth of seven places chosen for the deportation site for the Jews in the period before the final solution. The next to final solution was to move the Jews somewhere and they moved 50 Jewish families up to Matthews Ridge in the 1930's. Eichmann and von Bolschwing, as part of their deportation plans and for whatever reasons it didn't work out as an agricultural reality and then Israel was chosen and an agreement was made with the Zionists to set up Israel instead. This period shows that they already knew where they wanted to displace the populations that were giving them trouble around key resources and why did they want to move populations? 'To exploit resources' What the labor is worth to them is like the miners here in this country who were told in the 1930's that if the mine begins to collapse, push the mules out first because mules cost money to replace while there is an endless supply of human labor. It's that son of mentality, that this is expendable labor, *untermenschen*, useless eaters, and useless mouths. So the land is held by oligarchies, used for cash crops, the population starves or labors at a menial level and continues the corporate expansion. This was really the implementation of the Nazi programs in the third world, the 'camp' mentality and there were camps similar to Jonestown in Chile Colonia Dignidad, the German run camp that's there and implements the worst son of torture. Michael Townley Welch was there and did decapitations. It's one of the worst places in the world and is still in existence.

These secret camps existed throughout; the death squads existed and were trained in Nazi torture techniques. You may remember a rather infamous CIA agent brought that technology in and was eventually killed by the Tupamara guerillas. He's depicted in the [Costa-Gavras] movie *State of Siege:* Dan Mitrione. He was a boyhood friend of Jim Jones and they knew each other in Indiana earlier on and Mitrione brought these torture techniques, the thumb screw, all of the technology of the Nazi torture was adopted by CIA and then exported into these emerging fascist states. So pan of it was the anti-communism and pan of it was the exploitation of labor, but it was under those two rubrics that the Nazis could really function and that 'was their agenda anyway. So, they helped to put these key people in power. Their money helped to keep them there. They protected the Nazis and helped them continue to make their profits and explore the extension of fascism all around the world so that there would be no countries outside of the Soviet Union where they didn't have a stranglehold on the natural resources.

That's one-third of their plan for the end of the century. The second was to destabilize Eastern Europe, which is going on now, the reunification of Germany, the old Hitler dream, and the destabilization of Poland and the buffer zone between the Soviet Union and the rest of the capitalist countries. The third is what they call Air Land Battle 2000 or now they have a new name for the nuclear approach called SIOPSSeven where they'll try to go in and destroy the Soviet leadership in the bunkers with missiles that penetrate 600 feet under the ground, then the nuclear bombs go off. All these kinder, gentler technologies that make nuclear war more of a nightmare are being considered by Bush along with MX and the Star Wars and the Trident and all the first-strike capability for Air Land Battle 2000, which is the name they talk about in the army journals, it's full scale nuclear and chemical biological attack by the turn of the century and this idea of the winnable nuclear war you preserve a certain capacity of the population and the industrial potential and then you've won. That's, I think, still in the minds of these people. Despite what they say on the outside, that it's all *glasnost* and *détente*, that really they're going for broke in terms of eventually destroying the last vestiges of socialist or progressive rule anywhere in the world. They just can't tolerate it.

Even little Nicaragua, which poses no economic threat, the idea of a working model of socialism and self-rule anywhere in Central America is beyond what their fascist mentality can tolerate. If you took the people in the third world and Central and Latin America and their experience and got them into a world court and let them testify about what the United States had done, it would not be different from the old Nuremberg trials. What's different is that the technology of death has escalated. You no longer have to pick the Jew up and put them in the oven, you can drop the oven out of the sky onto the person. But the victimization and the horrors are the same and if the tables were turned, if those countries could speak the real history, we Americans would have to ask the same questions as the Germans had to ask themselves: How could it happen here? How could it go on without somebody saying something? Instead, we 're distracted by the consumerism, by the commoditization, by the sports, by anything that they can use to keep us from understanding what our moral position is in the world which is that we're continuing the specific tenets of fascism from the 1930's, whether it was in Germany, Spain, or elsewhere and the technology and techniques of that fascism were brought directly here and pervade almost every area of technology. The secret government needed even more money to implement their plans and the multi-billion dollar scale of drugs, control of raw drugs especially. What researcher Wendy Govier thinks we're seeing now is that they're going to move out of substances that you have to carry across borders into synthesizing the drug response.

This drug that's being looked at Yale and Harvard, Buprinex or Buprinephrine, which basically stimulates the same pheromones in the brain and stimulates the endorphins, gets that operating, becomes a replacement drug for both heroin and cocaine and can be synthesized. That's ultimately the tool, you don't have to carry anything in a package, you don't have to secrete anything, and you don't have to rely on a grower down in Colombia or what the politics of the situation are. As long as that's in place, then we're going to send U.S. troops in to make sure that we directly control the fields as we did in Turkey and Vietnam with the Meo tribes we paid off to grow the opium. But why go second hand and third route? It's cheaper and more direct to synthesize the response and addict people directly in other ways. They introduce and test these new drugs, crack, and ice, try out different things that can be developed here. But they control the labs, they control the routes, they control the origins, the U.S. intelligence agencies and the fascists and I think that they see these drugs as a simple way to have social control, exercise political manipulation, and profit beyond their wildest dreams, doing what was necessary in order to set it up. The specific links to the Medellin Cartel are that as you move historically out of the period of Barbie, the routes change from Bolivia to Colombia, but it's the same cocaine, it's not a different group. I mean these people, the teams, go way back. Theodore Shackley, who is central to the Contragate operations and the movement of the drugs for that enterprise, also ties in with the Nugan Hand Bank and the movement of drugs and drug profits during the Vietnam period. He goes all the way back with Henry Kissinger to the 970th Counter Intelligence Corps which moved Klaus Barbie out of Germany in the first place.

Corey Dubin: *In closing, John, then essentially what you 're saying, and this can be a short one, is that the United States' intervention in Colombia is designed to gain and retain control over the cocaine trade.*

John Judge: Yes. It's to have that control, 'control the routes and the profits of it and also the social benefits or social costs fit in terms of who's going to get busted and how it's going to be played out politically here in the United States. We know that the typical cocaine user is not a 17-year-old black youth. They don't have the money for it. The graffiti in the 70's [wrote that] cocaine is god's way of telling you that you're making too much money. It's more common with white professional males in the mid-40's range and that's the standard user. Crack, maybe, because it's more specific and more deadly, was introduced for experiment purposes in the Black community and a Black youth will more likely be a crack user than somebody at a different level. But it's a control that exists on every level - how much it's cut by, what price it has on the streets, whether it dries up for a period and is replaced by a different drug, and who deals it. The cost of dealing on the street is not money, it's not money payoffs to the police, it's political information about what's happening on the street, 'who's organizing and what's happening. So even if it were a random meeting between Huey Newton and some cocaine dealer that led to Newton's death, it doesn't mean that the government had no involvement.

H. Rap Brown tried to stop heroin coming into the Black community and that led to the shootout at the bar that eventually got him put into prison. One of the agendas of the Black Panther Party, Newton, and others was to get those drugs out. They were considered genocidal in the Black community. If these were just some Black opportunists living off of a drug trade they would have been pushed out of the community. It was clear that this was not what this was about, that this was entrenched, intelligence-run and had taken over. The independent labs had disappeared by the mid 60's; whatever there was of consciousness expanding or clean drugs was gone and chemical warfare was introduced - drugs laced with other things – and that's still the case. Worse and worse drugs, from the soporifics to cocaine, heroin, and the dependency drugs to PCP and those drugs that make people violent, get them social benefits - the crime that surrounds drug use is a benefit to them in terms of crackdown.

The violence gives them their excuse for going after people, but the basic operation is to control those drugs from point of origin in Colombia or elsewhere, to point of use. There's no other way they would do it. They're western, they're methodical and they're going to milk any given operation for everything it's worth, including involving and compromising potentially progressive elements that might feel they were doing something else by taking marijuana around or that kind of thing. They have got the political information on them and have them by the short hairs if it comes to pulling them off the street or compromising them or putting them over a barrel. So I think they get nothing but benefit out of that drug control and they've known it for many years. The British knew it with the opium trade in China and we picked up our intelligence skills from the British and followed the same patterns because they work.

THE FOURTH REICH

Speech by John Judge, San Luis Obispo, December 1989

The last few nights down in Santa Barbara I did a fairly extensive presentation but I thought since this was a smaller and a little more intimate crowd that maybe I would just outline some of the general themes and topics in Mae's work and my own and then we could focus more on questions and answers and see what people are interested in.

I started the work in this area with the Kennedy assassination back in 1968. I read a book, *Rush to Judgment*, which is not the book I'd recommend now, written by Mark Lane. Over the years I came to understand Lane was the official government critic planted in the case in order to distract attention from the real solution and who to this day will shrug his shoulders at you if you ask him who killed Kennedy. He ended up, among other places, as attorney for Jim Jones and, more recently, became the lawyer for John W. Hinckley, Jr., a case that I did quite a bit of work on, and the attempted assassination of

Ronald Reagan. But I started with the Kennedy assassination. I went through the 26 volumes of the Warren Commission Report and about 300 cubic feet of material that was in the National Archives. I began to see connections between those same figures and those names in the later assassinations - Robert Kennedy, Martin Luther King and Malcolm X. I began to follow the work of some of the other researchers like Penn Jones, whom I just had the chance to see in Texas.

I went down there for the November 22nd anniversary. About ten of us came out to the grassy knoll; it was raining out there. Penn comes every year. He was a feisty, independent, weekly newsletter editor in Midlothian, Texas, a suburb of Dallas, who was probably one of the first researchers on the scene. He began asking the right questions. He was at the Trade Mart waiting for Kennedy to show up for a luncheon there when he heard he'd been shot. He got in the car and drove down to the site and began to look around, see what people had seen, and talk to other news reporters. His major contribution to the work area, and we may get some of his archives at the Mae Brussell Research Center, one of our purposes is to serve as a repository for the real first generation researchers, but his major work was in uncovering the deaths of the witnesses in the case. He tracked over the years about 175 mysterious deaths just in relation to John F. Kennedy's murder.

There were hundreds of other deaths that surrounded the major assassinations and also the political scandals of the ensuing years, Watergate, Contragate. I didn't find out about Mae Brussell's work until 1972 when her article, 'Why Was Martha Mitchell Kidnapped?' was printed in The Realist. That article concerned the command structure behind Watergate at a time when they were still calling it a 'bungled burglary.' Mae named all the key figures in the White House staff and in the

Committee to re-elect the President, all the way up to Richard Nixon and how they inter related in the scandal. When Martha Mitchell began to talk about the reality that she lived in with John Mitchell and began to say that the country was going to go so far right we wouldn't recognize it, she was grabbed by L. Patrick Gray and some of his minions and dragged out to a motel room in California then pushed into a window when she tried to get on the phone, and then given painful injections from that point on. She died of the same rare carcinoma cancer that Jack Ruby died of in prison and told her doctor that she was being injected with cancer. In the ensuing four years of her life she was so totally surrounded and imprisoned that she never even saw her own daughter up until the time of her death and Mitchell closed the doors on family or friends viewing at the funeral home. But Mae caught on very early as to why she was kidnapped and had to be silenced, because she was talking about the dirty things and the behind the scenes reality of the Nixon administration and the secret government.

Mae started her work in 1963 when her daughter Bonnie wrapped up a teddy bear to send to Lee Harvey Oswald. She saw him beaten up in the jail and, somewhat reflective of Mae's compassion about the world, she wanted to send him a teddy bear, getting it wrapped just in time to see Oswald murdered by Jack Ruby in the basement of the jail. Mae as a housewife in Carmel from a relatively affluent family, the I. Magnin family, daughter of Rabbi Magnin, a prominent figure down in the Los Angeles area began to wonder what kind of world she was bringing her kids into and began with the newspaper and magazine articles in that first year on the Kennedy assassination. When the Warren Commission Report came out in 1964 she got a copy and spent eight years cross-reference indexing it – not just indexing it by names, but also correlating them. She has about 18,000 pages of typed material just on that in the Archive.

She worked for 25 years from that point on until her death. For 17-1/2 of those years she was a broadcast journalist on small stations in Carmel and Pacific Grove and she did a weekly radio show, if you can imagine 862 consecutive weekly shows, where she took the news of the week and what she was finding out in the research and broke it down and interrelated it. Starting with maybe week number 226 or 227, she started sending the tapes out to interested people, then eventually sent source sheets along with them. Initially she called this 'Dialogue Conspiracy' and later 'World Watchers International.' She came over that time to subscribe to 15 daily newspapers, 150 periodicals a month, and read hundreds of books a year, breaking down the information in them. So part of our task is not only to preserve that collection which is 6,000 books, 42 four-drawer filing cabinets filled with tens of thousands of newspaper clippings in order in her filing system, and her written works, but also to transcribe her words from those 17-1/2 years of weekly shows and to computerize them in a way that they can be easily indexed and accessed. *[This remains a goal, although the possibility of obtaining this material seems remote. The best online archive of Mae's material can be found in the late researcher Robert Falotico's website, www.worldwatchers.info. -Editor's Note]*

What she found in the Warren Commission documents were the names of the people central to setting up Lee Harvey Oswald as the patsy in the case; who it was that lied about him and got him the job at the Book Depository and moved him into position; who it was that said he owned a rifle and a gun when he did not; and who it was that handled and then destroyed the key evidence in the case and covered up in the autopsies and ballistic work and the legal cover-up later of the Warren Commission itself.

She went into the historical background of the Warren Commission members to find out what motive they might have had for lying on the Commission and the central theme that she developed- and it was for me the key theme that linked her work to mine.

In '72 when I first read the Martha Mitchell article I called Mae up right away because we were on the same track. I was living in Dayton, Ohio at the time. There was an article maybe this big about the Watergate break-in in the Dayton Daily News that named the four or five people that were arrested, but just on the basis of their names I phoned my mother at home in D.C. that day and said 'You should follow this story - these people that were arrested were connected with the murder of John F. Kennedy.' E. Howard Hunt and Frank Sturgis are among the central characters in the anti-Castro Cuban circles and Sturgis was the one who testified to the Warren Commission that Castro was responsible for killing Kennedy and planted one of the many stories that are meant to mislead people away from what actually happened on November 22nd, 1963 which was a covert, military coup d'état by the Joint Chiefs of Staff and the takeover of this country and the democratic electoral process... and those people have been in control of this country since that day. They jockey from time to time with each other about who's going to be on top when they go to outright martial law. They create scandals in order to do that jockeying and spill the beans on each other and we get a peek in the window at those points - that's what Watergate was, that's what Contragate has been orchestrated scandals.

But Mae noticed a pattern. Three things mainly: One was not only the witness deaths, but the murders of progressive people, of musicians, of labor leaders, of lecturers, of professors, of people who would speak out and organize against the rise of fascism within a democracy. This was a pattern that she also discovered historically in the Weimar Republic in Germany. At the end of the 20's and up into the early 30's there were a series of 400 unsolved political murders of these sorts of people in Germany that paved the way in silence for the rise of Adolph Hitler at the end of the Weimar Republic. The German government there said they knew the murders were politically motivated but they could not solve them. Then Mae began to track thousands of deaths here in the United States that she attributed to Death Squads operating here under the aegis of the U.S. intelligence agencies. So that's one main theme of her work and at one point she wanted to do a book combining many of the files. She has whole file drawers just called 'Deaths' that are about who these people are, how they died strangely, and what connection they had to the cases or to the politics of the time. She asked the unnerving questions that others don't ask about deaths of people.

Another major theme for her, and I think her central one, was the involvement of Nazi war criminals, Nazi scientists, spies, key figures in. both the German and Japanese fascist regimes and in the European revanchist elements. The czarist Russians (the white Russian community that formed an alliance with the emerging fascism of Spain, Italy and Germany in the 1920's and 1930's), the international grouping known as the Solidarists and the Eastern European revanchist elements that wanted to take their countries back from Bolshevik rule or Soviet domination, fed in quite conveniently to the cold war structure that Allen Dulles and his brother John Foster Dulles and others were creating here in the United States. The Dulles scenario called for continued world hegemony and the development of the national-security state, the military' industrial complex, the police-intelligence apparatus that has ruled our country since the late 1940s, and they killed Kennedy in Dallas, thereby putting themselves in an ultimate position of power today.

What Mae found totally surrounding the key figures in the Kennedy case were the top Nazi elements or the people that helped to cut the deals to move these Nazis into the United States and around the world at the end of World War II. Larry Flint printed one of her articles, 'The Nazi Connection to the John F. Kennedy Assassination' in Rebel magazine. By the second issue someone had come into the editorship that blocked her from putting any further articles in. But that, I think, is probably one of the groundbreaking pieces of work, this Nazi connection, and she went into it over and over and where these people were. She was still working at the time of her death on an individual in the Pentagon Plans Division for 30 years by the name of Fritz Gustav Anton Kraemer, who has the same name and appears to have the same history as a Fritz G.A. Kraemer who was a top lieutenant to Adolf Hitler and responsible (with Dietrich Pieper and others in the SS) for the Malmedy massacre.

His son, Sven Kraemer, is a key figure in the National Security Council. He was one of the two people who stole the Carter briefing books for the Debate gate scandal and Fritz Kraemer served at the top levels of the National Security Council for many years as well. He is closely related to General Daniel Graham, the Star Wars promoter who had several institutes for that purpose in Washington, D.C. which Kraemer was part of. Kraemer still has his little monocle and swagger stick and was a mentor for both Henry Kissinger and Alexander Haig, two people on what I call the 'George Bush team' that's in power now. They operate quite effectively behind the scenes to manipulate both foreign and domestic policy in the current era and were responsible along with Bush for pushing Reagan out of power March 31 1981 when they hit him and nearly killed him there in Washington, D.C. and Bush took over the government. Alexander Haig let us know that by coming out of the Situation Room argument that in part saved Reagan's life but not his presidency and announced that 'Gentlemen, I am in charge here until the vice president returns.' And that was exactly the situation. And when the vice president returned he was in charge.

When the Contragate scandal began to break, in the earliest testimony of MacFarlane, Meese and

Webster, all three identify in early press statements and before the Tower Commission the single day that they remember the first Presidential Finding being signed to authorize the shipment of arms to Iran in exchange for the hostages and that day is the 15th of July 1985. If you go back into the newspapers for that day as I did in my Reagan clippings, you'll find that that's the day when Ronald Reagan was in prostate surgery for nearly eight hours and there was an acting president of the United States officially designated George Bush. That's why I believe Reagan can't remember her signing it, because he didn't. That's why Bush's boy, Oliver North, had to shred it so that Bush's signature would never be seen. Bush is, I think, responsible for the whole tenor of the period, the dealings with Iran going back to what Barbara Honegger tried to expose when she worked with the help of Mae's files which she calls the 'October Surprise' the earlier arms dealings to hold on to the hostages in Iran until Reagan could get into office and so they were released right at the time of his inauguration.

These kinds of dirty dealings are nothing new for George Bush who has a history with the CIA dating, I believe, back into the

1950's. Oswald's CIA babysitter and controller in Dallas, long-time spy, anti-Bolshevik element, a white Russian, an oil magnate and geologist named George de Mohrenschildt, lost two personal fortunes to the communists - one in the Soviet Union and one in Cuba. George de Mohrenschildt, in his personal address books in the 1950's and 60's, included George Bush in Midland, Texas during his early oil speculation. Bush's connections with the CIA back to that time have been outlined in FBI memoranda and both of these memoranda are in connection with FBI debriefings concerning aspects of the assassination of John F. Kennedy.

Mae called him 'Killer Bush.' She, in fact, did leaflets about his relationship with the Cuban terrorists who came into the United States to plant the bomb that killed Orlando Letelier, the Chilean ambassador, in a car that was blown up in D.C., and tried to expose that. Mae was not the sort who would print that up and take it out to a small meeting like this, but instead she went to the Republican National Convention and tried to tell the Republicans who Bush was and passed it out there. She was able to see over that period the same lawyers, the same coroners, the same officials show up again and again, the same modus operandi in lying about the ballistics, the way the bullets went, setting up the patsies - the same pattern again and again in each of these major political assassinations.

Thirdly, I think Mae's other major work was to track other types of covert activity, including domestic operations of intelligence agencies, which is generally an area that little of the progressive press that criticizes the CIA and almost none of the current panoply of ex-intelligence agents that get up on podiums now and talk deign to mention. The idea that the CIA would spend $10 million to influence an election in Nicaragua or millions before that in hundreds of other countries since the end of World War II, probably billions altogether, but wouldn't spend a penny or lift a finger to make sure that the elections here in the United States came out right, are really matters indicative of the kind of American chauvinism that thinks that it happens in Third World countries but not here. But I think they just use the Third World countries to test the techniques until they find the one that works the best and then they bring it home.

Bill Moyers, in his Secret Government tape suggests that there's this legitimate government and from time to time to get certain things done they go out and hire these sorts of seamy thugs, killers, drug dealers, gun runners, that don't really represent the best democratic aspirations of the society but its underside... and they really shouldn't do that because these people go out and they operate on their own and discredit them. I'd suggest that the reality is the opposite, that those thugs, killers, drug and gun runners are the government and that they, in tum, with the huge profits they make, hire the boys in the three-piece suits that stand up in front of you and let you think you have a democracy in this country.

The reality is that whatever there was of a democracy, (and of course, that can be argued all the way back to the genocide of the native American people and the introduction of slave labor to build the wealth of this country and its continued exploitation of labor and resources around the world so that we can be 6% of the world population), consumes 30% of its resources and 60% of its energy pie every year. Even internally, wealth is concentrated in so few hands that under 2% of the population owns over 60% of all lands; if you talk just privately owned lands, it goes up to 95%. Over 95% of all the stocks and the lion's share of the natural resources in this country are controlled. Close to 80 to 85% of the corporate fronts that exist are in the hands of these families through interlocking boards of directors and corporate manipulation. So, the concentration of wealth is now worse even than when Ferdinand Lundberg wrote about The Rich and the Super Rich. The number of people living on anything besides credit is very small in this country because the dollar is worthless and they issue it on the basis of not even the inflationary gold and silver standard but on the whim of the Federal Reserve. They know that it's worthless.

The stock market would have gone last year had not the Bank of England intervened at the last moment and given unlimited credit to the leveraged buyers for the major stock houses. When they ran out of money as they did in the 1930's, the stocks collapsed and would have collapsed under natural conditions here.

The banks are showing themselves to be the paper money operations that they were set up to be and have been drained effectively. From time to time now the government has to step in and subsidize the bank failures in order that the reality of the domino chain doesn't happen. So these people have really gutted the economy. They own so much industrial and technological capability that they no longer need the labor that's represented by the vast population of this society and it's that concentration of wealth, commoditization of the human situation, surplus of either goods or labor depending on how you look at it. Naturally, the other side of the coin is that the same technology, if turned to human needs, could mean that we might work 2-1/2 weeks a year each and provide all the clothing and housing, cars, radios and televisions that anyone could live with comfortably. But the point of this society, its priorities under those people who are in a position of privilege, is not to have equity, not to have justice, not to have human dignity, but to have instead a hidden surplus, a hidden paradise that we could live in, expended and wasted instead on war preparation and the vast commercialization of society.

My friend Carl Chatzky in Baltimore says that what capitalism does is alienate all of us from every aspect of our natural human and community experience and then sells those things back to us in their most distorted form. And I think that's exactly what happens. Commercialization of the population took its toll in fascist Germany to the point that since the labor was expendable; they used to say to the mineworkers in the 1930's, 'When the mine is about to collapse, push the mules out first. It costs money to buy a mule. You we can replace.' That's certainly the mentality they have towards major sectors of this society and I don't think any of us can honestly say that we don't know which sectors of the society are expendable to them. I mean, all we have to do is look a little bit beyond the edge of our house, if we have one, and see who lives on the streets, who's institutionalized, who lives in the prisons, who lives in the psychiatric wards. These were the first victims of the holocaust in Nazi Germany, the first people to die began dying in 1937 1938. First vast segments of the society were put under a forced-sterilization program. Psychiatry and eugenics were the two major pseudo-sciences of the 20th century and they was hand-in glove in that period, so psychiatric conditions were diagnosed, were also held to be genetic conditions very directly and that language is back in the papers right now.

The term 'sociobiology' has been renewed, that's the title of Carl Jung's old journal in that period. 'Racial Hygiene' and 'sociobiology' were the themes of Jung who told his psychiatric students to read Mein Kampf and those psychiatrists determined that there was a genetic pool that was worthless, that it was 'life unworthy of life' and that they were expendable. And so, every major psychiatric institution had forms. They set up what they called a 'Public Benefit Transportation Society' of buses and vans to transport the psychiatrically designated 'incurables,' feeble-minded, retarded, whatever term they used, to six central killing centers. It was the psychiatrists of Nazi Germany, still respected, their textbooks still used today, many of them and their students came here to the United States or continue to practice there, it was the psychiatrists who invented the gas chambers, who invented the crematoria, and the technology of death that would eventually be used as they were brought in as the experts at Bergen Belsen and Auschwitz and elsewhere. The inmates of the institutions there were killed to the tune of 300,000 in a period of a few years. Seventy-eight percent of the inmate population would die in the first burst of holocaust fury.

In any given society, when wealth concentrates to certain point, when the industrial capacity reaches a surplus capability, that means that labor is no longer useful. When the dollar becomes essentially worthless scrip and the economy is undermined in that situation, fascism arises. It's not dependent on a little swastika on your arm or a goose step or a crazy person named Adolf Hitler. It's an economic and political reality that has to do with those arenas and it's objectively the condition that we live under after 40 years of fascist rule in the secret government and councils of this country. The specific Nazi criminals and Nazi mentality went into the top levels of the Defense Department and the CIA' s entire Operations Division was formed by 350 Nazi spies under the directorship of General Reinhardt Gehlen, the head of Hitler's Armies East for intelligence for the entire Soviet Union. They were brought here from 1945 to '48 basically intact through the Army Historical Division.

I found it interesting when I went into the National Archives that the person who actually wrote the Warren Report was on Technical Duty Transfer from the Anny Historical Division, the drop-point for the Nazi spies. His name was Otto Winnacker and he was one of 26 official historians for Hitler's Reich. Even the phony CIA-run investigative teams of the Warren Commission wrote internal memoranda criticizing every line of the Warren Commission report in the five investigative areas. 'Where did he get this conclusion?' 'What's the basis for this?' Because they knew that even their own trussed-up investigation wouldn't support the conclusions of Mr. Winnacker who came in to write the official version of history. But Gehlen and his spies, Werner Von Braun, General Dornberger and the rocket scientists, built NASA and the whole aerospace and munitions industry of the southern rim that came to dominate the post-war economy. Oil speculation, land speculation in the southern rim - a whole new class sector arose that was at odds with Rockefeller and Mellon and Scaife and the other old eastern-establishment monies. From time to time they either balance the electoral ticket so that they 're both happy or they get close to being on top and fight among each other.

Radio Free America, Radio Free Europe, the propaganda arms of the cold war were peopled with the entire Byelorussian government, the White Russian government that was a Nazi puppet state during World War II and then was brought here at the end of the war and given positions in the intelligence agencies and in the propaganda machinery of what I grew up under, being born in 1947. I was led to think that there had always been an Iron Curtain, a Pentagon, a nuclear capability-that these were part and parcel of history and human existence-instead of understanding that they came from concrete historical conditions and a failure to destroy the threat of the fascist state of Germany. So those fascist ideologues were central to the development of events here, but even more central was the concentration of wealth so that they're now back in the same position of being the paid agents of the American equivalent of the Ruhr Valley in Germany.

My friends ask me how I can think this country is fascist - we can walk around, we can watch television, we can do what we want and we live well.

Well, if you were a good German, if you went along with the Nazi program in Berlin in the late 30's and early 40's, you lived well. They were looting the art and culture of the whole world. They were developing the highest level of technological capability and inventions and you could live the dream. They thought they were free, they thought that they lived in an ideal society - as long as you were willing to look the other way, to not ask questions, to not ask 'Where are the labor camps?' 'Why are people dying on the street?' 'Why is the person in the house next to me being taken away?' If you were willing to look the other way and not be involved, you could delude yourself in the same sense that I think here you can be distracted by the social programs and the commercial values that you 're given for what the 'good life' is. Up to a point, because as the economy erodes, those people even able to buy things on credit eventually end up in the street. They hit the wall of the inflated consumer prices as against what the owners of the economy were willing to pay for labor right at the end of World War II and that's when they came in with what you may remember as 'Lay-Away' plans, the first name for buying things over time. Eventually a whole credit economy was established so that $7 trillion now are out on credit in this economy and $500 billion are in the banks and $5 billion are in the FDIC to preserve all that. So when that balloon bursts, it'll be quite a bit worse than the 1930's stock market speculation balloons and the inflation of those periods. It's going to be a very clear economic demarcation, since most people don't own their cars, they don't own their houses, they don't own many of the appliances even that they use day after day. You could stretch what a middle class is out to maybe 6 percent of the population in this country and, increasingly, the nature of who's going to be homeless includes families, single mothers with children, and broader and broader sectors of the society as the economy crumbles and is unable to productively employ the useless eaters, the people that take up the space.

The RAND Corporation, as early as 1968, estimated that in order to have an ideal and comfortable world where everyone could live as the rich live, they would have to go back to 2 billion people, cutting the population of the world in half. Figures are probably up from that period. It's what we're doing abroad and here at home as well, but certainly in the Third World countries in an aggravated way.

The technology of death is 40 years down the pike since Nazi Germany and more efficient, certainly more deadly. We make the Nazi Hohenzollern machine look like a rubber band affair with the current military apparatus that we have-and it's a genocidal apparatus. Vietnam was a genocidal war; the war in Central America is that, it's a war of the deaths of the civilian population who are 85 to 95 percent of the war deaths in any modern war that the U.S. is involved with. John Stockwell had the honesty to admit that at least 10 million people have been directly killed by CIA operations since the end of World War II and I believe that the real figures of the world holocaust are greater than that in terms of direct U.S. involvement.

We live in a society where we're obviously manipulated, disempowered, and made to feel that we can't do anything about the decisions that are being made in our name but those decisions are not different than the decisions that were made by the Reich and, in fact, some of the central characters of that Reich are still in positions or their sons or daughters or their underlings are in positions to determine that policy in the United States.

The current rubric is no longer anti-communism, which has pretty much shot its capabilities to get people excited even to the point that now we look at Gorbachev and the emerging detente or at least destabilization of Eastern Europe and reunification of Germany, two of Hitler's dreams being realized at long last, as a good thing. So, instead we 're told that what we need to fear now, the real terrorists, are the 17-year-old black kids in the community that take 'crack' they're threatening all of our lives in the same way that the boys with the pop guns on this year's cruise ship or the airplane that won't be allowed to land in Miami is what's supposed to get us shaking in our boots. Oliver North wants you to believe that he built a security fence around his house to protect his family from Abu Nidal! It's coming out in the investigation now of Pan Am 103, the crash over Lockerbie, Scotland, that the bomb may have been provided by a Syrian, Mansur Al Kassar, who works in the same offices with Abu Nidal. Mansur El Kassar is one of the numerous gunrunners who were used to buy guns for the contras by Oliver North and Richard Secord and the secret team. So they were funding the specific people that also arm Abu Nidal. I think if Abu Nidal came to North's house it would be to have dinner *mano é mano* and that the reason North put up the fence was because he was afraid that we'd figure out who he is and what he's done to the American democracy and how slimy a character he really is. Because they aren't afraid of the Soviet Union, they've been militarily ahead of them for many years. They aren't afraid of the Third World; they do genocide directly in the Third World. The only enemy they have left is 'us.

If we figure it out, then the gig is up. The last frontier that they have to conquer is what George Orwell called the... space between our ears.' And they're doing fairly well with it. They've got us to a point where we're a post-literate society. That's why the FBI, I believe, goes into the libraries to see who is still reading. The two or three percent of the population still that subversive that they haven 'just turned on the TV and given up thinking are fairly dangerous. No, I don't think they're looking for Soviet agents, I think they're looking for human intelligence, just as the Reagan administration came up with this interesting new idea of limiting access to documents that weren't themselves classified because they said that certain people using unclassified documents and putting them together could piece together a mosaic that would actually reveal national security secrets, sound like Mae Brussell?

I mean, I don't think they could believe what Mae was doing. They built a house across the street from hers that overlooked her house and she was warned ahead of time that it was for the sole purpose of spying on her. She went over once for 'hello to the neighbor and cup of sugar' and in the living room there wasn't any furniture, just a huge tape deck. And, when I went in to pack up her books while she was in the convalescent home dying of cancer, there were vans and trucks driving up and down the driveway of that house and there were hammers pounding and people talking day and night for about two weeks. I thought they were constructing something, but later I realized that they were dismantling the machinery of the house, because the morning that she died of cancer, at 7 A.M., that house burned to the ground.

The local Carmel Valley newspaper printed an article saying that the fire department refused to release the names of the owners of the house, the names of the current tenants at the time of the fire, and whether or not the tenants were the owners. 'State secrets in the fire department' in Carmel? I think this is fairly standard about how the secret government really operates. They can't let the connections be known and they block the news. So you have books that come out with holes in them or don't come out at all or come out briefly and are buried, not distributed. Jim Garrison's new book On the Trail of the Assassins about the Kennedy case has basically been bought up from the distributor and probably no more copies of that will get out. Books go out of print or they don't get printed at all.

Then there's just tremendous control of the media. The media is basically a corporate entity. ABC was bought not too long ago by Capital Cities, which was a major investment firm for William Casey and the CIA. General Electric now owns NBC, and Ted Turner is the only one that pretends to be some kind of an independent. I guess you can see from watching CNN News how independent he is. The newspapers were gone by the time of the depression, the corporate entities just bought out the competing ones. The wire services came in and it's easy enough to control the wire - no one else can afford to have foreign correspondents for the most part, so it isn't that hard to control. You don't have to buy out and compromise every reporter. You can do it with the assignment editor and the final copy editor on a newspaper to make sure that the wrong people cover the right story. The news is at this point little more than entertainment anyway and they're finally admitting it now. They have these, you know, docudrama sort of 'we'll recreate the news event for you with actors' and put little letters up so that you'll know that this is just the entertainment, so I think they certainly know how to manipulate that space between the ears.

They spent 40 years trying to perfect chemical means for it. They went to mass level at Jonestown on a slave population that they held at bay that was 80% black, 90% women, 30% children, elderly, psychiatric inmates, prisoners - the specific target groups that were named in Senator Ervin's report on The Government Role in Individual Behavior Modification (1974) as the potentially violent elements of the society, you know, the elderly, the women, and the ones they wanted to drag into the emerging California Center for the Reduction of Violence.

After Jonestown, both military intelligence and the international Nazis went to set up shop in Grenada for a long period and were, I think, responsible for continuing experimentation in the only building bombed in the U.S. invasion of Grenada, a mental hospital where 180 people were wiped out. The psychiatrist's left the inmates locked in their cells, the Air Force did the precision bombing, and then there was a mass burial.

The bodies in Jonestown were left to rot so that no one could tell that they had all been murdered and that there wasn't a single suicide. But the Guyanese grand jury, relying on the testimony of Dr. Mutu (?), their main pathologist, knew that the victims had been injected in the back of the left shoulder blade in 80% of the cases and the remainder were strangled or shot, every single person was killed. Nobody drank cyanide out of a cup because there was no cyanide pathology and there weren't 'bodies on top of bodies' that kept them from getting the count straight. Their first lie was that the Guyanese didn't know how to count, that's how they explained the rising body count. But the truth was that 700 fled into the jungles surrounded by

British Black Watch, American Green Beret and Guyanese Defense Forces whose officers were trained by Dan Mitrione, a rather notorious CIA torture trainer who was a boyhood friend of Jim Jones. Those troops over the period of ensuing days, five to six days, murdered them in the jungle and dragged the bodies back into Jonestown.

In the photographs the bodies are face down, they are in calm repose, they don't show any signs of cyanide rictus or splaying of limbs that you get from cyanide, which is a cholinesterase inhibitor. Had they been autopsied, they would have shown massive drugging. There were enough drugs on site in Jonestown to drug the entire population of Georgetown, Guyana, over 120,000 people for a period of a year. These drugs were being used daily by the sixty nurses and one doctor there, Dr. Schacht, on that population, different combinations of drugs, torture techniques, public beatings, and sexual humiliation, public rape, a variety of techniques that they used on the children and adults in order to create a slave labor camp. They were trying to build in a suicide response, but when push came to shove and the people knew that it was the real drill and not a phony one, they revolted and fled into the woods, but they were captured and killed over the ensuing days and they were left to rot with no fluid autopsy.

The Air Force Pathology Division planes and the American doctors who arrived on the scene told Dr. Mootoo that they had forgotten to bring any medical bags or equipment with them, so they couldn't even do a fluid autopsy. The American Council of Medical Examiners wrote an open letter to the Army saying that they'd totally bungled the chance to find out what killed these people. They brought the bodies back in a condition where they couldn't even be identified, much less autopsied, and they did mass burials and covered up.

They were trying to create a batch of slave labor there in the Guyanese interior: Matthews Ridge is the site of manganese mines. There's manganese, copper, uranium, gold and some of the richest mineral deposits in the world in the jungles of Guyana near the Venezuela border in the Orinoco River Valley. Most of the gold mines are at Five Points and the others surround Matthews Ridge. In fact, as soon as the massacre was over, the evangelical community re-populated Jonestown with the Laotian tribes that grew and helped fly the opium out of Southeast Asia for the CIA. The Meo tribes, 12,000 people were brought in and then they were moved to Surinam.

That specific site, Matthews Ridge, had been populated continuously since 1909 with different labor schemes that began with the Nunan-Luckoo plan of that period. In fact, it was the sixth of seven sites chosen for eventual and final relocation of the Jews before the Final Solution was developed at the desk of Otto Albrecht Von Bolschwing and Adolf Eichmann. Fifty Jewish families were moved to Matthews Ridge in the late 1930's as an attempt to develop a site. The final one agreed on by the Nazis and the American Zionist community was Israel and the Jewish relocation happened with, in part, the collusion and collaboration of the fascists and the Zionists in that period. Matthews Ridge as a site saw a lot of use: Blacks from the UK were enticed to come back in there. It was a site where they wanted to see whether the thirty years of individual modification they had tested could be used on a mass group and in many ways it was successful and in some ways it was not, but it was done as a medical experiment. Larry Layton, the only person brought to trial here in the United States for the murder of Congressman Ryan, didn't shoot him but certainly was clearly part of the collusion that led to his death. Layton's father was head of all chemical and biological warfare research at Dugway Proving Grounds from 1956 to

1963. Dr. Lawrence Layton came out here to California afterwards, apparently something to do with the development and the research on the AIDS virus. His wife, Lisa Phillips Layton, was the daughter of Hugo Phillips who was the stockbroker in the 1920's and 1930's for l. G. Farben. The largest Nazi drug and dye cartel which helped to finance Hitler into power, it was eventually broken up as a cartel, but all of its subsidiary elements are now richer than l. G. was at the beginning and its largest American subsidiary is Solve Drugs.

The major stockholder in Solvay drugs was the Blakey family out of England whose son, George Philip Blakey was one of the top lieutenants to Jim Jones and married Debby Layton, Larry Layton's sister, at a posh English boarding school that she was sent to. So these people were not unconnected to the top levels of the military. Terry Buford, one of Jones' key lieutenants in setting up the international banking accounts was the daughter of Rear Admiral Buford who headed up Navy Intelligence for the whole 6th Fleet out of Philadelphia. They didn't just walk in off the street as drug addicts - they came from the top families in the same way that the women who were drugged and manipulated in the Charlie Manson scenario by military intelligence in order to discredit the counter-culture, came from top military intelligence families themselves and were expendable or 'throw-away' children.

John W. Hinckley, Jr. also fits this description. He wouldn't go along with the family program like his older brother Scott, who was scheduled to have dinner with Neal Bush the night of the Reagan shooting and they canceled their dinner plans. The two families have been very close financially and socially for many years, the Bushes and the Hinckley's.

When Hinckley, Jr., sat down in the basement and plunked Beatle tunes on the guitar and wouldn't get with the program, they sent him to a psychiatrist named Rappaport who put electrodes in his head and programmed him and sent him out to be the bang-bang man in the Reagan shooting. None of his bullets hit Reagan, none of Sirhan 's bullets hit RFK, Oswald didn't fire a gun that day. About the only patsy who really did it was Mark David Chapman his bullets actually hit John Lennon - but he was just as programmed and set up as the rest of them, trained in the same circles. He got his military stance from Wilson and Terpil in Beirut, the two CIA arms dealers and gunrunners. And so, when you go into the background or ask questions about the deaths of these people, you find out that there are motive and means and opportunity that relate back to the international fascist networks and the U.S. intelligence agency. That's their little oyster, and their machinery.

On the other hand, I don't feel that the situation is hopeless. I feel that individuals like Mae were able to break the code of the 20th century's hidden secret. I think it's possible for us to understand and expose these people and I think that the reason they expend so much energy on that space between our ears is that we ultimately have a power that they don't understand and that they don't know how to control. But that has to do with re-establishing human trust and human decency between each other by understanding what Malcolm X meant when he said, 'If you read the newspapers long enough, you'll end up hating the people being oppressed and loving the people who are doing the oppressing.' It has to do with changing your relative position to the privilege that's been concretized in this society and renouncing that privilege and pulling that corporate consumer junk line out of your arm and relying no longer on a dying eonomy. What I was suggesting in the most recent World Watcher newsletter in my article 'Technology of Democracy' is that the idea of a representative democracy - and I won't end this talk by suggesting that you write to your congressperson - dates to the 1700's when travel was limited to a wagon or a horse, when several hundred miles was a matter of several weeks in terms of time that it took to get back and forth. When a meeting in New York or Philadelphia concerned dealings with people in North Carolina, there was only one alternative and that was to pick someone usually the person you liked to have around the least, put them on a wagon and send them up to be the representative so that you could hear what happened later and they could put your point of view across. We now live in the 20th century. We have instantaneous travel and communication. We have 98% of the population plugged into electronic media. They license those airwaves through the FCC because they are common property they belong to the people. They're right now under corporate control, but at least 30% of all airtime on electronic media ought to be paid for out of the tax dollar and reserved for full public debate on the issues that matter to us in our lives. The struggle that we have to wage right now, day in and day out, starting in the home and going out to the work place and the organization and the community wherever we live, is the struggle to establish democracy again.

Democracy is not what Bush and the press mean when they talk about the students in China or Lech Walesa in Poland, who was given $50 million by the 'Pope (who worked at Auschwitz for the Solve Chemical & Rubber Factory there and was one of the minions of the Nazi regime). Lech Walesa's father, in fact, was in charge of deportation of the Jews from the whole sector of Poland where he lived. Democracy in the verbiage of the cold war and the current media means any system that preserves privilege. And any system that threatens privilege in that doublespeak is called 'communism.' And that's all they mean. They don't mean anything about Marxism or philosophy or anything else. They mean a system that allows economic and capital penetration and privilege to exist and corporate manipulation and control: that's democracy. And anything that furthers that is what we're supposed to believe we want in the world.

But we no longer live in a democracy. We live in the illusion of one. What a democracy would do, it seems to me, is that any particular social decision that affected people would have to be made by those people that are affected. To fight for democracy or democratic rule is to constantly expand that definition to further include or more directly include all those people. Even the founding fathers, 'who were certainly more democratic than George III, preserved a class structure for the landed gentry and white males who were still in the privileged position of that society. Not everyone was accorded or allowed a vote, even up to the current period. And, in case the popular vote put the wrong person in, fairly early on they established the Electoral College so that by manipulation of the electoral votes they could change the results and put somebody else in. That's, in fact, how John Kennedy got in, Nixon won the popular vote and Chicago Mayor Richard Daley, the old family friend, changed voting machines and Chicago carried Cook County, which carried Illinois, which carried the Electoral College and took Kennedy into the presidency.

That manipulation along with, of course, many others, have been used to ensure that there isn't total or real participatory democracy in this society. But we're smarter than they were, hopefully, this many centuries down the pike (if history isn't retrogressive), and we can figure out that there's got to be more participation, not less. Five or six hundred representatives in congress don't even attempt to represent the vast hundreds of millions of people that live in this country. Have you been approached by them lately to find out what you think about an issue so that they can proportionally split their vote up to represent the electorate that put them in office? Or isn't their position that once they get the electoral mandate of a majority they are the people, and they'll make the decisions according to whim, lobby, whatever? And if they make the wrong ones, the military-intelligence community certainly has the money to blackmail them, or bully them, or bribe them, or bullet them into compliance.

It's not that big a job to take care of Congress, certainly not that big a job to take care of the presidency and if they get out of line, we've been given the message that they can kill them. In fact, the message that we were meant to get from the Kennedy assassination after the transparent lone nut Oswald thesis inevitably fell apart is, 'Yeah, we killed the S.O.B, what do you want to do about it? If we can kill the president we can sure as hell kill you.'

If we take that message to heart, if we take the message they give us day in and day out that we have no power to change anything, then the system works. But when we realize who we are and what we are and what we can do, then we could say no, we don't want representatives anymore. Let those congress people go out and do an honest day's work. Take them off salary, take back the media, debate issues, and have public referendum from local issues on up. I don't think it's necessary to have an income tax because you could take a 1% flat tax of corporate gross in this country and end the national debt in a year, besides, their black budgets, their narcotics profits pay for what's necessary. I think the purpose of personal income tax is merely to make us compliant and threaten us, put us all in a position of subservience. If we pay individual income taxes then I suggest that there ought to be a final page at the end after all those other figuring's that you do where you can draw your own pie and directly allocate your own tax money.

They, of course, won't allow it, but that's no reason for us not to, in a given community say, send out a letter to every residential P.O. box and address with a brochure that explains where the current tax dollar money goes, has a return envelope, and has a three-pan carbonless form. One pan you can keep at home to remind yourself how bad things are after you finish filling out how you want your taxes spent, one you can stick in with no legal status at the beginning with your tax dollars or lack of dollars, (however you file when you file it), and then the third you can send in to show how you want to spend your money to the address the envelope came from. An organization can tally those results, compare them to the local representative's voting record on tax allocation, hold a press conference, and let the representative explain why he or she is better at spending that money than you are. At least you will have planted the seed of an idea that I think a lot of people would like to think about, which is why shouldn't they be allocating their own tax money? These aren't things that have to be begged for and shouldn't be begged for from Congress at a national level. They are things that could be implemented and done, at a local level to start, as models, to spark the imagination of people. I think that most people in this country don't vote or participate because they've been convinced by this system that they have no power to change anything and, in fact that's true ' given the way that this system is rigged. If voting could change something, it would be illegal.

So I say put democracy back on the agenda. Figure out not only what kind of a system you live under, but what kind you want to live under. Take back control of your own life. Address the class privilege and the racism and the sexism that pervades the issue of personal support that I think is critical to understanding how to change society. Who gets support in this society and why and who doesn't and why not, is really an issue that's obfuscated and covered by that vast industry known as psychiatry which replaced personal politics with a 'professional' You know, we have an advice column in the national newspapers from Ann Landers and I find it ludicrous that it's even called an advice column because the only advice you get is to see a professional! The psychiatrists like her so much they made her an honorary member of the American Psychiatric Association. You see a professional because you've got an illness and when you go into the medical model you don't deal with why people might be doing drugs in this society, why kids might be running away from home, what's not functioning about this social structure.

Instead of facing those personal realities and the issues of support and the politics of that, we're told instead to blame the victim. The 17-year-old kid-selling crack to survive on the street is somehow the terrorist of the 1980's and 1990's that threatens us all. So we have Bennett, this American proto-fascist, the Joe McCarthy of the current period, foaming at the mouth about how 75% more prisons need to be established along with curfew laws, take people's drivers licenses and jobs away, force urinalysis in all the workplaces. They're setting up the fascism and they're even invading other countries. I mean, in any other analysis don't you know that American warships going to Colombia means that the U.S. is invading Colombia? But they tell you it's to stop the drugs. As Paul Krasner said at a recent lecture, 'Bush tells us 'just say no.' He tells the CIA, 'just fly low.''

They don't want to stop drugs. Drugs make them a million dollars a day in heroin alone just in Harlem. They produce the drugs, they create the drugs, and they control the drugs from the point of origin to the street. They no longer have independent labs in the United States. They no longer have independent dealers; nobody deals except the drugs they're supposed to. They replace and reduce the drugs on the street; they decide what they cost; and they run the whole operation top to bottom. They take the profits and pump them into the fascists for the overthrow of other countries, and then they want us to jump up and down thinking that there's this drug problem that's totally out of control and we have to understand the worst kind of measures, have the police go into the ghetto. They admit that the standard profile of a cocaine user is a professional white male in his mid 40's, but they keep looking for him down in the ghetto!

That's not what they're concerned about. What they're concerned about is an excuse that will work to let them establish more and more totalitarian control, something they can wave over here while they stab you in the back with this hand, distract your attention. We don't have to be distracted. We're not all so thick that we don't get it. But they've got a lot of us hooked into not trusting each other, trying to grab the little crumbs of the rotten system for ourselves, maintain ourselves one rung above each other on some little ladder that they've built, instead of understanding that we can withdraw from them, demand back control of our own lives. We can't issue monies as the economy goes to nothing, but we could issue credit. Credit is All American Sears everybody has credit, right? So we could form a public benefit corporation and issue credit to each other on an ethical basis. We could save the lives of a lot of people in this society when their phony money goes, because you don't need money. Money isn't wealth. Money is a means of exchange and communication for an economy, but it's not wealth itself and it doesn't represent it. The day after the stock market crash there wasn't any less labor available, not any less raw materials, not any less technological capability or factories or tools or equipment. The means of production were in place...

To say, 'You can't work today, there's no money' is like a carpenter saying, 'You can work today, there's no inches.'

So I say, re-establish the credit 'ourselves. We can issue it based on a non-inflationary standard: We could buy 30 different commodities on the world market, that's Borsodi's model, (an economist from the 30's who figured out the depression back then and went to alternate economies and rural revival). Thirty different basic commodities don't fluctuate in worth, so it's non-inflationary. You can issue it based on that for the initial part, and people establish credit. You can computerize it at a local level or otherwise, set up fairly simple barter systems. They rely on what the counter-culture of the '60's threatened part of what the fascists had against the counter-culture was that people shared houses and goods. They didn't all sit in individual units and each buy 16 lawnmowers per block, 16 washers and dryers, 16 televisions, you know, so that they replicated the little consumer model. Unfortunately, even the progressive groups do the same thing. Somebody last night asked me why we don't have a national newsletter. Instead of all the individual political groups putting out a newsletter, why don't they put out one newsletter? I said I'd fall over if even half the groups in this country would agree to do that. I don't know any group that doesn't want every page of the paper to be their news. I don't know groups even in a progressive community like Santa Cruz, who would put their resources together to buy even one set of top of the line computer equipment that could facilitate all of them because they couldn't agree on how to use it, how to give each other time. I mean, we've really been taught not to work together. Even when I grew up there were neighborhoods: Admittedly they were ethnically isolated and oriented, but they were neighborhoods.

There isn't even that now. There is no social cohesion and they wonder why kids are lost. They don't have jobs; they don't have a visible future. I mean, I figured out when I was ten when they tried to get me to sit under this little desk to avoid an atomic weapon that I was among crazy people and was in danger and wouldn't get under the desk! Whatever the bomb was I knew it was big enough that that desk wasn't going to save me. And then I realized that I was in a room, my little ten-year-old life in the hands of an adult that I couldn't trust because they'd have such a weapon.

Kids certainly realize that in a concrete way today; the nihilism that creeps in comes from that because there aren't other alternatives. There's nothing else visible. And we aren't even telling them the history. I mean, anyone in this room who knows the history of the 1960's, the anti-war struggle, the racial, women's, and gays' equality struggles, ought to be out talking to young people right now about those struggles. Otherwise they'll know as little of them as I knew of the extensive struggles in the 30's until I got to be almost an adult and found out some of the hidden history.

The young people are smart and they think quickly. They can keep up with all the images on TV. But they're isolated. They live in an historical environment and history isn't even required in school anymore in most of the states. They don't want the kids to remember that this is even supposed to be a democracy, much less how we got here. They want them to think that things have always been thus and to relate to the images of the stars and buy the right thing. So I think it's our responsibility to turn that consciousness around for ourselves and for others and to begin to relate to each other because if we do figure it out and do refuse, then they don't know what to do about it. I grew up in a generation that stopped a war into Laos and Cambodia, a much wider war than was originally planned. They got done with the Vietnam War.

They planned the Vietnam War as soon as Kennedy was dead. My mother was five levels above top security in the Pentagon; she was the highest-paid woman civilian employee of the Pentagon for 30 years. She was a manpower analyst for the Joint Chiefs of Staff, Deputy Chief of Staff for Personnel, and she determined and projected the overall national draft-call figures. They'd give her a current force level and a projected-force level. They'd give her a number of combat deaths expected for the period, and she had tables that would tell her how many would die of non-combat deaths in that period, how many would discharge under each category, how many would retire, how many would re-enlist, how many would enlist again, and therefore how many did you have to draft each year in order to come up with the projected force level figure? She had to project the figure for drafting that was given to the Selective Service System for breakdown into local board quotas. I asked her, 'When did they tell you they would escalate in Vietnam?' because she had to be among the first to know. (In October of 1963, Kennedy had put out a National Security Memorandum that called for withdrawal of all U.S. troops and intelligence personnel from Vietnam by the end of 1964. On October 10th, he said that he would 'scatter the CIA to the four winds,' which meant that he would move Bobby out of Justice into CIA and clean out the Gehlen network and the Nazi spies. He and his brother had threatened the oil depletion allowance, a tax write-off that even in 1963 meant $27 billion a year to the oil industry and financed electoral results in this country. He was pushing racial integration too fast for the southern rim. He was talking about detente with the Soviet Union and an end to the cold war. He was normalizing relations with Cuba and had refused to allow further attacks on Castro by those who wanted to kill him from the Cusanos community of anti-Castro Cubans. He was pushing arms limitation talks as well and an end to the nuclear arms race. He had broken with the agenda.

She said, 'Late November, 1963 they told me.' I said, 'The last week in November?' because the 22nd on Friday was when they hit him. 'The Monday following the assassination.' I said, 'A few more troops or advisers?' She said, 'I couldn't believe the figures.' She took them to the Joint Chiefs and she said, 'These can't be right.' But they said, you'll use them. 'This was November 25, 1963, probably the first civilian protest of the war in Vietnam.

They told my mother the war would last ten years and 57,000 Americans would die. 'Exactly on target, they know where they're going and what they're doing. But they planned an even broader war into Laos, Cambodia, the whole Southeast Asian sector, and that war my generation stopped. It stopped it here at home and it stopped it on the field where officers were getting fragged or shot by their own troops to a level that second lieutenants had a shorter life span than paratroop medics for a period. Soldiers sat down and refused in whole units in the field and the brass had to choose between a military that functioned and a war that they couldn't win and they brought the boys home.

The American GI movement that I was part of organizing was one of the central factors in the victory of the Vietnamese in that war and the eventual end of U.S. involvement there and in what George Bush and Ronald Reagan and those circles know as the 'post-Vietnam syndrome,' a syndrome of refusal that they're still afraid of that they were so afraid of happening in Grenada that they wouldn't let the U.S. press come in and film it. And it happened! The black troops in the 82nd and 101st Airborne are crack troops and refused on the field. An invasion that was supposed to take six hours took three days because the troops wouldn't shoot other English-speaking blacks. They switched over to the light-division concept, a primarily white troop, but they're still afraid that they can't take the American population and the American GI's into another war like Vietnam. We established the idea that there's such a thing as a bad war and we established that there's a right to say no to a bad war.

Those were fairly radical ideas that even two or three television generations haven't completely wiped out, but they'll wipe them out eventually if they can. And they'll go where they can and when they can under any cover that they can and any lie that they can invent. Aeschylus the Greek said 3,000 years ago, that the first casualty of war is the truth. It always is. We live in a society where, as William S. Burroughs said; 'If Magellan was an American and he sailed around the planet now and found out it was round instead of flat, we wouldn't tell anyone so that we could attack from the rear!'

We live under the aegis of someone like Henry Kissinger, who, in The White House Years says, 'History, to be successful, must be negotiated in absolute secrecy.' They make the decisions now behind the closed doors of the National Security State, but I say it's time for us to realize that those decisions belong not to them but to us and to take our history and our lives back.

Questions and answers

Abbie Hoffman?

I believe and have said for some time (and just recently got attacked as a 'nut case' in the Nation for saying) that Abbie Hoffman's death was not a suicide.

Abbie Hoffman got printed the only article about Bush's 'October Surprise' in any national publication he got it in Playboy before the election of Bush. He had good details because his source, I believe, was Jimmy Carter, silently through the aegis of his daughter, Amy, who was friends with Abbie and got arrested with Abbie protesting the CIA in Massachusetts. It's politically too hot for Carter to say himself, but this was a way to feed the information through Abbie. He was coming out with a book. It'll be interesting to see if the book ever surfaces, called Preserving disorder that is supposed to have more on this.

When he went to deliver the manuscript to Playboy Abbie had an automobile accident he ran into the back of a truck and he was still suffering up until the time of his death from injuries from that accident. He told his friend and long-time fellow activist David Dellinger, that his brakes had been tampered with in that situation. The last book he wrote was 'Steal This Urine Test' which had to do with a beginning political analysis of the upcoming war on drugs and the way it would affect people.

I don't agree with every aspect of Abbie's politics, but Abbie was clearly a symbol and a voice that remained radical from the 1960's period when Bush was coming into office and when they could ill afford it. In the same way, I believe, they could ill afford John Lennon coming off his heroin addiction and making albums and going to demonstrations as Reagan and the warfare machine came in in the 1980 election and had to wipe him out. So, I think it was as much symbolic as it was that Abbie posed a particular threat, although I think his connections with Carter posed the pressure that Bush would be further revealed in the October Surprise matters.

You don't, if you're smart about drugs (and Abbie was), take 150 capsules of phenobarbital to kill yourself. That's enough to kill 15 people. The coroner in the case could have determined an alcohol and phenobarbital overdose in a matter of an hour with a simple fluid autopsy. We didn't get a final read until five days later from a lab with a full toxicological schedule. You don't need that to determine that cause of death. It's fairly common and has some signs you can see in the situation, one of which is not what was noted in the original autopsy report, a trickle of blood under the nose.

It's too many Phenobarbitals, the alcohol level was tremendously high, and it was .6. His son said that Abbie was the kind of guy who, if he were going to do it, would wrap himself in the flag and jump off the top of the ITT building. Why would somebody who communicated as much as he did in his life not leave a note? He had plans to speak at several universities. He had just bought an airline ticket to go visit his mother. He had just written to Dave Dellinger a few days before saying it was a great time to be alive, that the campuses were active again and that things were happening.

The psychiatrists, of course, want us to believe that he was manic-depressive and they had him on a lithium substitute which itself might have been deadly enough in combination with those drugs, or by itself, to have killed. Many of the lithium salts corrode the entire blood, heart and artery system after a short period. So that could have killed him and they buried that in the autopsy. The specific coroner there in Bucks County for New Hope where the death happened is Mr. Roscoe, who also covered up the death of Jessica Savitch, another case that I worked on some years before.

She had produced three shows on Front Line one about the death of a top official in the NFL who

I believe was killed by the mob. The next to last show she did on Front Line was 'God's Banker' about the murder of Roberto Calvi, the head of the Vatican bank who presided over the movement of Vatican bank money and the scandal there that rocked the whole Italian government. She fingered in that show as the killer an individual named Francesco Pazienza, who at that time was not even under indictment for other financial dealings that led to his being jailed. Pazienza was openly a friend of Michael Ledeen, Henry Kissinger, George Bush, the NATO circles and P-2, the secret fascist government in Italy. So he was a character central to what was happening there in Europe under Kissinger's auspices and he was somebody who was dangerous at that point to finger. She showed that two thugs hired by him had been with Calvi in the last hours of his life before he was found hanging, supposed suicide, under Blackfriar's Bridge with $18,000 in his pocket. Now even the British government admits it wasn't a suicide.

Then came her last show on Front Line, and I was calling Mae each week as these came out saying, 'You're not going to believe what was just on TV,' because these were hard investigative shows. Savitch had been on cocaine up until about six months before, gotten off, and started to work hard on investigative journalism and on her career. She was bucking for a position as an anchorwoman and into her life walked this fellow Marvin Fishbein, who later died in the car with her. He was the hatchet man for Rupert Murdock, who himself is tied to CIA and Australian intelligence circles. Fishbein is the one who bought out the New York Post and the Boston Herald for Murdock. He was vice-president of the Post at the time and their story said that he was going 45 miles an hour with her on a rain-slicked highway and lost control and went into the Delaware River, an entirely false story.

The car was upside down in a little historically preserved canal off the parking lot of a Chez Odette restaurant where they went frequently. I talked to the waitresses. The couple hadn't had anything to drink. They left at 6:45. The neighbor woman heard the car crash at 10:00 p.m. 'Why didn't they go over the little bridge? They knew how to get out to the road with the car had it been driven by them at that point. Instead the car went to the other end of the parking lot and over a little gravel driveway near three residences. There are signs up saying 'No Vehicles Allowed' and supposedly they fell accidentally into the canal. In each of the seven other accidents in the canal that I researched, the car stayed right side up, it's a fairly narrow canal. The roof of their car was dented into a 'V', from front to back. There's nothing in the bottom of the canal to do that, just mud. So I think that they left at 6:45, they were ambushed at some point on the road or back at the motel, drugged, put back in the car. She was in the back seat. She couldn't have climbed back there; the roof was caved in too much. No signs of struggle by either one. He was strapped into the drivers seat and the car was upside down for several hours before somebody came home about 12:30 to empty trash and saw the car sitting there. The neighbor woman who heard the crash didn't go out because it was raining too hard.

I think they took the car up the gravel driveway, turned it over; it hit the edge of the canal as it went in which is what smashed the roof that way. This is the same coroner that ruled it was an accidental drowning and death there and Jessica Savitch is gone for trying to tell a little bit of the truth about what was happening. The last show she did was on the 'rat line' and the involvement of the U.S. Army Counterintelligence Corps 970th

CIC Unit in the movement of Klaus Barbie and the other Nazis out of Germany. That unit included among others, Henry Kissinger and Theodore Shackley (one of the key figures in the Contragate case). I just heard last night from somebody who is reading the new book that's out about them by Sayers, the Unit also included J.D. Salinger, the literary figure who is such a recluse.

So I think that Abbie was murdered. I don't think he took phenobarbital and alcohol. The coroner told his son prior to the first press conference when they said they didn't know the cause of death that there was nothing in the stomach. Then five days later we're told about the residue of all these pills. But there was no way at that point to do a second autopsy because in the interim he had been cremated. We have a number of these cases that one of my friend's calls 'suicide' by the system. So I think you have to be suspicious and take the time. Penn Jones used to say, 'Take any one thing and research the hell out of it.' Take the time to go and look and see what Fassbinder was doing, what movie he had made or was about to make. Who was around him at the time? Do the circumstances of the suicide seem real? Take a look at the autopsy reports if you can get them. I'm trying to get Abbie Hoffman's family to release the autopsy report to one of the decent coroners who worked on the Kennedy case over the years and see if I can get a real coroner to take a look at Roscoe's work because I think it can be broken open. But one of the family members is blocking doing anything with it, unfortunately.

Round Up!

It has a long and seamy history that dates back to martial law plans that were worked on under the Reagan administration at a time when Thomas Turnage was head of the California National Guard. Louis Giuffrida, who headed up the State Guard was put into control there, eventually headed up FEMA, Federal Emergency Management Agency, and his liaison with the Pentagon in those years was Oliver North. The two of them worked on the REX-84 plan that the Christie lawsuit has revealed, a plan for a national roundup of Central American people and also U.S. dissidents in case of a full-scale invasion of Central America. Giuffrida wrote a plan for the army in 1970 to round up all blacks in America, 22 million Blacks into concentration camps. Ed Meese was also involved in the Guard in California in that period. There was a national program called 'Garden Plot' and the California derivative was called 'Cable Splicer.' The Guard involvement was under the rubric 'Golden Bear' and one of the State guard units still uses the title 'Golden Bear.'

There's still an extant California State Guard which, when it's mobilized, will be trained here at San Luis Obispo at the camp, and issued [45 caliber] side arms, and other weapons. Anybody can be drafted into it, but they recruit it primarily in the survival magazines, the far right wing, the Aryan Brotherhood, and others. They serve as a civilian back-up and replacement so that when the Guard is used as the front line troops in Central America and taken out of the state in order to control the local dissidents the governor will mobilize this civilian State Guard, which will be ill-trained, ill-equipped, but properly motivated ideologically to go after anybody who's making trouble. The elements of that guard and who's in it and how it's being recruited have been exposed in several states, Utah and Virginia and other places, and it's been much restricted. There was some move by the California State Assembly recently to put some restrictions on it and by the end of the next fiscal year they're going to have to answer some questions about where their money goes, who is in it, and what they do. The Specialized Training Institute was the site for both police and guard military training in California for repression of civil dissent and basically how to set up a martial law situation here. So any research that can be done about it, any infiltration of it, anything that can be found out in the current period would probably be useful.

My friend Wendy Govier has been researching what she calls the 'War On Drugs.' In major cities new railroads are being built, and the track sections and the railroad yards go right into the stadiums, same with the new military bases that are being built. They Closed 83 bases, but they're re-opening bases with multi-million dollar budgets for the drug war stuff. They have a commission on alternative uses. Health and Human Services, DOD, and Thornburgh 's justice department (if you can call it that) are working together looking at all U.S. military lands for three things: where to put the homeless, where to do the drug-rehab boot camps, and where to build the new prisons. And they want 75% more prison space. C-Span had Bennett on the other day foaming around about prisons in Utah. He said they've got enough room there, they can spread the prisons out, and they don't even have to stack them.

His version of the future is that just about everybody ought to live in prison and one of the things they're doing now is the Drug War Bonds Act, which will go into schools and replicate the old War Bonds 'Schools at War' program from World War II. The classes and the students and the schools will compete with each other for how much lunch money they give and try to raise $4 billion a year or more to build prisons. At the same time, all of the federal funds that are 80% of what's being diverted out of the OMB revision of the 1990 budget into the Drug War come from education, from social services, from housing, from anything that might give another option to young people besides either going into the military or starving or selling drugs on the street. So they're going to make these kids now, while they're in school, compete to pay for the place where they'll have to live when they get out of school.

Chappaquiddick and Good Hope?

Mary Jo Kopechne supposedly drowned and the family had questions. I think it was the same exact modus as in the murder of Jessica Savitch, except that in this case Ted Kennedy wasn't even in the car. Even Leo Demore, the author of the book Senatorial Privilege, had to admit that Ted wasn't in the car. He claims he opened the door and jumped out at the last minute, which is ridiculous because the windows are shut, and the doors locked on that side. If he were in it, he wouldn't have bothered on the way out to lock it or even shut it. So, I mean, its just nonsense. But then Larry King asked Demore what he was doing now and he said, 'Oh, I'm writing a book with Oliver North.'

Mary Jo Kopechne came from George Smathers employ, George Smathers, friend of Bebe Rebozo and the Nixon mob. She was an infiltrator into the Kennedy camp. She thought she was taking him out to be killed, I believe. He was drugged at the party. He was ambushed, taken out of the car and back to the motel. He didn't have any wet clothes. He didn't swim anywhere that night, and he wasn't in the car. He was in a jovial mood the next morning. He didn't know anything had happened. They came to him and told him, 'She's dead in your car and we have blackmail letters signed by her. We can make it a murder rap or a manslaughter charge,' threatened his children and his life, and got him to lie about it. The Judge turned to the Kennedy table at the end of the trial and said, 'You're all lying through your teeth.' Deputy Look saw the car outside the water hours after Kennedy said that they accidentally went in, in the phony story that he concocted. And the car went off at tremendous speed. Lines show evidence of the car dragging along. They killed her. She had blood all down her back and her blouse, but it washed out during the night and didn't show up until chemical work was done on her shirt. So I believe she was already unconscious or maybe dead by the time she went into the water and she was upside down in the car. They drowned her and framed him and made sure that he can never be president without their bringing up Chappaquiddick.

There was a $10,000 payoff to Tony Vlaczewitz by Jack Caulfield mentioned during Watergate, for that summer called 'Operation Sand Wedge.' It was never explained or asked about. I think 'Sand Wedge' was 'wedge the Oldsmobile in the sand' in the little pond there and take care of Tony Vlaczewitz, who was up on the island. Local people in Martha's Vineyard I talked to said it was crawling with Nixon's men the day before. Lasowitz said that he got a phony press pass to ask embarrassing questions of Ted Kennedy at the press conference afterwards. But the date he said he went to get the press pass was before the accident happened. So what was he going to ask about? And he didn't show up at any of the press conferences. This was all nonsense. He was up there with the bag money ready to take Teddy out. But yeah, I think it's the same modus operandi.

E. Howard Hunt?

A.J. Weberman used to say that Hunt was one of the three tramps arrested in Dealey Plaza and he had these comparison photos and I said I don't do photo comparisons. I said if you'd get me a Kirlian photograph of the auras at 12:30 eastern standard time he's there in spirit.

Reverend Jim Jones. Is he Dead?

I'll answer the last one about Jim Jones first. I think he was killed quite a bit before the massacre. He himself said he had doubles. I don't think a religious leader wants a double. I don't think Christ or Buddha wanted a double running around. But for an intelligence operation you have doubles. The body that they said was Jones, they claimed to have identified by taking the fingerprints and the way they said they did it was they cut the skin off the fingers, put it over a rubber glove... I mean, you know, try and take that one into court. It's just not a way that they could have gotten a print. They said they checked it twice, which doesn't make any sense because it's like weighing something twice on an accurate scale. If you can't get it from that you'd go to the teeth. Then also the tattoo on Jones's chest is missing on the photographs of the body and there are other reasons to believe that wasn't Jones there. I think he was killed probably as soon as they got down there because he was merely the recruiting agent. They didn't need him on site. They needed somebody that could pose as him, perhaps, but in any case he and the operation were expendable as soon as Leo Ryan wanted to go down there and investigate. Ryan had authored the Hughes-Ryan Amendment, which was to force the CIA to tell congress ahead of time what it was going to do for covert operations. In fact, I just saw this interesting little article from the London papers in October, saying that Bush was complaining about new secret regulations passed by the Senate Intelligence Oversight Committees that would require, strictly read, that foreign leaders who we were going to kill or stage a coup that would endanger their lives, would have to be warned by the CIA in advance. Bush specifically noted Noriega, (this was back in October), as an example, if we were going to do a coup against Noriega we'd have to warn him in advance that his life was in danger. So, at least you can rest assured that the secret regulations that the intelligence oversight committees are making in your behalf are being followed to the letter I guess. They have to tell them ahead of time before they kill them. I'm sure that's the case. Not that we'd think of killing anyone, but if we did we'd certainly 'warn them, wouldn't we?

Telling the Truth?

I found out most of what I know from people that I've talked to. I don't think people are so dumb. I think that people know quite a bit but don't talk about it. I find that when I talk about the U.S. doing genocide it often puts off white audiences, but if I say that in a black church in the community there, everybody nods their head because they live under it. So l think different people in different positions of privilege know parts of the lie and what's happening. People are more or less powerless or feel powerless to do something about it and people are easily distracted, but I think that if we decided, all of us, to tell the truth even of our own lives, our own oppression and our own silence and sanction of that oppression of others, the institutional realities and lies that we've worked under and worked with, that everything would come out. Just two Christmases' ago I was at my cousin's house talking to him about a notorious American psychiatrist by the name of Dr. Freeman, who was the major proponent of what we call 'trans orbital lobotomies' in the United States. It was a special knife that he developed that would go around the eye in the socket and then cut the ganglia from inside so you didn't have to do major surgery. You could do it in a matter of second's, trans orbit the eye and go up into the brain and change the emotional effect to nothing. He performed personally 5,000 lobotomies. He's the psychiatrist that lobotomized Frances Farmer, the actress that's depicted in the film Frances in front of all these students, brought her out and did his little gig. In fact, I was told by his assistant who spoke at my college in the

1960's that Freeman carried a gold-plated trans orbital knife in a velvet pouch on his belt and made jokes about doing it at home or at the drop of a hat. He's quoted as saying that men don't do very well afterwards but women make good housewives.

My first connection with psychiatry was in my neighborhood, which was Pentagon NASA NSA Navy Intelligence DOD employees, asking my mother why many of the wives in the families acted strangely and she told me that they had been lobotomized. It was a kind of 'Stepford Wives' community out there in the D.C. suburbs. If the wives acted up, the CIA boys would take them down to the local psych ward and have them fixed and don't think they don't do that at the top level today. Methods may be a little different. But I was talking about Freeman and what a bastard he was and my Aunt Jay was there, she was a clinical nurse most of her life, my cousin's mother- and she pipes up and says, 'Oh I knew Dr. Freeman, I was his scrub nurse.' So my aunt, for years in D.C. prepped these people for these little trans-orbital operations! So if in our own families and among our own neighbors we were to stop now and to tell the truth of our own lives, we would break this system wide open.

The Reality Within Us

I said last night I'm so negative it would probably take six crystals to cure me, but I come from the East Coast where we look at reality and I'm just a transplant out here in California so I haven't got my vibes positive enough yet not to mention Auschwitz when I see it. I think that the history is there and I find it out because I go and talk and somebody comes up to me and says I have this piece or that piece, so we have the reality and we know it within us. We have a lot of denial and we have a lot of shame and a lot of us have made compromises in our lives in order to have the wage slavery money that we need to survive. But that doesn't mean that we couldn't turn around and tell each other about it as my mother finally opened up to me after years in the National Security state and told me, among other things, that standing armies don't stand, they move. She learned that in 30 years in the Pentagon.

Why Watergate?

To take Nixon out, it was a scalpel operation in order to get Nixon out of office and put Ford and

Kissinger and that circle back in. Nixon represented an independent threat to them and they orchestrated a scandal. Woodward and Bernstein came from military intelligence and CIA backgrounds. Deep Throat was Mr. Bennett from the CIA Mullen firm where E. Howard Hunt worked. His father was Senator Bennett from Utah and he did PR for the Mormon Church. He's the only one that they've ever categorically denied was 'Deep Throat.' They basically cornered Nixon. If you'll remember, it was Jaworski and Haig who came out with the smoking gun tape at the last minute when the House committee was on the edge of deciding whether or not to indict him. Also, it was to re-establish the idea that even if the government wasn't credible, which everyone knew from Vietnam, that the press would save us and we could rely on them to be the credible element of the society and that 'democracy would out' even among the worst of thieves. And, of course, it was to give the president a chance to tell us that he wasn't a crook!

Mark Lane?

Penn Jones, in his volume *Forgive My Grief* has several articles on Mark Lane and who's pulling his strings and Mae Brussell in some of her tapes worked on exposing him. It's only by inter-reaction over the years with Lane that I came to see what role he played. His book *Rush to Judgment* that was made into a best seller at the time and became the official critical book (when there were better books out that didn't get any play) was printed by Holt Rinehart & Winston. Holt Rinehart was controlled by the Murchison oil family, which among other things, had meetings the days before the assassination with J. Edgar Hoover and Richard Nixon, planned the hit on Kennedy and put up money on Kennedy's head. Lane went to work for Marina, Oswald, came and told her he'd be the attorney. She fired him after a brief period of time.

I think that the 'planted critic' is going to make those kinds of claims and, in fact, the government is going to appear to suppress things in order to build their credibility. I think you have to look at Lane and his overall history, his Air Force intelligence background in World War II and the role that he played during the Vietnam War with Jane Fonda at the Covered Wagon Coffee House; his willingness to be an attorney for a slime bag like Jim Jones and to go physically to Jonestown and not blow the whistle on a slave labor camp; his ability to walk out of the Jonestown massacre with Charles Garry into the jungle of Guyana and get back to Georgetown with no trouble when everyone else escaping was murdered.

I think if you and I went out to the bathroom now and then came back and everyone in the room but two people were dead, we'd ask some questions wouldn't we? 'How do you get out of there? How do you preside over that and be allowed to walk and then do you do what Lane says? Tear up your underwear and tie it to the bushes so you won't get lost?' Its like Hansel and Gretel in reverse, making a trail for the witch behind them to follow them and kill them. They heard gunfire behind them. Do you think you leave a little trail of underwear so that they can pick up on where you are? And how did they find their way? Jackie Spears didn't trust them. Leo Ryan's attendant, Joe Holsinger, who spoke out finally, came to the same conclusions that we had that it was a mind-control experiment, that the top levels of the DIA were involved and that the people were murdered. These were Holsinger's conclusions. He was horrified. He's a conservative businessman, a real estate agent from Ventura, but he came to see the implication of what happened. He realized that Lane helped to set Ryan up in the situation.

Lane shows up as the attorney for James Earl Ray, but instead of trying to bring Grace Walden Stevens (one of the key witnesses who knew that the man in the rooming house that's supposed to have shot King was not James Earl Ray) to the House Select Committee investigating the matter, instead he made arrangements for Terry Buford to bring her down to Jonestown. There were memos found in the rubble concerning giving her a false passport from Maxine Swaney, one of the women killed in Ukiah who tried to defect from Jones' camp. They still had her passport and were going to use it to bring Grace Walden Stevens down there to the death camp instead of testifying to the House Select Committee.

I've learned from going to conferences over the years that Lane played an instrumental role in blocking appearances or invitations to Mae Brussell at any of them and continually attacked her work. I saw him at an NYU Conference pounding on the table, saying it was totally irresponsible to talk about mind control in relation to assassinations and then ten years after that talk at Madison he's up on stage with Don Freed talking about the programmed assassins. It was ten years after Mae spoke about them and it's irresponsible to mention it. Mae said, 'Yeah, they say I'm crazy. What they mean is I'm crazy to talk about it.' So, I knew from conference organizers that he tried to keep her from having a forum or a podium for her views.

I know that to this day that he hasn't read the Warren Commission Report, his volumes are in mint condition while Mae's are dog-eared. He does the same lecture verbatim year after year; he doesn't change a joke, and you can't ask him who killed Kennedy. He says he'd be as irresponsible as the Warren Commission to say so. Well, I say 26 years into it, if you've got a brain you can figure it out! I looked at the documents when I was fairly young and it's not that hard to tell who killed him once you understand the backgrounds of the people that set Oswald up.

Was the Secret Service In on The Kennedy Assassination?

Elements of it had to be. They went against orders in changing the route of the motorcade for the double turn. They left the bubble top off the car at the special meeting with Elizabeth Forsling Harrison and Jack Puterbaugh at the Sol Bloom Agency where Oswald worked for a period when he was at Jagger Chiles Stovall (he did his photographic work there). They hit the brake instead of the gas when they heard the shots and slowed the car down. They aren't involved as one faction currently suggests by saying that Greer turned around from the driver's seat on the left and shot Kennedy in the head. That's not true. But they were involved in the cover-up and also in violating simple security procedures in the route.

The Dealey Plaza Shots

According to my analysis, the fatal shot comes from a storm sewer to the right front of the motorcade. It's a .45 slug and it lifts Kennedy up out of the seat. If Jackie hadn't been holding him he would have flown back out of the car over the trunk, I believe. I've watched the Zapruder film hundreds of times. It slams him back at over 100 miles an hour to the left and lifts him up, which a shot from above on the grassy knoll would not have done and a shot from his left would not have done from Greer in the front seat. It was a shot from the right front of the motorcade, an upward shot. I've been down in the storm sewer; it's a good military location, it's hidden you do it with a silencer. The motorcycle cop to the left rear, Hargis, was hit so hard with brain fragments that he thought he'd been shot and got off his motorcycle.

The next guy over, Martin, was also covered with blood. The brain fragments went back on the left of the car, Jackie climbed up and grabbed one of them and another one flew 30 feet behind to the left south side of Elm Street and was picked up by one of the bystanders. The bullet itself, a .45 slug, was located in the grass south of Elm Street by Bill Decker, the sheriff's deputy, and by an unidentified man except they say he's FBI and we have a photograph sequence of him leaning over, picking it up and putting it in his pocket and destroying the evidence. So that's what I say was the fatal headshot. It came from the sewer to the right front.

The shot to the back, I believe, came from the top of the Dallas Jail Building from Deputy Harry Weatherford, who had that week, bought a 'high-powered rifle'. A 15-year-old researcher Mickey Cohen questioned him, he used to go around and ask questions of these guys because it would disarm them, he's just some young kid. But he had read the Commission Report and understood it and he went to Weatherford and said, 'Did you shoot President Kennedy?' and Weatherford's response was 'I shot lots of people, you little son of a bitch.'

So I think he's one of them. I think the shot was interfered with by the back brace, which is why it is not an exit wound. It's five inches below the neckline and it goes into his back. They probed in to the second knuckle at Bethesda and there's no more to the wound. I think that bullet fell out in the car, fell out in the stretcher somewhere.

As for the throat shot, I tend to agree with Cutler, that it came from the front, from the umbrella man. I think the umbrella was a concealed CO_2 cartridge weapon and this was a flechette dart, little darts, self-propelled tubes that go into the body and put in a paralyzing or lethal drug. That's why it makes a small hole: It was under 3cm according to the Parkland doctors. It was obliterated and expanded by first a tracheotomy and then what appears to be an even larger cut in the neck. By the time the Bethesda photographs are shown it's completely obliterated and the neck sliced half open. But they did probe in there and took out a missile from the chest cavity in the neck area. The FBI signed for it at Bethesda and that bullet disappeared as well. So there are two entrance shots, one in the throat and one in the back. There's the fatal head shot which blows off a flap on this side because it's coming at a low angle into the right temple, it blows the flap up here, blows out the back of the occipital bone in the right rear and throws Kennedy back into the car.

Then there are at least two shots that hit Connally, one a through-and-through chest shot at a different angle and a later point than the shots that first hit Kennedy. It can't be the same bullet, though the whole Warren Commission depends on it being the same bullet, but the bullet through the chest is not the one that hits the wrist because he's still holding his Stetson after that. The bullet in the wrist severed the tendon on his thumb that would allowed him to do that, so there has to be at least one other shot, that one breaks his seventh rib. It's at frame 238. They said it was a delayed reaction. The other bullet broke his wrist, went through and cracked the bone in there and then that shot, or another one, buried itself in his left thigh.

The Warren Commission moved the back shot up to the top of the neck, said it was an entrance wound in the neck that went through and came out the throat at a downward angle, at an angle that had to be more than 26 degrees to the right not to hit bone, hit only flesh. So it's coming downward like this with Connally over here in front of him, has to go back up, back over to the right, start back down again at a 45-degree angle into Connally's chest, come out the front of his chest, turn itself around again, wait a second and a half between these two points when Kennedy is obviously hit and Connally is obviously hit, hang in the air, and then come back down at another angle and go through his wrist, smash the wrist bone, go into his thigh, and then not even be found in his thigh, but be found on a stretcher upstairs at Parkland Hospital on the second floor after an individual meeting the description of Jack Ruby kicked the stretcher and a pristine bullet appears that's missing less metal than the grains of metal left inside Connally's wrist or removed from his thigh by the doctors that day. That's what the critics know as the 'magic bullet' Commission Exhibit 399. I'd suggest if this is true, it was probably that same bullet that took off again, hit the Pope, hit Ronald Reagan and just keeps going around the world doing the dirty work! 'One single bullet' for all of them.

Presidents & Their Bang-Bang Men

I think the .45 'slug may have been an exploding, like a frangible bullet. I think that there were a lot of metal fragments in there, but they never did even a simple sectioning of JFK's brain to see what direction the bullets went. They destroyed Kennedy's brain they destroyed the photos. I think these photos that you're seeing now in Lifton's book aren't even Kennedy. I think they killed somebody else and put 'them on the autopsy table. The guy who did the funeral home embalming of what was supposed to be Kennedy's body, maybe it was, and they used the other body at Bethesda because two caskets showed up at different times. But that guy in the funeral home that embalmed him also was used to embalm Howard Hughes. Is that because they don't have a funeral home in Texas? Or is it because you use the same embalmer to go from key case to key case covering up who the dead are and how they died. I think they have an embalmer somewhere in Texas they don't have to come to Arlington, Virginia to get one, but nobody is allowed to see these bodies except people who are pre-selected at the time and they come in and they debrief them and the wounds are hidden.

Witnesses, I believe, to the wounds in Martin Luther King were killed. A.D. King, his brother was there that day and his mother who saw the wounds later at the hospital where they declared him dead both of them were murdered in strange ways and couldn't be witnesses to those wounds at the appeal trial of James Earl Ray because of their deaths. I don't think you're supposed to see the wounds. I think the bullets are all just as phony. I don't think any of Sirhan's bullets hit Robert Kennedy. I think all the bullets came from behind, from Thane Eugene Cesar's gun and I think you will find the same thing when you go into detail in each of these cases that this is how it happened.

Reagan was also hit, I believe, by a flechette, a razor-edged little disc that left such a small hole underneath his arm that the nurses in the trauma unit at GWU took 15 minutes to figure out he wasn't having a heart attack and that's not because they've never seen a bullet wound in GWU in the emergency room. Believe me, in D.C. they know what a bullet wound looks like. But he didn't have anything except a little razor cut line and a little bit of black blood under there. One of the nurses finally saw it and thought something went in, told the doctor, and they did three x-rays. They couldn't find it. She squished the lung around and they were just about to close him up when they felt something in the lung and pulled it out. He described it as 'round and flat as a dime, a little disc' and he put it in a cup, which the Secret Service disappeared with and that's the end of it.

Hinckley, who was firing a .38, not a .22, blew out Brady's brains with the first shot, then hit Delahanty, a D.C. cop, in the shoulder and threw him to the ground. He hit McCarthy, the Secret Service agent, in the groin, a 160-pound man, lifted him up and threw him up to the other end of the car. That's not a .22, that's a large-caliber high-velocity weapon. It was a .38 he bought, just in case you didn't get the message, on Elm Street in Dallas, the street where Kennedy was killed, at a pawnshop there.

They changed the two guns. I've watched the film sixty times to get how they did it. You can see the .38 as you 're facing it to the left side of the crowd that's surrounding and holding Hinckley. The .38 is on the ground. A Secret Service agent with his back to the wall sidles over while they're hustling Hinckley and reaches into his pocket and pulls out a handkerchief, bends down, picks up the .38 and pockets it. Simultaneously, a D.C. cop in a rain slicker runs down with no purpose after they've got Hinckley under control, goes to the edge of the Secret Service crowd holds his arms out like this and goes back and forth for a minute, puts one arm up under the rain slick and just as he does that you see the .22-drop out at his foot. And that becomes the official murder weapon because they needed a smaller caliber weapon hours later to explain this 'non-hole' in Reagan's arm.

If Reagan had been hit with a .38, nobody would have wondered whether he was shot or not. He didn't know what had happened to him, but it's clear that he's hit and Time magazine and all the newspapers show him hit at the point where he raised his arm to wave and they say, 'Mr. President' and he raises the arm like this. On the cover of Time, the hair is mussed, the cheeks blown out like Connally's when his lung collapsed. Reagan's lung collapsed, his mouth is grimaced, and he's clearly hit, but that's simultaneous with the Brady shot by Hinckley and Brady and Deaver are in the way of Hinckley's bullets until the end of the sequence when Reagan is pushed into the car.

At that point they came up with this phony story that a bullet that went into the trunk instead ricocheted off the car, you can see the hole into the trunk, went into the hole between the door and hit Reagan as he was going into the car. Had it been that bullet, it would have hit Parr, the Secret Service guy, not Reagan. But you have Brady, Delahanty, and McCarthy, which are three shots. You've got the window on the back door, you've got the bullet hole in the trunk and you've got the shot into the Universal Building across the street. That's the six bullets in Hinckley's .38. You have to get a seventh bullet to get Reagan and it's this little flechette, from up above on top of the retaining wall. Dr. O'Donnell says it's a downward angle 45 degrees left to right, back to front, exactly opposite of where Hinckley's standing down over here to his left. It comes from the Bushy Knoll.

Why Was Reagan Shot?

Bush, coming into office and taking over the government. That's the motive. Pushing Reagan out at a point when their policies didn't agree. Several days before Bush had been put in charge of crisis management and at a press conference they asked him 'What does a crisis mean? How do you define it?' and Bush said, 'The president will know it when he sees it.' And he did, and he said 'Get me the demographics on that kid!' and when they got the demographics on John W. Hinckley, Sr., it led directly back to George Bush!

Did They Mean to Kill Reagan or Just Scare Him?

Well, I think you kill him and you've got more problems. They did mean to hit the heart, I think. It deflected off the seventh rib and came within a quarter inch of the aorta. They may have just been planting something that would cause a later disease cancer or something, I don't know. I think they meant to kill him. You do have additional problems if you actually kill him, but I think they wanted to. When they didn't, they sent him to Bethesda in the limousine that had been parked 40 feet down the curb to put him out in the open. The Secret Service had not made a diamond around him, they all filed out to his right so his left side was open to the gunman. They told him to leave his bulletproof vest off that day and set him up for the hit. But they shoved him into the limousine, they yelled, 'Rawhide is okay!' they were expecting to say, 'Rawhide is dead.'

They turned to the right when they hit Connecticut. If you 're going to the White House or to GWU you tum left. When you turn right off Connecticut off, of T Street you're heading north and you 're going to connect out to Bethesda Hospital. At that point the Reagan loyalists figured out that he wasn't coming. Brady, who was still lying on the ground for five minutes, beat him to the hospital by 15 minutes. Reagan walked in and Brady came in on a stretcher and got there first even though he was left well behind because they were taking Reagan up to finish him off at the Navy hospital. But the loyalists in the situation room started screaming and so they said, 'Alright, we'll leave him alive, just tell him to shut up and get out of the way.' And then Haig emerged for all to see, forgetting the 25th Amendment as if that applies when crisis management comes into effect, it doesn't. But the press wants us to think he just didn't know about the 25th amendment what presidential succession is supposed to be. Haig emerged and said, 'Gentlemen I am in charge here until the vice president returns.'

Bush was in a jovial mood according to people on the plane. He wasn't sure he was even going to come back to D.C. when the incident happened. He thought he might fly on from Houston to Dallas. He's out there in Air Force One flying around and then he comes home eight hours later and from that point on Reagan goes out and watches movies at Camp David with Nancy and grins at the press and waves his hand and pretends he can't hear them over the helicopter. If you'll remember, he was making so many bad statements at the beginning they kept jumping up in front of him and saying, 'Well, what he meant to say... ' They even had poor old Kissinger doing that but his German accent was so thick that they got rid of him after a while. Then they put this thing on the side of Reagan's ear for a while with the presidential seal about the size of a Danish and they said it was a hearing aid, it was stuffed up the side of his head, you know. That's 'control central,' but that proved too obvious so they reduced it and put it discreetly inside the brain so that he could get messages.

Remember when he went to the high school and the little girl asked him something and he started talking about the contras and Nicaragua? Sometimes they get the answers mixed up for him, you know. Recently they said he fell off a horse and he hurt his brain but there were no symptoms for a month. I could believe that! They took him into the hospital and they had the brain drained. It took an hour and then he came out and probably couldn't remember who George Bush was after that.

At the time of his second inauguration Reagan had 14,000 police, that's how scared he was! On one day he hired 14,000 cops! It was the most police ever to guard a president at an inauguration. They sealed the manhole covers (you see, they know how they killed Kennedy at Dallas). They sealed the manhole covers for blocks; they put the Secret Service up in every building in all the windows. They even had a guy next to him all day with a surface to air missile! You go to the White House now; there are concrete bunkers all down Pennsylvania Avenue. You can't drive anything into the White House. There's barbed wire on the roof and troops. The whole place is an armed camp, in 'totalitarian' Nicaragua where the horrible 'communists' rule, Daniel Ortega goes out and passes guns to the people. Can you imagine Bush or Reagan walking 15 feet down the street passing out guns and surviving in this society? Instead they live in an armed camp! So he's back there and they have a bulletproof specially built podium and a bulletproof vest: You can bet he learned how to wear it after March 31!

He still didn't come out. He decided it was too cold, he said, so people wait out in the street for hours and they never have the ceremony outside. But that was the day that the Marine Corps band marched into the White House and a guy in civilian clothes went in with them and nobody noticed him. Well, I'll tell you, you do anything funny near the White House or go to the gate and ask to see the president and they take you up to St. Elizabeth's. They have about 20 or 30 a year, they call them

'White House cases', and they even have a special psychiatric diagnosis for them. They're delusional because they think the president of the United States is going to help them!

Nobody walks in with the Marine Corps band in a civilian outfit. They know how many are there and who's going to come in. But this guy goes in the White House and supposedly no one notices. He walks around the dining room and bedroom until finally somebody comes across him and takes him out and he's just some good old' boy from Texas, just wandering around to see what he could see. That's the message to Reagan. 'Go ahead and put 14,000 cops around your ass and when you go to get your pajamas we're going to jump out and blow your damned head off!' Then he goes to stay with the Queen of England, you know, at Buckingham Palace, and they're having such a grand time until that night the guy comes in and sits on the Queen's bed! That guy, it turned out, was the nephew of Rudolf Hess, the last surviving Nazi war criminal in prison at Spandau. The nephew of Rudolf Hess comes and sits on the Queen's bed. Well, you know if someone comes and sits on your bed at night how much your life is worth and they told Reagan time and again. For instance, when he went up in the helicopter this plane almost hits him and the guy said, 'Oh, I was looking for my contacts.' Then we learn he's from the Army and they said he was AWOL but he said at the press conference, 'I'm not AWOL. They're embarrassed.' I mean you can get the point if you listen. And what was the allegedly AWOL pilot doing. He was flying some corporate guy to meet with Donald Nixon, the Nixon brother who took Howard Hughes' filthy money for the Nixon election years before. They don't come from nowhere.

So they kept giving Reagan his warnings if he was stupid enough to think he was really the president. Bush is the president. This is his third term, it's Alexander Haig's fourth term and it's Kissinger's fifteenth term in the White House and that's the team that's in there. It includes Ledeen and Kirkpatrick and Bush and the rest of them. They just pushed Reagan out and now they're coming back in full force.

Bush and Secret Societies

Bush is part of a secret society from Yale called Skull and Bones and unfortunately so is John Kerry, which is why he won't talk about Bush's full involvement in the drug operations. I'm sure they have them out here. I know the Tacos are down in Guadalajara - that's one of the World Anti-Communist League societies. I don't know this particular one you're mentioning, but a secret society or Satanist group or UFO contactee cult is a good breeding ground for assassins and for training. They operate as the intelligence agencies do on a need to know basis, with concentric circles of initiation. Ellsberg said 'he was 15 levels above top security and he thought every level he got to it was the top one until he got to the next. So they are good breeding grounds. They usually have you perform some criminal act as your initiation rite and then they have you by the shone hairs for the rest of your life. Like they had the Skull and Bones go and dig up some historical figure and rob a grave. Prescott Bush dug up Geronimo and George Bush is said to have dug up Emma Goldman. I don't know. I hope not. I hope she bit him.

Coups d'état

I think they killed Kennedy in the open in order to show that they had that power. I think it was a military coup d'état that involved the DIA more than the CIA although CIA elements were involved. The CIA was basically, as I suggested, compromised from its beginnings by the Nazi spies that ran the operation division and that it helped build the lie for the cold war. Kennedy wanted more civilian control over the Defense Intelligence Agency and the CIA. The elements that were used to kill him interrelated more with the Pentagon and DIA structures, although some segments of the CIA community were pulled in.

Kennedy realized that the CIA had lied to him about the Bay of Pigs and about Vietnam and he had begun to change his whole foreign policy based on what he understood was distortion. He wanted more civil control over the Pentagon as well and he was angry about being treated by Pentagon errand boys as somebody to take orders from the Joint Chiefs. He didn't like it. He had said publicly that he'd scatter the CIA to the four winds and he meant to put Bobby in and name a special task force to clean it up. They were going after the Mafia too. One segment of the old Mafiosi had stayed with J. Edgar Hoover, but the other, the new cross-ethnic syndicate, Lansky, Luciano, Bugsy Siegel and that crowd and eventually Giancana and Roselli and the others took up with the CIA elements. They had had dealings with the OSS at the end of World War II.

This was a coup from the top level of the Pentagon, not from the Mob. There is no Mafia goon from Carlos Marcello or anti-Castro Cuban or pro-Castro Cuban, there's no oilman from Dallas and not even any CIA boy that could touch any of those. The Mafia was nothing but shoeshine boys and errand carriers. This story now that we're being told that the Mafia did it and could walk away with impunity from it is nonsense. They used the Mafia's gunmen, but the Mafia sure as hell couldn't plan it and they couldn't touch those codebooks. Those books involved 16 hands on passes in order to put them on and take them off at a regular interval and change the codes and effect the immediate nuclear response and security of the whole nation. The only people who could have ordered them off the planes were the Joint Chiefs of Staff! The entire communication grid in D.C. for the federal phones failed for two hours as soon as Kennedy was shot!

They used a corporate firm, Permindex, 'Permanent Industrial Exhibits,' up in Toronto to coordinate the mechanics and 'schlepper level,' (as Mae Brussell used to call it) the people who do the killing and carry the money. That involved several groups, one of which was the largest internal police force in the United States, the Defense Industry Security Command (DISC) started as a security command guard for the Manhattan Project, the Tennessee Valley Authority and David Lilienthal and expanded into the largest police force totally under hidden governmental military control, no civilian control. They still exist as 'DISCO'. They have headquarters in Columbus, Ohio and Mussel Shoals, Alabama. Among other things, they were the ones that surrounded and radiated and killed Karen Silkwood. Also involved was the American Council of Christian Churches, now International Council of Christian Churches, headed up by Carl McIntyre and an evangelical organization down in Mexico that was a front for the training of assassins headed by Albert Osborne. Their current replacement is a group called 'World Vision' which since the 1950's has recruited assassins from refugee populations across the world. The chairman of the board of World Vision for many years was John W. Hinckley, Sr.! One of their employees out of Fort Chafee with the Thai refugees was Mark David Chapman, the person that shot John Lennon. Also involved was a syndicate gambling group between Miami, Florida and Havana, Cuba that was known as the syndicate. It wasn't the whole syndicate, but it involved Bobby Baker among others, the scandalmonger in the LBJ administration and Cliff Jones from the Democratic National Committee.

The anti-Castro Cuban groups operated under the aegis of E. Howard Hunt. William Reilly of the Reilly Coffee Company funded the Cuban Democratic Revolutionary Front out of New Orleans where Oswald worked for a brief time. Those specific anti-Castro groups were used, along with segments of the Mafia, through that gambling group and also through Operation 40 and Operation Mongoose and included Giancana and Roselli 's boys who were on hire. But there were also other shooters Billy Seymour, Emilio Santana, and others from the Oaxaca, Mexico training camp.

It involved the security at NASA for Werner Von Braun and General Walter Dornberger, his mentor who worked at Bell Helicopter Systems and employed Michael Paine. He and his wife, Ruth Paine, housed Marina Oswald - some of the few along with George De Mohrenschildt and his wife to testify falsely that Oswald owned a weapon of any kind. Ruth Paine got him the job at the Book Depository to set him up as the patsy and Michael Paine worked directly under General Dohmberger who thought up Star Wars in 1963. He talked then about satellites circling the globe with nuclear weapons that would go around every 90 minutes and threaten the rest of the world and also developed the ideas for the shuttle which was originally to be a weapons carrier for the Nazis back in World War II.

Dornberger was supposed to hang at Nuremberg but McCloy, stepped in with Lucian Clay. John J. McCloy the Rockefeller banker, acted on behalf of Werner Von Braun who said he wouldn't build any rockets unless Dohmberger was saved. The Nazi general was never prosecuted, but instead brought here to the United States. McCloy, of course, sat on the Warren Commission later along with Allen Dulles who cut the deals with the SS's Karl Wolff and Reinhardt Gehlen to bring Nazi intelligence here. The Operation Overcast deals to bring the rocket scientists were affected by the capture of Werner Von Braun and the Peenemunde group in Switzerland by General Thurston up in that sector. His aide-decamp who actually arrested Von Braun and these rocket scientists was Clay Shaw, the guy who later sat on the Board of directors of Permindex and who Jim Garrison tried to prosecute years later in New Orleans. So these people fold through the history.

One of the people who buried prosecution evidence at Nuremberg, later moved the Nazis under the aegis of the International Red Cross and then went into Texas with J.M. Kaplan Fund (a CIA conduit for years), was the liaison between the Texas State Police investigation of the murder of Kennedy (which couldn't be carried out because they stole the body) and the Warren Commission, later was also the person who investigated Koreagate and Watergate and was considered the most trusted man in America - namely, Leon Jaworski, who as I suggested before went in with Haig and pulled Nixon out in the middle of Watergate and effected the fall of the regime.

So you have key figures that are central to the cover-up: just about every member of the Warren Commission was compromised. Ford was too dumb to raise a stink and followed orders since he was the CIA's man anyway. McCloy and Dulles were the evil geniuses of the group. John Sherman Cooper had been an ambassador to Germany and helped hide the Nazis-Krupp and others. And Russell and Boggs were about the only ones who asked any questions, but they were consistently shut up when they said anything.

All of the lawyers were chosen at a secret meeting. The meeting where they chose the lawyers is still buried in the archives 75 years by Johnson. This phony Blakey who ran it buried the House Select Committee evidence for 99 years. Very little chance to get anything real out of the government except what we learned on the news that the House Select Committee believed that there had been a conspiracy to kill Kennedy and a conspiracy to kill King but then they closed operations. So you got the news item 'Revealed today by the House Select Committee on Assassinations, a conspiracy was involved in the death of John F. Kennedy. Now the sports.'

More on Jonestown

The Daily World was the only paper that printed any information in the left papers on Jonestown. Tim Wheeler did exhaustive work with Joe Holsinger and got some of the real story out about Jonestown and they've consistently had fairly good coverage of different scandals involving the intelligence agencies. They're more willing than most of the left press to print stuff that really reveals the true nature of the system. Of course, they're the party paper of the communist party USA and so they push their political line, but they do have fairly good investigative reporting and they do reveal things that even other left and progressive papers don't.

The RICO Statute

G. Robert Blakey, who headed up the House Select Committee, originally thought up the RICO Statute. He made himself a friend of the Christie Institute by filing amicus curiae brief on their behalf for the first civil RICO suit, which allows them to look for a pattern of criminal activity in the Christie case. I think it's an interesting approach for a court case. Of course, it's open to abuse from the other side if they start going after other types of political groups besides the Mafia. It could lend them an air of credibility in looking at a long-term history of a political organization or a labor union and claiming a pattern of criminal activity to go after them.

Like any other law, it has two sides to it. I don't know what the basis of the repeal action is, it may be that they don't want it used against government operations and so somebody's put pressure in that direction. But the legal systems in this country is constructed, I believe, to have enough laws so that nobody can live without breaking them and then decide who to bust.

Quayle

Yeah, well I certainly think he's health insurance for Bush and impeachment insurance. I think he was Bush's concession to the farther right and usually they balance the ticket. His parents were very close with Robin Welch who founded the John Birch Society. They were regular listeners, when Danny was young, to the tapes of Carl McIntyre and the Council of Christian Churches and they're far to the right. The mother's family is the Pulliam family, which runs the paper not only there in Indianapolis but also the Arizona Republic. When an investigative reporter for the Arizona Republic, Don Bowles, began to unearth Goldwater's connections with Willy Bioff and the mob, illegal land deals and speculation there in Arizona, the newspaper wouldn't print his stories. Then Bowles was blown up in his car and they wouldn't even investigate that. A group of reporters had to come in from around the country to try and find out who killed Bowles. It was Goldwater who called the National Guard unit in Indianapolis to make sure that Dan Quayle didn't have to go to Vietnam and got his position there. So the family relates to the right wing. Even Quayle's wife, Marilyn, is apparently tied in with some rightwing evangelical preacher that she listens to the tapes of, but Quayle is essentially a dolt.

What would be the grounds for impeachment of Quayle?

I think the impeachable offense for Quayle is what was the relation of his staff assistant Rob Owen to introducing North and the illegal funding of the contras through their operations with the Indiana backers. Quayle came in under the auspices of drug money that was pumped into these right-wing organizations that were trying to kick out anybody who had been on the Senate Oversight Committees on Intelligence during the 60's and 70's and had created any problems for them. Steve Simms ousted Frank Church in Idaho by that right-wing money which was basically funded through North and the contras, the funding for the electoral campaigns to kick them out. In Indiana, it was Birch Bayh that they wanted to get out and they replaced him with Dan Quayle, so he was part of the rightward shift of the Reagan em. Also, apparently there were some illegal dealings that involved his father in Bush's drug operations the laundering of some $4 million through an Indianapolis bank that his father was connected to that 'was drug money from Bush's operations. I haven't gotten more than sketchy details on that, but I'm sure there's dirt. I mean, there's dirt in the Pulliam family itself if you look hard enough, on the mother's side, and the father's probably not much better. I think he says he basically stands by his misstatements: He's pretty much a good reason for them not to take Bush out and a concession by Bush to have somebody of their ilk. There've been some strange meetings where Bush and Quayle and their respective wives have met with some constitutional lawyers talking about transfers of power should something happen to Bush. They were asking Quayle early on in the press conferences what would he do if something happened to Bush and he became president. He dodged the question a couple times and finally he said was 'Well, the first thing I'd do is I'd pray,' and one of the reporters in the back said, 'So would we!'

Noriega

(Editor's Note: Please bear in mind that this talk occurred just prior to the U.S. invasion of Panama.)

When Bush was Director of the CIA, Noriega was a CIA asset in terms of intelligence in the area. Also there were drug dealings through Panama. 'Panama was central to their canal strategy and some other things, so I think that when Noriega says he has the goods on Bush he's talking about from that period on when he knows Bush was involved in the drug dealing and in the Contragate scams. I think Noriega flexed his muscles a little bit and became somewhat independent and they don't like it, but on the other hand I think he's still got enough clout that they can't treat him the way they've treated the last string of little tin horn dictators to basically send someone in to tell them to move out of the way while they put in the 'liberal alternative.' And so it's got Bush in kind of a frothy dilemma.

You remember he used to attack Reagan for being weak on Noriega and say he ought to get him out? But now he's in there by the short hairs and he can get revealed. You know, you talk about National Security... I mean, if they can blackmail the president at that level, and god knows who else has dirt on him, the Iranians and everybody else for all the dirty dealings over the years, who knows who is really pulling other strings or at least holding his hands on the international level? They're worried about somebody that's gay over at the lower levels of the CIA, but I mean whatever blackmail potential that has, if it has any, is nothing compared to Bush and all the dirt he's done. So I think that Noriega's acceptable enough so long as the U.S. retains control of the canal. But if that isn't going to happen, then we've got another story coming. But the Panama Canal isn't big enough for the super-tankers. They really want to blow one through; they've been planning it since the 60's, with nuclear weapons or some other alternative, through Nicaragua that's a little bigger.

KAL Flight 007

Cutler and Chubb have written about this among others, Fletcher Prouty, other researchers. The best evidence shows that KLA 007 remained on course along the R20 route and never strayed into Soviet air space, that another Boeing plane, a Boeing design, an RC-135 Ferret which had a similar radar pattern, flew on the course with it as part of a regular figure eight loop they do out over Anchorage for intelligence purposes. It kept going along the route and became one single radar blip and then, using Stealth technology and testing that technology against the Soviet radar system, it flew into Soviet air space and eventually flickered in and out of its radar contact.

This brought up two interceptors at one point who couldn't find it, which to me suggests very much that it was a Stealth plane. It had no radio contact: The radar blip when it was seen had no electronic ID tag. It was basically a drone and they related to it militarily because it could have been automatic, filled with weapons, whatever.

The second pilot, by chance, saw it, ran up and wigwagged it, backed off and fired at it when he didn't get any response except an evasive action. But when he fired at it and said, 'The target is destroyed,' he didn't mean that he followed the missile and waited to see it blow up. He got it into his electronic cross hairs and hit his computerized button and sent his heat seeker out, and then he veered off to come home because you don't want to run into return fire and you don't want to run into the explosion. When the CIA and DIA listeners along the route in Japan heard that transmission, 'The target is destroyed,' they simultaneously pushed a radio signal and detonated a bomb on board KAL-007 and blew it up over the Kiral Trench, which is why no parts of it were found, it's one of the deepest areas of the Pacific.

The first search teams from Japan headed towards the trench because Flight 007 was last reported by KAL-015 behind it at the Noka Point out there over the trench and still on course. They knew that the Soviet defense radar system would be lit up by this exercise, so in addition to testing Stealth they were going to take a full look at how the Soviets defended their border at that point because the Soviets were about to do an ICBM test off of Sakhalin. The first report generated by the CIA was that the plane had not crashed but had landed safe at Sakhalin and that report held through Thursday morning, giving hours of time to Oliver North and Jeanne Kirkpatrick to doctor the Soviet pilot tapes to come in with the 'Evil Empire' scenario to the United Nations later. They ended up with about twenty hours of lead-time before they had to actually present the evidence. So they got an extra bonus of watching the Soviet defense system from both the Shuttle Challenger that was looping along the route in the same direction and from the main geophysical spy satellite that the U.S. had. The person in charge of positioning both those vehicles at that time was National Security Operative Oliver North. Secord had also used the KAL plane to fly the arms to Iran and probably knew the pilot; the pilot of the plane was the personal pilot for the head of the Korean CIA, which is our CIA there in Korea.

I don't believe that Larry McDonald was aboard the plane. I believe that McDonald got off the plane in Anchorage. There were six people on the manifest who didn't switch over. He told the rest of the people traveling on the plane before he left that he wasn't going to get on that one because the KGB thought he'd be on it. This is what he told his friends. I guess they knew he was nuts or paranoid enough that they didn't have to listen to him so they got on the plane that he said would blow up because the KGB thought he was on it. I don't think he ever got on the plane. His wife showed no emotional reaction. They were calling her the 'ice lady' in the Atlanta press. She read the party line: she dyed her hair in the hours between the time she heard of his death and went out to make her official statement.

The 'safe on Sakhalin story' I felt was not only to buy time but also to create a scenario where McDonald could emerge some years hence from the terrible Soviet gulag and tell us again about the evil empire. And, interestingly enough, in last December's American Opinion magazine, that's exactly the scenario that the John Birch Society is pumping for. They're saying that the first story was true and the plane was safe and McDonald was captured by the Soviets. We'll see if my speculation about McDonald comes true, but they had to get him out of the scene, whether they killed him or not, because his Western Goals Foundation was in the middle of a civil suit out here in California. The ACLU was suing it for having gotten hold of all the criminal conspiracy section records of the LAPD, which consisted of records from every red squad in every city of the country that spied on the left in the 60's. These 'red squads' sent their files down through the LAIU to the criminal conspiracy section. Those files, which were ordered to be destroyed, were instead stolen by Jay Paul, a detective, and given to his wife Mary Love in Long Beach, who put them into a $100,000 computer that belonged to Larry McDonald and Western Goals Foundation.

Threatening to open that up might have also opened Watergate West, Operation Golden Bear and Cable Splicer and the whole

Reagan and Turnage and Meese connections. And so, William French Smith, whose law firm was defending the LAPD, left the Justice Department, ran to California, and got a $2 million hush settlement on the suit so it didn't affect Reagan's election and Meese instead went into the Justice Department. Turnage went into the Selective Service and then the VA, and Giuffrida moved into the FEMA and the change was affected.

There was a book written two years before that describes the scenario with the Stealth plane and all the different aspects called Flight 209 Is Down by Barry Schiff who writes for Aviation Week magazine. It outlined the scenario. The senator that they put on the plane to blow up is a thinly disguised version of Scoop Jackson. Scoop Jackson died of a heart attack the day of the KAL 007 crash and his administrative assistant, Richard Pearl, went into the NSC to work with Oliver North. Alexander Haig replaced him on the board of Boeing Aircraft. Henry Kissinger, who is still there determining Central America policy right now under Bush, replaced him on the Foreign Intelligence Advisory Board of the President's Central American Task Force and Carl Spitz Channel, the main fundraiser for Oliver North, replaced McDonald in the presidency of Western Goals. So there was a nice little transitional shift of the Bush team into the key positions that were affected. KAL 007 had not only the desired effect of getting the Soviets to believe that they'd destroyed a plane and made them into the barbarian empire that we didn't become by born bing a 'Soviet airbus out of the sky later with our pushy little ships in the Persian Gulf. Nobody thought we were barbarians because we 'accidentally' (with the most sophisticated equipment on earth) couldn't identify a civilian airbus from a military plane going up instead of down.

This poor ship must have thought they were attacking so they blow it but then it was an accident. Before it was that 'no modern radar system could ever mistake a civilian airliner and the Soviets just didn't care, they blew it out of the air.' That was the story. So they got that bad rap and for a while they believed it. I think they eventually figured it out, found the plane in the Kiral Trench, got the black box, and have it as a bargaining chip in the current period against the U.S. But I think at the time we fooled them and we fooled the American public and so a one-third cut in the defense budget failed in congress the week after. The end to nerve gas and chemical and biological warfare monies failed, the MX got funded, the Stealth bomber got funded, and generally the cold war was re-established and that's basically the case whenever this system has tried to move toward detente in any serious way.

The John Birch Society

The Birch Society, I think is basically that Welch was an industrialist and it was a smokescreen for the emerging southern rim money of the military-industrial complex to point the finger solely at the Rockefeller end of the class and the eastern establishment and to call them commies and to go against them. H.L. Hunt, who had more money than the Rockefellers, but didn't know how to use it, used to say 'When I go east, they treat me just like a stable hand.' So they didn't like the old eastern establishment, the banker boys and the established capital. I think the Birch Society was basically a way to catch people who began to realize something was fishy, some conspiracy existed in the society, and divert them instead into thinking it was a communist plot that involved the Rockefellers and the eastern establishment and to hide the Nazis and the military industrial complex.

On Uncovering Hidden History

I think there are always murders that you can focus on. Penn Jones said to take any one thing and because of the significance of the black genocide operation, but also because by the time it came up, many young people who hadn't been alive at the time of the Kennedy assassination didn't remember it, but 98 percent of the population had heard the Jonestown story so I used some of the media tales that I knew were false to get in the door, to throw the dirt on the floor for the vacuum salesman. It's that kind of a thing. You go with what you know. If you go out to people and start discussing the Knights of Malta and Skull & Bones they don't know what you're talking about, but if you say remember Jonestown, did you ever think about the story another way, you know that this is what you were told, but this is the reality, you've got a foot in the door and you've got some frame of reference. The shooting of Reagan is one of the stories most researchers didn't work on, but it could have revealed Bush all the way back in 1981 for what he is. I think focusing on practically any aspect reveals the Bush team in murders and the drug dealing, but I think it's up to all of us to do the picking of what's important. The people that are still trying to do the grassy knoll, Dealey Plaza, or the Ambassador Hotel without finally naming who the guilty people are who are doing these killings and who's in control, but instead still focusing on the bullet holes in the pantry wall, or whatever, I think are engaging in a kind of nostalgia. I can remember years ago talking to somebody about the Kennedy assassination on a street corner in D.C., near an older black man, who finally looked and said, 'Kennedy, he died.' He is dead. And the history is dead. It's not a reason not to talk about it and there's a certain level of recognize ability, but history has moved on. There have been thousands of deaths since and there are many current things that we need to be exposing and looking into. Any one of them can reveal the whole, but there's also no reason to look into them forever without saying anything except the official version is wrong. Even the government has told us the official version is wrong. That's no longer a mystery.

How do people generally respond to the information provide? What kinds of reactions do you get?

I find people receptive. I get on radio and I get across the country sometimes in different kinds of radio formats and whenever I do I get a lot of people who've never heard any of this stuff before and they react like people thirsting in a desert. They want the information. They want to understand what's happening. They feel that the analysis makes sense and I put the analysis out, not because I want you to follow me down the street and say John Judge knows the truth, but because I'm trying to at least give you a different paradigm to look at reality and look at what's happening in your current history. I think that if you got even the gist of the analysis from me tonight, based on my own and Mae's research, that now when you read the papers and see a certain news item, things will begin to click for you and make sense in a different way. Hopefully you'll raise some questions that you haven't before. To me 'that's the goal: to make people alert and give them a different way to look at the situation so that they can use their own imagination to solve the cases. But if you don't look, then you might as well not hire a coroner or a homicide detective or anybody to figure out how someone died. You might as well just bury them and go on.

The Fascist Agenda for the 90's

I've said for several years in my lectures that there's a three-pronged program for the current period going into the turn of the century. One prong is to get a stranglehold on all natural resources. They know where they are, they've known of them from satellites. They knew in the 50's where most of them were. Most of their motive for going into Vietnam was not the genocide of the Asian people there, although that was a side bonus to send a message out to people not to get out of line, but it was because offshore oil was discovered in 1954, larger than the Texas Panhandle, because tungsten couldn't be gotten in that volume anywhere else in the world which is why we funded the French, because we knew the day after Pearl Harbor (when 98% of our rubber supply was cut off because the Japanese closed the southern rim of the Pacific to us) there were specific strategic materials there that we wanted to control and have access to.

That's really the basis of the game, starting with oil, which is often the most important element in the whole history, the secret history of oil, and then later uranium. But oil is the major source that has to be protected, also gold and other things. There's enough raw material in the southern tip of Africa, from the northern border of Zimbabwe down, to keep us at current consumption levels for another 500 years. This is why we back the current apartheid regime there and don't want local rule and will do whatever is necessary - genocide, intervention, or exploitation of malleable labor to control those resources and deny them to the Soviet Union.

The second aspect or prong of the fascist agenda is to establish by the end of the century a first-strike capability of nuclear weapons. That's what MX and Trident and Star Wars are about - to give us first strike capability and the idea of a 'winnable' nuclear war, where we have 15% of the industrial capability and at least 5% of the population left. That's enough for them to call it a win. They 're going to be down in the underground bunkers anyway, and to go for broke they have a thing called

Air Land Battle 2000. In Army Times magazine they talk about it. It's full-scale chemical, biological and nuclear attack on the Soviet Union by the turn of the century.

But the Soviets are no longer in a position to wage the nuclear arms race and the cold war because it's bankrupted their entire economy to the point that they've got a huge internal domestic problem. So Gorbachev is playing re a/politic in a clever way that at least partially embarrasses the United States into dropping some of their defenses. But at the same time Bush talks about going to the Malta summit and having a 'kinder and gentler America,' he's developing a new program of next generation nuclear weapons called SIOPS 7, with nuclear bombs that burrow 600 feet into the ground and blow up the Soviet command bunkers. They've got just one step after another going ahead with the program.

The third aspect that I've talked about for some time is the destabilization of the eastern European buffer zone that was set up between the fascist and monarchist states and the Soviet Union. The whole history that I talk about really began in 1918 with the Bolshevik revolution and the reaction of the monarchs and the industrialists around the world, the fear that that might happen someplace else. Herbert Hoover served as a central element in collecting money from the monarchists and others under the International Red Cross. He delivered food and monies that were supposed to go to the starving people in Russia to the Vasilov White Russian armies and counter revolutionaries instead and fed and financed them to try and destroy the Bolsheviks. He spent years and years collecting monies from the remaining monarchies and a secret fund was established that was pumped into post-World War I Germany to finance the secret rearmament of Germany from 1918 to 1932 and the eventual rise of Hitler and the Nazi war machine.

The main purpose of that war machine's development was to get back the Soviet Union. They failed in 1943 at Stalingrad at a cost of over 20 million Soviet lives; the Soviets won the war in that sense at tremendous cost and stopped the drive and in 1943 Allen Dulles and the others knew that they had to go back underground and regroup and work again for the rise of the Fourth Reich and international fascism which is what we live under and are fostering in the current period and the Soviet Union is again the target. But part of that would be Hitler's old dream of the reunification of the German state, which is what they're trying to portray with the Berlin Wall change, although the politics internally in East Berlin are not that different and the people that came over mostly came over to get a free Coke and $50 in free shopping money and went back the same day.

They always like to talk about all the people running from communism, but usually reality is a little different. They like to say that the Soviets put up the wall to stop the brain drain, but 1 think that the reality was that they put up the wall to stop all the Nazi agents that weren't taken out of the post-war German military and intelligence structures from coming in and easily infiltrating and destroying their attempt at a socialist society. I think that the main people involved in these eastern European changes are the old revanchists, the Radio Free Europe people. The Nazi sympathizers are being invited back in.

I talked earlier about Lech Walesa. Everybody thought he was so noble when he got $1 million from the Nobel Peace Prize and gave it to the Vatican. Well, he's just paying interest on the $50 million that the Pope, whose family name is Wojtila, gave to him in order to help effect Solidarnosc and the Polish disruption there. But they're doing an effective job of changing the nature of the buffer job and destabilizing it and I think its just part of the program. By the end, some of these people want to go for broke. They want to go to martial law and total armed control here in the United States.

MOVE AND THE MILITARIZATION OF THE POLICE (1985)

Short History of a Principle

The principle that there should be a split between the functions of the military and civilian branches of government dates to the earliest years of our formation as a country. The Declaration of Independence complains of excesses by King George's troops, and the Bill of Rights establishes rights against abuse by militia. The Constitution is even clearer on how military forces are to be set up, governed and used.

Since that time, however, the principle has been eroded in practice. By 1792, George Washington had ordered the use of troops to quell the Whiskey Rebellion. Even then, it was made clear that stopping insurrection with militia was not the same as responding to riots. Unfortunately, this distinction was to fade into history as the national military force grew.

As labor began to fight for its demands, owners and managers began to hire private strong-arm agencies to bust the strikes. Infamous in this regard was the Pinkerton Detective Agency, which grew into our current National Guard. Federal troops were used to smash demonstrations for human and civil rights, such as the Veterans March on Washington following World War I.

Soldiers and Strikers

The labor struggles of the 30's and 40's saw the regular use of National Guard troops to enforce the will of the rich. John L. Lewis, one of the first national labor leaders complained bitterly of the use of such forces and their role as scabs in the mining strikes. "You can't dig coal with your bayonet," was a popular slogan of the time. By the 1960's and 70's, National Guard involvement in opposing (and sometimes creating) riots and in strikebreaking efforts was commonplace. "Operation Graphic Hand," a scabbing operation to counter the nationwide postal strikes used active duty Army troops to deliver the mail.

Democracy+ Military= Coup d'état

The continuing encroachment of the military into such civil affairs threatens a democracy. The first aspect is a loss of civil liberties. This is often accompanied by great secrecy about policy-making, spying on civilians, censorship, unsolved murders and disappearances, and conscription. The final stage in any uncontrolled growth of military power is coup d'état, the military overthrow of the state, and martial law, total suspension of civil liberties during "emergencies." History does not hold much hope for these being temporary conditions, as the history of much of the Americas demonstrates.

Until recently, at least on the books, the idea of any military role in law enforcement or police functions was considered taboo. The Posse Comitatus Act, used following the civil war to stop the excesses of federal troops during Reconstruction, banned the military from making arrests. During World War II, and especially in the years that followed, police and military functions began to become centralized, tasks overlapped (such as guarding the borders and controlling contraband), and a new era of close cooperation was born.

Still, people spoke of the dangers. The dreaded Nazi Schutzstaffel (SS) units, that carried out the bloody genocide against partisans and Jews. And their Death's Head Gestapo police were a fearful example of the combined function of military and police forces. Eisenhower warned of the encroachment of a vast military-industrial complex at the end of the 1950's. Like many other concerns for traditional civil liberties, these fears took second place to the orchestrated anti-communism and "red scares" of the McCarthy era.

From 1947 on, foreign and domestic policy was manipulated to insure both international control and domestic production and profits. We inherited a permanent war economy, a police intelligence state, and a national security apparatus. What was to grow into the largest police force in the country, Defense Industrial Security Command (DISC), completely under military control had its roots in the Tennessee Valley Authority police, set up by David Lilienthal to guard the Manhattan Project scientists developing the atomic bomb. DISC currently guards all military contractors, certain bases and installations, Voice of America, and the nuclear plants under control of the Atomic Energy Commission. Such "national security" projects continue to confuse who needs guarding from whom.

The Chickens Come Home

Perhaps the earliest example of direct training and cooperation of both military and police forces came in the 1950's, at secret CIA camps in Georgia, when police from many states were covertly instructed in anti-riot techniques. By the end of the

1960's, as Malcolm X put it following President Kennedy's assassination, "The chickens [had] come home to roost." The rising civil rights and anti-war movements of the 50's and 60's put the public in the position of an "enemy" to the emerging security state, and the war in Vietnam came home. The Defense Intelligence Agency (DIA), with budget and manpower ten times that of FBI and CIA combined, began to spy on anti-war activists, keeping dossiers on over 8 million civilians. As veterans returned from the war, many used the training they got to land jobs in local police departments. At the same time, police were being openly trained with the same weapons, tactics and techniques used in urban counter-insurgency wars abroad by the U.S. military. They began to develop the same arsenals (including tanks, gas, and other anti-personnel weapons), intelligence methods and personnel.

Martial Law & Internment Camps

Even the language began to reflect the reality. The small village of Wounded Knee, South Dakota, site of a confrontation between federal police and activists in the American Indian Movement over native people's rights, was referred to in almost every press account as a "hamlet," the term used to designate small villages in Vietnam. The underlying implication was clearly that the people inside were military targets. Another example was the open declaration of martial law in the streets of Washington, D.C. on May Day, 1970, an attempt to stop demonstrations against the war. Using methods eventually declared illegal by federal courts, the military and police rounded up thousands of people in mass arrests and drove them into a barricaded stadium for detainment.

Civil liberties and rights were suspended.

During the McCarthy era, Senator Pat McCarran had set up internment camps, similar to those used during the war to round up Japanese Americans. These are available in times of war or "emergency" for mass arrest and confinement (without appearances before judge or jury, and without rights of habeas corpus). Interstate highway systems, in use since the 1950's and projected for completion in the 1990's, are actually under military control, and will close to public use come the "emergency." Army and Marine units have been specially trained to effect civilian round-ups overnight, and planning extends to the neighborhood level. We have promoted and paid for similar martial law and internment operations in many countries abroad, with Chile as a striking recent example.

By the late 60's, the Rand Corporation had studied the "feasibility" of martial law in several foreign countries, including Vietnam, Canada, the Philippines, Chile, South Yemen, Pakistan and Iran, everywhere, in fact, that U.S.-backed coups and dictatorships made it a reality. They also studied how to create conditions here that could lead to acceptance of martial law by American citizens. Specific martial law plans included one set in motion just before the shooting of demonstrators by National Guardsmen at Kent State University in Ohio. Eighteen camps were open and ready for prisoners, had students escalated their demonstrations in response. Instead, many were frightened into silence. Senator Sam Ervin revealed what he called a "fascist" plan for martial law during the Watergate Hearings, referred to as the "Houston Plan," but details were never made public. "Turnsole," "King Alfred Plan" and other exotic names refer to plans aimed at Black Americans for internment in camps, and "vaporization." Secret presidential orders suspend normal constitutional rules in times of "crisis management."

Spying on Civilians

The National Security Agency (NSA), also under DIA control, is the largest spy operation in the world, monitoring every electronic communication in the world. Under "Operation Harvest," the NSA set up listening posts in American cities that could simultaneously record 450,000 phone conversations. These tapes were then played back at high speed to computers, searching for key words or phrases, and repeating patterns. Only small fractions were then singled out for human ears, and certain lines put under permanent surveillance. The NSA declassifies so much material each day that they use the paper in their furnaces to heat the building.

Each of the military branches has it's own intelligence units under the DIA umbrella as well. Anny intelligence used ROTC units on campuses to spy on anti-war and other progressive activities and organizations. Navy intelligence, among other projects, tested "desensitizing" methods to make selected people into assassins who would respond on post-hypnotic command. Strapping their heads into position, and pulling open their eyelids (like the famous scene in "Clockwork Orange"), the Navy drugged them, forced them to look at pictures of violent and brutal murders, and distracted their attention with other details until they became indifferent to the shock of the violence shown.

The military spying was but one piece of a much larger effort on the part of all U.S. intelligence agencies to disrupt and destroy the anti-war and civil rights movements of the 60's. The FBI's Division V, Domestic Operations, began "COINTELPRO" (Counterintelligence Program) to discredit, divide and smash the New Left. The CIA, though legally prohibited from operations inside the U.S., had a similar program called "Operation Chaos." Intelligence was gathered through local police "Red Squads" as well, and coordinated nationally by a computer system known as "Law Enforcement Intelligence Unit." The central gathering point was the infamous "Criminal Conspiracy Section" of the Los Angeles police department. These files were eventually stolen following Watergate revelations, and collected into the computers of Western Goals, a neo fascist operation under the control of Congressman Larry McDonald, the John Birch Society, and a board of reactionaries. Western Goals is currently directed by Carl Spitz Channel, the indicted bagman for Oliver North 's operations.

Beyond Surveillance - Provocateurs

At one point, J. Edgar Hoover, former FBI director, claimed to have dossiers on more than 200 million Americans, and insisted on "closing the gap." In addition to surveillance and infiltration of groups, these operations included "black bag jobs" (burglaries of office files and homes), disinformation in local papers, letters and threats, forged communications to create distrust, phony organizations set up or manipulated to cause disunity, kidnappings and murders, and classic "provocateur" operations (using police agents and materials to encourage violent or illegal activities by groups or individuals, setting up traps for police arrests or attacks).

Perhaps the most notorious, and the most effective of these provocateur actions was the so-called Symbionese Liberation Anny (SLA) in California. Almost every member of the group was a police agent. SLA leader Donald DE 'Freeze had served as a police informant in Cleveland and California. William and Emily Harris and Angela Atwood were a "mod squad" of narcotics cops working at University of Indiana in Bloomington, before migrating to California. Colston Westbrook, who ran the SLA recruitment program in the

California prison system, and owned the "Peking House" where the other agents lived, had worked in Vietnam for Pacific Corporation, a CIA subsidiary, and was part of the murderous "Operation Phoenix." Police and DIA provocateurs were also used to spark police riots against demonstrators in Chicago in 1968.

Militarized Police

It was in this context, using the SLA as an excuse, that the first Special Weapons and Tactics (SWAT) team was created and used in California. Trained by a weapons expert from the Van Nuys police force (also the first husband of Marilyn Monroe), and by local ROTC officers, these militarized police unit's spread across the country for use in hostage situations and against "terrorists," the new bogeymen for the sophisticated 80's. Out of those teams grew special military and civilian forces called TNT (Terrorist Neutralization Teams). The ultimate provocateur scenario will be a "nuclear terrorism" inside American borders, scaring people enough to justify an end to civil liberties and martial law. One of the current planners of such martial law operations is none other than Lt. Col. Oliver North, also considered to be "counter-terrorism ex pen." Under that rubric, many of the excesses of Contra gate were committed, and more are likely to emerge.

Provocateurs serve to escalate the violence and mistrust, and to insure public acceptance of police abuse. Other methods include constant television programming that makes all police into heroes, especially those who use, illegal and unconstitutional methods to stop "vicious criminals" (we see the targets committing the crimes as the show starts, so there is no question of innocence, or doubt of guilt), who are supposedly using the rules of law to succeed in living outside the law. In addition, certain authors and moviemakers develop elaborate plots years in advance to pre-condition acceptance later or to send up "trial balloons" to gauge public reaction.

Final Solutions

Part of the "Watergate West" operation under then-Governor Ronald Reagan in California were state-wide martial law and internment plans known as "Operation Cable Splicer," and "Garden Plot." These were aimed directly at using National Guard and state and local police against the growing progressive movements of the 60's. Key characters in these plans later took positions in the Reagan Administration, notably Ed Meese of the Department of "Justice," Louis Giuffrida, a former director of the Federal Emergency Management Agency (FEMA)-perhaps you can guess what they do? And Thomas Turnage, head of California's National Guard round-up plans ("Operation Golden Bear") and later director of both Selective Service and the Veterans Administration. In keeping with this trend, the recently (1990) appointed director of the Selective Service is former C.I.A. Executive Robert Gambino. In 1970, at the Army War College, Louis Giuffrida drafted a plan for the mass arrest and internment of 20 million "Black Americans." He later worked with Col. North on a joint FEMA and Pentagon plan for martial law and arrest of Central American refugees and American dissidents called "Rex '84," set to go into operation when U.S. troops invaded Nicaragua or El Salvador. The names change, but not the intent.

As my mother, a Pentagon analyst, used to say, "Standing armies don't stand." Plans have a way of implementing themselves. Beyond surveillance and disruption, and even beyond the now well-publicized attempts by FBI blackmailers to get Martin Luther King to commit suicide, was murder. At the first level, it may have consisted of failures to warn political figures of impending threats known to the intelligence agencies through informers. Later, it included standing aside while KKK and other neo-Nazi organizations pulled the triggers on demonstrators lacking police protection, or failing to investigate or prosecute those responsible.

Outright patterns of murder became clear in the deaths of many members of the Black Panther Party. Political assassinations of both national and local figures escalated, with the system denying either "conspiracy" or "foul play" before the evidence was in. Neglect of human and civil rights in general led to the deaths of thousands of disenfranchised people, the poor, the institutionalized, and the powerless.

Posse Militarus

The 1980's also mark the final erosion of the divisions between civilian and military roles in law enforcement. A direct attempt is being made to undermine the provisions of the Posse Comitatus Act, and to have it taken off the books. This time the excuse is interception of illegal drugs. The tactics of arrest and intervention continue to escalate the military role at every turn. Regardless of the reason used to overturn this protection against military abuses, the outcome is not likely to limit itself to "curing" a single social problem.

In the final analysis, the civilian oversight needed to make democracy a functional reality, and the secrecy of our national decision-making process can't co-exist. One or the other has to go, and democracy is in a much more vulnerable position than tyranny. Attacks on the least popular among us are attacks on us all. As Malcolm X once said, "If you read the newspapers long enough, you'll end up loving the people doing the oppressing and hating the people being oppressed."

MOVE Was Nothing New

What happened in Philadelphia in 1978, and again in 1985, when police targeted and attacked the organization known as MOVE, was no isolated instance. Many, if not all of the factors discussed above came into play.

There were comparable instances in recent history, but not in the popular history we are taught in school or shown on TV. This was not the first time in American history that a black neighborhood was bombed during a period of unrest. During the police attack on Chicago Black Panther organizers Fred Hampton and Mark Clark, police fired nearly 400 rounds into the house before two rounds were fired in return. We know this because work with ballistic rods at the murder scene proved it in court. Fearing a repetition of this, a special Philadelphia "police demolition team" razed the MOVE house to the ground within 24 hours after the 1978 shooting incident, destroying the evidence.

MOVE and the SLA: A Comparison

Perhaps more telling are the comparisons of two seemingly unrelated instances, or "scenarios," the attacks on MOVE and the attack on the SLA house in Los Angeles in 1974. These were both domestic military operations involving violent responses and psychological warfare. I would argue that both were also provocateur scenarios, planned and brought on by police design. The history of the characters in the SLA, and their activities, made clear their role as provocateurs to any objective observer. The backgrounds of MOVE members (many of them Black Panthers, though they were infiltrated heavily with police agents as well) do not make as clear-cut a case. Survivors, however, are sure that at least one or two of the group's members were police agents. Perhaps their most important role had been to isolate the group from the Black community and the progressive white organizations as well, making them an easy target for attack and an "example."

To compare the situations, I have divided the information into nine categories that shed the most light: planning, isolation, participants, military units/personnel, city administration, operation/press coverage, evidence, denial, and purpose. Taking them one at a time:

Planning

Scenarios for intelligence purposes are planned well in advance, linked to some plausible "trigger" 'incident, and usually completed only if several "bonus" goals are reached with a single operation, including disruption, propaganda, change of policy, and elimination of opposition. As early as 1972, prisoners in the California prison system and elsewhere were being approached and recruited for the "Symbionese Liberation Army," offered early release in exchange for commitments. Some radical group was obviously not doing this recruitment systematically, it was acknowledged and supported by the system itself.

That same year, a pornographic novel appeared called Black Abductors, from a bogus publishing firm. In the novel, a bi-racial group kidnaps "Patty," the daughter of a major west-coast publishing figure, and "seduces" her through forced sexual initiation. She changes her name to a more radical one, and the group demands the release of political prisoners as ransom. Milton Caniff, who gets his material from military intelligence contacts, and draws the comic Steve' Canyon, admitted cancelling an entire strip because it was "spooky." Apparently, it predicted the Patty Hearst kidnapping, and he feared the family would be embarrassed (and presumably he would be as well).

School superintendent Marcus Foster challenged the use of a student ID plan cooked up by his assistant, a Vietnam veteran. The plan was the same one used to identify Vietnamese victims of the deadly "Operation Phoenix." The local KKK attacked Foster in flyers as a "Mixmaster" (i.e., racial integrationist), and a week later he was shot to death with cyanide-tipped bullets. His assistant, wounded in the same incident, survived in part because the bullets striking him were not toxic. This murder was the first public act claimed by the so-called SLA, and was performed by two Vietnam veterans. The SLA further confused the incident by claiming they killed Foster in retaliation for his support of the ID scheme!

The real history of the SLA is that of a well-planned agent provocateur group, directed through the LAPD Criminal Conspiracy Section, and the CIA-linked Law Enforcement Assistance Administration. Donald DE 'Freeze, or Field Marshall Cinque of the SLA, was a paid police agent, cultivated by Colston Westbrook of the CIA, and released from prison to stage the operation. Another LAPD agent, Louis Tackwood, in his book The Glass House Tapes, revealed much of this history.

The "trigger" incident was the kidnapping of Patty Hearst, the bank robberies and murders. The final "shoot out" was triggered by a phony "tip off' call to police, who first surrounded and terrified the people in the house next door with bullhorns, until a youngster came out to tell them the people they wanted were "next door."

Similar advance planning is evident in both the MOVE incidents. The "trigger incident" in 1978 was a health inspection for rats, supposedly reacting to neighbors' complaints. MOVE members, reportedly armed, stopped the inspector at the door. This terrible violation supposedly led Mayor Rizzo to state publicly that MOVE should "Get out or die!" The police first set up 24-hour surveillance using the Philadelphia Red Squad, then called the Civil Disturbance Unit. Police presence escalated until a steel-link fence was erected around the whole neighborhood, public access restricted, business disrupted, and local residents forced to carry special ID (sound familiar?) and be escorted to and from their homes by police "protection." The neighbors began to carry signs demanding, "Cats, not cops!" to solve the alleged "rat problem."

One month before this siege began I located an issue of Vigilante magazine, from a far right organization, which had photographs of the MOVE house, identified members as "dangerous urban terrorists," and called for police or vigilante attacks before the situation got any worse. This publication was sent regularly to police departments and Red Squads around the country. I passed it over the fence to MOVE as a warning of what might come.

The pattern repeats itself in the 1985-bombing incident. Neighbors' complaints are· again used to "trigger" a response. One month before the attack, the national fascist group, "The Order, announced that the whole country would soon look "like Vietnam." The special "counter-terrorist" Philadelphia police units, left over from Rizzo years, spent 18 months at a U.S. Army base in New Jersey practicing with helicopters and "explosive devices" to perfect their aim. When the C-4 bomb exploded in Philadelphia, catching the MOVE house afire, police and fire officials did nothing to put out the flames for nearly an hour, endangering human lives and burning a Black neighborhood to the ground. This was no accident.

Isolation

Important to both the secrecy and success of intelligence operations, isolation from existing groups is a critical aspect of such plans. When Donald DE 'Freeze was first released from prison, he approached Vietnam Veterans Against the War, Venceremos, and other left groups, offering his services as a "hit man." Perhaps initially designed as a recruiting ploy, these actions insured the isolation of DE 'Freeze and the SLA from coalition or cooperation later. The SLA operated like a religious cult, with layers of control and secrecy. Early recruits from the legitimate progressive community left the organization's public functions because of these practices. In addition, the membership of the SLA had an unknown history, and members who had almost no community or organizational background.

MOVE shared a history of hostility to other groups, and some disruption of community meetings. By the time the police became involved, they were isolated from most of the Black community due to their beliefs, and from the progressive white left due to their practice. They were reportedly drawn from the ranks of the decimated Black Panther organization, but they had no pattern of cooperation or consultation with other groups. Led by John "Africa," they operated as a political sect, and a religious cult. These factors assisted the police in their attack, since much of the left and the Black community failed to come to the defense of MOVE, unless they saw the more important principle of opposing fascist police tactics against all people. It was easy to blame the victim.

Participants

The SLA was made up of "migratory birds," coming into California from elsewhere, people whose earlier histories would not get in the way of the operation. They were, almost to a member, police agents or collaborators, and unbeknownst to them they were ultimately expendable. Donald De'Freeze and Thero Wheeler, allowed to leave the California prison system, were protégés of the prison programs run by Colston

Westbrook, an employee of CIA subsidiary firm Pacific Engineering. The "migratory birds" flocked around Westbrook, and he established the "Peking House," taught Black Lexicon at the California state college, and held "radical meetings" in the prisons. William and Emily Harris and Angela (D' Angelique) Atwood had no history of progressive organizing in Indiana, but they did have a history of setting up students for drug busts, and testifying against them on behalf of the State Police narcotics intelligence units.

DE 'Freeze himself had a long history of collaboration with police in California and Ohio, working as a provocateur to avoid charges and prison time. One of the guns he used in a bank robbery was linked by serial number of police stockpiles of confiscated weapons in Los Angeles. In the final shootout, the Black members and the two women who had done some political work, Hall and Solystik would die the Harris couple would survive.

MOVE set up house in West Philadelphia by grace of a University of Pennsylvania graduate student, who was white and who owned the house they lived in. He was later to surface as the main witness against John Africa and others on weapons charges in 1978. Did he play a role similar to Westbrook's, housing them while he set them up to be discounted, discredited and killed? In the final siege in 1978, when SWAT units opened fire on the house, and police to flood the house used a huge fire hose, a police officer was killed.

Most of the members were wounded, beaten or imprisoned. It is not as clear, in 1985, whether the police had someone on the inside. It is important that the survivors and other members have said in public that someone served as a provocateur. In the end, the victims and the dead are Blacks, women and children.

Military Units/Personnel

Superintendent Marcus Foster's assistant, Colston Westbrook, and the Vietnam veterans Ramiro and little of the SLA who shot Foster had multiple connections with the CIA assassination plan "Operation Phoenix" used to kill indiscriminately in Vietnam. The recurrent theme of the

Phoenix ID program in California and Philadelphia stretch coincidence. These operations clearly involved military units. Another military aspect in both operations was the presence of the Special

Weapons and Tactics Teams, SWAT. Trained by special ROTC and active duty units, these militarized police included veterans of Vietnam. In fact, it was the burnout of the SLA in Los Angeles that served as both the first "trigger" excuses and public act for SWAT in America. The FBI, whose Division V (Five) Domestic Operations group was dominated by Navy intelligence agents William Sullivan and Catha Deke DeLoach, was used to create and to cover up the reality of the SLA. In 1978, a police agent named George Fenci was busy carrying out the FBI's COINTELPRO operations through the local Red Squad. SWAT was in place in Philadelphia, and provided an arsenal for the attack on MOVE. Following the shootings, a Special Police Demolition team razed the building. Were these also SWAT or military units? No such organization has been cited since. By 1985, the militarization was even more evident. Despite changeovers in city management, the same unit, and even the same officers led both attacks on MOVE. Mayor Goode was taken out of town just before the incident, and did not arrive on the scene until it was too late to avert a tragedy. The Philadelphia City Manager Brooks gave the green light. He was a former general in Vietnam. SWAT and special helicopter police teams trained at nearby bases led the attack, using C-4, an explosive legally; restricted to use by U.S. military only.

City Administration

Strangely enough, the SLA and MOVE burnouts, though they happened thousands of miles apart, and over a span of several years (1974-85), both occurred in cities during the terms of their first elected Black mayors. Racism was the theme in 1978 as well, when Rizzo openly called for whites to "join hands and unite" on Election Day. His famous "Get out or die, quote came in the middle of an election campaign, as did the siege. Special police intelligence units in each case controlled the operational level: LAPD Criminal Conspiracy Section (now called Public Disorder Intelligence Di vision) in 1974, Philadelphia's Red Squad in 1978, and the same unit in 1985, then renamed as the Civil Disturbance Unit. In two of the cases, the Black Mayors were only informed of the plans at the very last moment, making it impossible for them to either change the course of events, or to avoid the responsibility.

Operation/Press

Fire fighters were deliberately kept out of the area during the shootout/burnout of the SLA. Hundreds of rounds were fired into the house and adjacent houses, threatening innocent neighbors and damaging their homes.

The first attack on MOVE involved oven fascism in the Black and student area of Powellton. Police set up an armed camp, complete with surveillance, fences, ID cards, and hundreds of police and paramilitary troops. The literal destruction of all evidence, when the house was razed, marked the most oven fascist act, but drew little attention in the press. The 1985 bombing ("incendiary device") started a fire almost immediately in the MOVE house. A huge water spray hose was already positioned across the street, and had been turned on to drive the MOVE members out. However, police ordered fire fighters to stay clear of the equipment, even when the fire was clearly spreading to surrounding homes. Falsely claiming that fire fighters were in danger from MOVE members, the police let the fire rage for 45 minutes before allowing any action to put it out. By then, people inside the MOVE house had burned to death, and the homes for several blocks had been consumed by fire.

At the SLA event, press representatives were hand-picked, and the incident was handled as a public relations event for SWAT by J. Walter Thompson advertising, a CIA-linked firm that did public relations for Nixon's election and for Chile's dictator Pinochet. Similarly, the press was kept at bay in the 1978 MOVE attack. One reporter hid in a nearby abandoned house inside the police blockade, and surprised the Rizzo administration by getting photos of police beating and kicking an unarmed MOVE member, Delbert Africa, as he emerged from the house basement. One of the few local reporters to tell the truth about the event was Mumbai Jamal, a co-founder of the Association of Third World Journalists, who was himself framed in the shooting of a police officer shortly after that. Press and public alike were blockaded from the 1985 MOVE bombing, but what was happening soon became visible outside the police-controlled area.

Evidence

The constant pattern with evidence in these intelligence operations is one of destruction, alteration or concealment. The bodies in the SLA incident, were destroyed by fire the first count was inaccurate. The bodies of Camilla Hall and Patricia Solystik were not "discovered" for three days. In fact, the death certificate for Camilla Hall places her death at a separate address, raising the question of whether they were killed earlier and elsewhere, and dragged to the site. The corpse of Donald De'Freeze, if in fact it was his body, returned to his family in Cleveland without head or hands (removed for purposes of identification, according to Los Angeles authorities). No trial was held for these crimes, since all were presumed dead. Ramiro and Little, the Vietnam veterans who murdered Dr. Foster, were the first in the country to ask for a televised trial in their cells, rather than being present in the courtroom.

Psychiatric "experts" from the CIA's MKUL surrounded the living witness, Patty Hearst TRA (mind control) program, Dr. Louis Jocelyn West and Robert Jay Lifton, claiming as they did for the U.S. prisoners of war in Korea in the 1950's, that Patty was a victim of "brainwashing." Patty's victimization and control was much more sophisticated, involving sensory deprivation (living in cramped closet), rape and forced sexual humiliation, drugging, and forced involvement in criminal activity. During the trial, her family was threatened and her phony lawyer, Melvin Belli, told her to "shut up" about the details of her abuse. Belli has handled many important cases for the intelligence community, not the least of which was the "defense" of Jack Ruby in Dallas for the murder of Lee Harvey Oswald.

Ballistic work was impossible once the MOVE house was destroyed in 1978, but the community raised no outcry over these tactics. Officer Ramp, who was killed during the final siege, was clearly shot from above and behind by all available ballistic evidence. The MOVE members were below him and to his front, what was behind and above was the SWAT teams. Why this aging officer, off the streets for years and nearly retired, was involved in the frontal and open assault with a fire hose against MOVE has never been explained. Did the Rizzo administration need a dead cop to move public opinion? Was Ramp targeted by SWAT for some other reason than saving the cost of his pension? 'Following capture, and clearly presumed guilty at their "trial." Seven different people were convicted for the murder of Officer Ramp, none of whom could have been proven as even a suspect using ballistic evidence. The Philadelphia police took pains to make public display of a so-called "arsenal" supposedly located at the site, but the weapons displayed contradict all other witness and ballistic evidence of what few guns MOVE members had. Such "arsenals" are often constructed after the fact from confiscated weapons stores.

In 1985, a MOVE house was once again destroyed by, allowing it and the people inside to burn beyond recognition. The first claims of an "arsenal" of machine guns and explosive weapons there proved to be fabrications by the police. Destruction by fire makes autopsy work difficult. Forensic "experts" used by the Philadelphia police, including one who had identified remains in Paraguay as those of Dr. Josef Mengele (another cover-up), first identified bullets in the bodies, and then decided that the metal fragments were not bullets after all.

Denial

DENY, the first four letters in the CIA alphabet, is the modus operandi in these cases. Planted stories and disinformation are prepared in advance (e.g., false "sniper" story following military murders at Kent State, or "murdered by inmates" story after police assault at Attica State Prison), and serve to hold the press and public at bay while a more formal denial is worked out. Witnesses that count are either jailed or end up dead. "Doubles" of the main characters frustrate investigation and confuse events (E.g., Jim Jones and Lee Harvey Oswald both had doubles). Special lawyers, psychiatrists and "experts" lead the "official" investigations. Officials in the key agencies lie to cover up the real story.

Planning for the official lie in the SLA story began with FBI agent Charles Bates, who said, "All you need to start a revolution is a tape recorder," referring to SLA taped "communiqués." Bates and others maintained the myth that the SLA were "revolutionaries," and that the members had a "radical" past in fact, members were police agents, provocateurs, CIA operatives, topless dancers at Howard Hughes' Vegas casino, narcotics cops, university employees in Indiana and California, people with no history of political consciousness or development that might have Jed them to "pick up the gun." Both FBI and CIA agents hid Patty Hearst during her captivity and travels, in "safe houses." The FBI agent who revealed this was locked up in a mental hospital for "alcoholism" when he spilled the beans. Donald De'Freeze had an exact double, close enough that the man lived with De'Freeze's family for months before revealing his identity to them. An exact double for Patty Hearst ("down to the moles and scars") was arrested and released in Ohio. A check of high school yearbooks in the small town revealed that the story was false, but this event could have provided an escape for Patty. If the wrong agency spotted her, or local police arrested her, she could play her own "double" and be released with the confirmation of the FBI.

Witnesses were either dead or in jail by the time the story went to trial. Patty "converted" to Born Again Christianity and married her 'prison guard. Similarly, Rizzo lied and distorted facts and events to justify the open martial law he declared in the MOVE neighborhood. Police officer Ramp's death was falsely blamed on MOVE. Key witnesses were shot at the Philadelphia Roundhouse after arrest, as was journalist

Mumbai Jamal, apparently. These witnesses ended up in jail. Lies about "machine guns" in the MOVE house in 1985, or that a "can of gasoline" accidentally started the fire were used to cover up the military escalation and bombing tactics during the event. City officials later lied, and Jack Brooks resigned. The National Association of Chiefs of Police for the bombing and endangering the public roundly condemned Philadelphia Police Chief Saunders. The real reasons for death, the discrepancies in body counts and parts, and the possibility that more bodies were added later as in the SLA action, were never fully investigated by the official panel that looked into the MOVE incident. Witnesses were mute burned to death, or shot.

Purpose

Such incidents, long in the planning, execution and follow-up, usually involve more than one purpose. Some of the purposes are to discredit political dissent or alternate lifestyles, frighten the general population, justify increased repression, escalate militarization, test public response, and realize the "bonuses" of related deaths or imprisonments.

The SLA was set up politically to discredit the left, the anti-war and anti-fascist groups working for social and political change in legitimate ways. The scenario was a sort of soap opera for the rich. The incident fed into general public fears of being kidnapped or taken hostage. This orchestrated panic, fed by CIA-staged hijackings and hostage events, also allowed the government to cause certain people to "disappear" under cover of the general escalation of "terror." The SLA was also engineered to bring in militarized police, the SWAT teams, and gave that added fascism its excuse. This was among the earliest incidents that introduced the idea of a right to use "deadly force" in police operations. The SLA 's demand for a public food program was a litmus test for their credibility with the left, and many legitimate groups were fooled into cooperating. Indications are that the food may have been botulized or poisoned. Delivered and distributed by street criminals and police agents, the food distribution points were often the scenes of provoked rioting, another method of discrediting the poor. One such person led into the trap was Prisoner's Union organizer "Popeye" Jackson, with the help of an FBI agent posing as a "radical," Sara Jane Moore. Not surprisingly, she was later used as a patsy in an attempted assassination on Gerald Ford. She shared a jail cell with Patty Hearst, and later was sent to the same prison with Lynne "Squeaky" Fromme of the DIA-led Manson gang. Moore admits that she set "Popeye" Jackson up to be killed. Other "bonuses" included the infiltration before and after of the California prison system by SLA recruiters and members, and the murder of progressive community leader Marcus Foster.

Like Manson and the SLA, the MOVE attacks were used to discredit alternative lifestyles of any kind. MOVE, a semi-religious cult, refused to kill any animals, were strict vegetarians, and believed that toilets polluted the water supply. Rizzo was successful in stirring up racist fears, polarizing the white community against MOVE. This allowed public acceptance of the massive police and SWAT presence and the armed camp in Powell ton. Bonuses in 1978 included the death of Officer Ramp, Mumbai Jamal's imprisonment and the successful election bid by Rizzo. By 1985, the purpose had changed to discrediting "terrorism," a term openly used to describe MOVE activities. The burnout put neighbors on notice that there would be tremendous cost to allowing such groups to live among them. It declared an "open season" on Blacks and militants, as had been done in Greensboro, N.C. and in the incidents in Atlanta, New York and Buffalo since then. The escalation to bombing marked the early shots in an all-out war, since this was the second time in U.S. history that a Black community had been bombed. Since the incident, police in Maryland in a Black neighborhood has used another incendiary device. Besides the deaths of many MOVE members not already imprisoned, the final "bonuses" will probably come clear from the Philadelphia investigation report.

Racism and Black Genocide

The central role of racism, and the broader purpose of the systematic deprivation and destruction of people of color in this country are evident in the MOVE attack for those who will look. Not only would the incident not have happened in a white neighborhood, but also it could not have happened to white children without a much greater response in the community. MOVE was considered "strange" by both the Black community and the white progressives, so they were shunned. Immediate support was not forthcoming in either incident, although the Quakers did offer them rural land to relocate.

The left is rarely concerned with domestic intervention, even in such glaring examples as this. What we would see immediately as an example of fascism abroad, or as genocidal in the Third World, we see as an "isolated incident" or an "aberration" here at home. But as James Baldwin said, "If they come for you in the night, they will come for me in the morning." The system looks for this response, but such silence is consent. Are we saying that groups like MOVE are fair game? Do we buy the cover story while 900 Blacks die at Jonestown, or a whole neighborhood burns here? They are bringing it home. Was it "murder suicide" in Jonestown? Was it an "entry device" in Philadelphia? These were both military escalations by special police squads and intelligence agencies. They were Black genocide operations, and they are not isolated, nor things of the past. They will expand in relation to our indifference.

As wealth concentrates into fewer and fewer hands, and the technology creates capital surplus that is eaten up by war production instead of used for human needs, the population itself serves no purpose for those who run the society. Their labor, at some point, is superfluous, and these poor, mostly women, children and elderly, and people of color, become the modern-day "useless eaters" that were rounded up and exterminated during the Nazi 's Third Reich for the same reasons. The racial and class bias of the society involved determines the targets. Those on welfare, the chronically unemployed, the homeless, the institutionalized, the disenfranchised and powerless are the victims to be both blamed and eliminated. These are the people who constitute the "Third World" inside America. They fill its courts and prisons, its military and combat positions, its psychiatric hospitals and "homes." To those who run this country, they are expendable. If we ignore the attacks on unpopular groups like MOVE, then we cannot be held blameless when they escalate to more of us. This is how fascism works, targeting the vulnerable and isolated first. The first victims of the Holocaust were psychiatric inmates, by the tens of thousands. Few stood up for them or their rights.

We have already had martial law in this country; we already maintain concentration camps and have used them against Native Americans and Japanese, and more currently against immigrants; we know what genocide is, having "discovered" an occupied country; we began mass sterilization in the United States in the 1920's, long before Nazi psychiatrists implemented its use there, and we sterilized the same people; our technology of death is more advanced now, we do not pick the body up and put it in the ovens, we drop the ovens from the sky in the form of napalm and white phosphorus, weapons used in Vietnam and Central America.

If the countries of the world where we have staged coups, assassinated popular leaders, propped up fascist dictatorships, manipulated elections, stolen natural resources and exploited or killed laborers could take us tomorrow into the World Court, would the testimony be so different than that of the Nuremberg Trials? I think, in fact, it would be worse. If Aryan Germans wanted to turn their heads and avert their eyes during the Nazi years, they could Jive well and comfortably: Not all were terrorized by fascism, only the victims. They, too, plundered the wealth, the art, the culture, and the produce of the world community into a few hands. Berlin represented the most advanced technology and cultural expression of the times.

As one study title says, "They Thought They Were Free." So do we. We ask ourselves, how could the Germans have let it happen? Perhaps, if we can look at the truth of America today, we know.

CONTRAGATE AND THE INVISIBLE GOVERNMENT

Excerpt From A Speech by John Judge, 7/4/1987 at the Women's Building in San Francisco

Since I spoke on Barry Scott's show last Saturday, there's been this tremendous feedback to me, this outpouring of interest and I've been wondering all week what it was that I said, but I must have struck a nerve someplace.

I just wanted to say a special thanks to friends of mine here who were nice enough to come tonight and help sell some of my materials and a book that I edited somewhat and indexed. But the main credit should go to my friend Lenny Lapon who was the author of the book and self-publisher because he couldn't get anyone to print it, even in the progressive circles. It's a very, very important book and we have some copies here, called *Mass Murderers in White Coats: Psychiatric Genocide in Nazi Germany and the United States.*

It's a history of the development of the fascist techniques for murder by the psychiatrists in Germany who were the ones that developed the gas chambers and the killing methods and then were brought in as the experts to Auschwitz and the camps in order to set up the technology of death for the wider holocaust. But the first pan of that holocaust was the death of 300,000 psychiatric inmates in the late 1930's in the psychiatric institutions. These victims were considered to be "useless eaters" and expendable parts of the population in much the same way that the homeless community, which is also being identified as mentally ill in most of the press, and which in the polls taken by people who work with them on the streets, show that 70% on the east coast. I imagine it's a similarly large figure of there-and about 40 to 50 percent nationwide of the homeless are veterans many Vietnam veterans and other veterans with less than honorable discharge. With continuing drug and personal problems from the fascist nature of the war the genocidal nature of the war that they were asked to participate in, many of these veterans are just trying to survive.

The AMA and the APA are working on "lock-up" laws currently to make it easier to lock people back in the psychiatric institutions, force them onto the drugs. In Philadelphia, the Mayor there starred the "cold rule" whereby after the temperature got to a certain point, the homeless could be forcibly rounded up and taken into shelters. The first night that that was done in Philadelphia the shelters they went to forced them on to the Phenothiazine's and the psychiatric drugs. You can't stay overnight in a shelter in Philadelphia without getting on the drug regimen and that's going to spread. The APA and Ralph Nader's group, the liberals in Washington working on public health issues, want 24-hour psychiatric intervention in the shelters. If they don't get that treatment, instead, the homeless were taken into a community here on the West Coast, the Rajneesh commune, in busloads by the thousands and given injections. They didn't know the purpose or nature of the injections. They were given drugs every day and the community there was visited by the California Psychiatric Association and given approval in the national APA Journal as an alternative psychiatric and therapeutic model since they were using the Phenothiazine's and other drugs and 80% to 90% in the Rajneesh commune were psychiatrists, psychologists or some other form of therapists.

I know it's rude for me to bring this up in the Women's Building where I guess quite a bit of therapy goes on from what I hear, but l 've been an anti-psychiatry activist for many, many years (removes his sweater to reveal a T-shirt that reads "Psychiatry Kills"). (Applause)

I also wanted to thank the other people that have been an inspiration to me in this research and work for many years, including the indefatigable researcher Mae Brussell who has done tremendous work from the inception in 1964 and '65 when she began clipping newspapers and collecting magazine articles. None of the research community that I am aware of can hold a candle to the volume of material that Mae goes through - 15 newspapers a day from all across the country - I'm lucky to get through two a day, about 150 periodicals a month. I subscribe to 60 for my work and about 1000 books a year that she clips and cross-files and breaks down into categories and updates the current news and connections.

Although I've done a great deal of independent work and I did five years of research before I heard of Mae Brussell and came to the same general conclusions that she had, she has always been an inspiration to me. Tom Davis, who I also want to mention who has made available for many years the books that are central to this research field and there's a flyer in the back that you can pick up that's the back page of his catalog and send him a first-class stamp without the envelope in the mail and he '11 send you the full catalog, hundreds of titles which alone would educate you in terms of what's going on in this country, even if you didn't get around to reading them, but reading them is worth the effort if anyone here is still not post-literate in the TV generation. I suggest that as an antidote too much of what the current system puts out. I also have in the back two other pieces of paper I printed for tonight, this one, which is Conspiracy, with an exclamation point so that you get the idea, is from me. It's the list of the articles that I distribute.

"Conspiracy" is from the two Latin words "conspire" (to breathe together) and some people have worse breath than others. I also have a printout that Tom Davis was nice enough to make available today with the names and committee members of the three other committees who are not being broadcast on TV, the Senate Subcommittee on Narcotics, Terrorism, and International Operations with John Kerry, the Judiciary Subcommittee on Crime with William Hughes, and the House Select Narcotics Abuse and Control Committee with Chairman Rangel. The members and their phone numbers are here. These are the committees that are looking into the underpinnings of what really moved the Contragate situation in terms of the drugs, the hidden finances, and other things and have much more potential to shed light on the real nature of Contragate than the current orchestrated scandal, and I believe phony investigation that we're seeing day in and day out on the TV.

I'd like to get an idea before I get started because our time is limited, how many people already heard me speak on Barry Scott's show or have otherwise had an occasion to hear me speak in general. Okay. If I could have those hands down, for how many of you is the first time you've seen my mug and somebody you know dragged you in here, you don't know how you got here. Okay. Well, we're about half and half. And then would the people who were paid to come here and report ... Almost 'got him! (Laughter)

There's not a lot in the papers out here. I don't know what happens as you go west. (Laughter) I'm from D.C. so there's a little bit more. This is a nice thing. "President Reagan signed legislation for homeless into law to set up a federal oversight board, $1 billion in government aid for the problem in 14 months," and the measure directs the head of the Federal Emergency Management Agency to establish a board that would oversee the expenditure of money for the food and shelter programs. We'll talk a little bit later about who the Federal Emergency Management Agency is, but they're the people that will handle the detention centers for everybody else besides the homeless. (Laughter)

There was some news that Roici Sasakawa has begun to finance the battle against AIDS. He's having some meetings with prominent people about it like Pope John Paul II. Roici Sasakawa describes himself as "the richest fascist in the world." He was connected with the axis and fascist banks in Japan. He made a fortune since the end of World War II, but despite that, he seems to be quite welcome in many of the liberal and civil rights circles and his funding and other things aren't being contested, although I'm sure they're manipulating people. He was the keynote speaker, unfortunately I felt, at the birthday party anniversary for Martin Luther King, sitting up at the table with Coretta Scott and the other people in King's entourage with this self-describe multi-millionaire fascist, Roici Sasakawa playing this other role.

He, like many I might mention tonight, have hidden identities and come from murky backgrounds. Lest you doubt that there are fascists in the United States, this is from one of your local papers. Louis Trager just the other day. It says "Bomb Victim Calls Ex-Husband a Domineering Ex-Nazi." This is a woman who was delivered a plastic pipe bomb in a bouquet of dried flowers by her husband's lover and the husband she mentions made anti-Black and anti-Semitic remarks, displayed Nazi memorabilia, had family in Germany, had known Hitler and other top Nazis, was a member of the Hitler Youth and had sabotaged Allied tanks with explosives. His name is Peter Pulaski. Apparently this happened out here in San Francisco. So they're right here in town, in case you're missing them.

This was a nice headline the other day, S.F. Examiner on the 23rd "Transplant Research Explores a New Frontier: The Brain" I won't tell you where that one goes. This was S.F. Chronicle, Tuesday, July 14th. There's this interesting looking little bracelet and it's an article about how a slum lord here is going to be forced to live in this rat-infested building that he had where he did his exploiting. They had an almost exactly similar article in the Washington papers when l left about a month and a half ago about a Boy Scout leader who was accused of molesting children.

The point that's missed in here is that this little bracelet is called "Electronic House Arrest." They have these now in twenty states! They're computer linked electronic bracelets that are put on to the people on parole or in these special court-ordered situations, and the computer goes off if you try to leave the situation. Thousands of people already have these for use. It may sound like a good idea to somebody because the people they put them on, they make sure you don't like them from the start and they're people that have done some awful crimes or have been accused of them, but you miss the point if you don't understand that that's the beginning of techno-fascism down to the local level.

Here's another hidden fascist. "Service for William Casey Marked by Protests. "This is Bill Casey's funeral. There's a nun out there with one of the little white crosses that's used in the Central America movement, listing one of the dead, Mumerto Hereto (?), and there's two people there and I can tell by their ties, but also their buttons are the same, from the same outfit. One says "North, our American hero" (but in the background the little bumper sticker says "Support Freedom Fighters" and there's swastikas on either side of it, so it's just behind the scenes. You know, what's wrong with this picture? Look for the duck in the tree. (Laughter).

Another piece of this techno-fascism was the awful Supreme Court decision about the service member who was experimented on as part of the MK-Ultra with the acid and the Supreme Court said they couldn't sue the government. There was no wrongdoing, its just part of your service duty to be experimented on. Of course, it always has been, but they finally made it legally official.

This item is nice too; it says "TV Radio Shows Are Censored for U.S. Troops." We're not allowed to hear about them and they're not allowed to hear about us. The Press is only allowed to go to war if they sign up beforehand and they decide who can come.

Here's a nice one. A scientist in the Herald, Thursday, July 9th: "Scientist's Way to Avoid World Run by Robots." Become like them.

I've done work since 1968, almost daily work, on much of this, starting with the Kennedy assassination and the Warren Commission Report, and went backwards from there into the history of the intelligence agencies, the government lies about Vietnam, the international heroin traffic which finances many of the covert spy operations around the world, international sales of arms, the permanent war economy, with watershed years after the war in 1947 and 1948 which is actually the originally title of George Orwell's novel. Harcourt Brace changed it to 1984 in the first American edition in 1949. It is the year I believe he describes in the novel; the technology is current to that year. He wrote it in 1939, and that's the year that televisions were introduced into American homes. It's the year I found 400 parallels after 12 years of work in the book by just re-reading it. I hadn't read it since high school to what actually were set, the technology and the methods and the lies and everything else to the way the system was operating. Of course, it's post Orwellian now and, I believe, post-Huxleyan, but we're certainly in a "brave new world" with "brave new heroes" out there.

I found the same names, the same money, the same operation going on every time I looked behind the scenes in the major and minor political assassinations and began to follow the murders and the deaths that had political implications. There was a similar string of deaths in the Weimar Republic just before the rise of fascism to power. There were 400 unsolved political assassinations in Germany of labor leaders, musicians, progressive people that might speak out, politicians who might opposed fascism were murdered or supposedly committed suicide. The murders were covered up. The police knew that they were murders but said they couldn't solve them. Then the fascism was able to rise. So I found a similar pattern over the last period from the 60's into the 80's, starting with the assassination of John F. Kennedy. These studies gave me enough of an overview and enough of a cast of characters that the day of the Watergate break-in, when I was in Dayton, Ohio and the only news was two inches in the newspaper that day, a little column with the names of the five people arrested in the building. I called my mother in Washington that day and I said, "These five people are part of the Bay of Pigs, they're part of the team that killed John F. Kennedy, and the fact that they were even arrested is important. You should look at this story."

She clipped Watergate for three years in Washington and mailed it to me in a package every week and politically educated herself. At the end of it she said, "Three years ago you told me that fascism was coming in the United States and I thought you were crazy. After doing this clipping and looking, now I understand what you were talking about." Because when you look at any aspect of this, and these are windows that open up from time to time, they let you see into Contragate or Koreagate or Watergate, they let you see into the structure for a moment and the lines, the divisions within the class, the operatives, the histories, come to bear and the same names reappear and the people who investigate the scandals are the people who are tied to the scandals which we'll talk about.

The scandals are orchestrated, the electoral politics are manipulated, and the murders are done in order to make sure that the whole truth doesn't come out or the wrong person doesn't get into power. But it gave me enough of a context so that I could analyze from an earlier period, not because I'm psychic but because these people reappear. If you went through my work you'd think there were only six lawyers and about three guys that do autopsies and four that embalm the bodies, because every damned time the same crew shows up. They do the work and then they disappear again. It's not that I'm so brilliant I can see ahead into the future, it's just that once you understand the context and the players, then you can unravel what's happening and that's what I'm hoping to do in the talks that I do and tonight as well as on Barry Scott's show last week and tomorrow. Whenever I speak, I distribute the articles to give that context so that you don't all have to run to a hall on a Friday night when you might want to go see Bob Dylan if you had that might money. Because I'm not interested in being followed around for the rest of my life to talk to hundreds of people. I mean, it's an interesting thing, but if 500 had come tonight I probably would have sent a tape. The point's not 'Gee that fellow John Judge, he knows it all, so let's listen to him." But hopefully all I did was figure some things out with a little hard work and I pass that work on to you and then you can do your own work. I get a lot of letters saying, "This happened and I thought of you." Then maybe the next time it'll be "This happened and I thought of what I thought." The idea is for you to begin to use your own analysis and trust your confidence in what you feel and what you see rather than what this system tells you day in and day out to believe.

The broader context, I believe, for Contragate that I'm going to try and go through quickly now, has to do first on the international and geopolitical level with oil, with the movement of oil, with the oil market, with the created shortages of oil, with the manipulation of oil available to Europe, especially to Japan and Germany, the capitalist competitors of the U.S. in the current period. They have no internal oil sources, and with the phony oil prices that are manipulated and raised up above market levels by this manipulation and by limiting and delimiting the oil flow and what amount of crude oil is refined and how much is charged for it a very real control is imposed... I believe that that history is a secret history that goes back probably to shortly after the time oil was discovered as an energy source and concentrated into certain wealthy circles.

That concentration came around land ownership or government manipulation or, like Howard Hughes made his fortune, because his father invented the oil drill bit, the rock-bore bit. He had a patent and a good patent lawyer and they couldn't grab it from him, so they had to pay him for every time they drilled and bought a bit. That's how Hughes cashed in and moved up.

The history of oil is a secret history; it's the history of the Rockefellers and the histories of top ruling class families. It's also the secret history of war. It's the accepted energy behind war.

The second level is nuclear and that history is almost as well hidden as oil's or perhaps more hidden how the nuclear industry operates and how it concentrates and what it moves and who controls it. But these are energy sources in times of war so they are critical to nation states and international policy. I think that on the mega-level, what you're seeing is a struggle to keep a war going in Iran and Iraq, to manipulate situations in the Mideast that control the flow of oil out of those countries, that manipulate people like King Faud and others who were trained by the American CIA here and then sent back in to form OPEC. OPEC was not an independent Arab oil machination. Rather it is part and parcel of U.S. international oil policy, used at that point to help create the phony shortage and cut off Japan and Germany from that flow and the rest of Europe so they could get a stranglehold on Europe and, under David Rockefeller's Trilateral Commission, drag Japan and Germany into continued U.S. hegemony over oil.

All the resources of the world are critical to them, especially since the time of World War II when they had the technology to locate all of them to get cheap labor near them, to get hold of the lands around them. Now, if neither of those is possible they kill everyone in the area and go in with whatever they have left. That's one of the reasons I say as an aside that people should take a look at what resources are in the area of the Chad border near Cameroon. Because for that many people to have to die- and it certainly wasn't a bubble that came up out of the lake that killed them the area not able to be to be repopulated, and the bodies mass buried at once by the Israeli-trained troops there, the cover-up completed. The scientists aren't able to come up with an explanation even that makes any sense. That means there's probably something there, Uranium, gold.

There were gold mines and manganese and bauxite mines and uranium mines in the interior of Guyana at Matthews Ridge where the Jonestown massacre happened. There were attempts to repopulate that interior from 1909 on. In 1937 that area was the area chosen before Israel by Eichmann and Otto Von Bolschwing as the location to put the Jewish world community. It was the sixth of seven choices, Israel being the seventh and the final negotiated choice.

There were plans to move Dominican Blacks to Matthews Ridge. There were plans to move Guyanese who had gone into the U.K. and other Blacks from the U.K. and repopulate the Blacks there, move them into the interior where no one lives and use them as exploited labor. The Jonestown situation was an attempt through mind control to develop a slave labor population that could be manipulated electronically or through drugs or other manipulation techniques as slave labor batches.

The real history of much of hidden politics is the history of resources and where they sit. The resources south of the northern border of Rhodesia, known to us, would keep the U.S. at its current consumption level for the next 500 years. That's why the politics in South Africa are so central and what's going to happen in terms of the liberation of Black peoples or Third World peoples. Their plan from here on out until the turn of the century is to put a stranglehold on that labor and those resources, to cut it off from every competitor and certainly from the Soviet Union. If that means genocide in the Third World, they're doing it and they'll continue doing it with the AIDS virus, with warfare, with "natural disasters" that they can create, but that's the first agenda, get their hands on those resources. If there's exploitable labor, leave it in place. If not, eradicate it and move in technological equipment and monopolize that.

The second piece of the agenda from now until the turn of the century is to de-stabilize the buffer zone that was set up at the end of World War II between the Soviet Union and the rest of European countries. This military buffer zone was set up as insulation against a return of the monarchists and international fascist elements to take over the Soviet Union and set back the Bolshevik Revolution in 1918 that came under attack from that year on. They failed at Stalingrad in 1943 and they've been regrouping since, so the second part of the agenda is to de-stabilize. The third part is to build first-strike nuclear capability. With the MX or the Trident or Star Wars.

Star Wars is not just nuclear. None other than General Walter conceived it as nuclear Dornberger, the mentor for Werner Von Braun and the rocket scientists who developed the idea for both the space shuttle and the Star Wars technology in the 1940s, not the 1980's, and who envisioned by the 1960's satellites filled with nuclear warheads circling the earth every 90 minutes, they could rain those warheads down. But you have to understand that if they have technology sophisticated enough to track an ICBM missile through space going at 5,000 mph, or whatever it does, they can certainly track an individual. They can certainly target a town, and they can certainly bring down enough heat to set cities on fire or to alter the environment or to change the weather patterns with these satellites.

So it's not merely a nuclear technology, but part of it is to expand to first-strike nuclear capacity. I'm not taking these things out of my head. You can go and get Army Times, any of the D.O.D. publications that discuss their strategies. They commonly refer over and over again to something called "Air-Land Battle 2000." This was a plan for full-scale nuclear and bio-chemical attack on the Soviet Union by the turn of the century. So I think that oil, as one of the key resources to international movement and on a petroleum-dependent machine-based economy and technology, is central to the manipulations that have been happening since Reagan came into office and before, but the first thing on his agenda was the Iran-Iraq war.

People wonder why do we fund both sides or why do we arm both sides, or why do we misinform both sides by saying we want to end the war when everything we did kept it going and fueled the situation. It blocks key pipelines for oil and oil production in that sector, it keeps oil production and flow in the hands, like we're going to go "protect" the Kuwaiti ships.

We're going to go control the Kuwaiti ships. You have three bullet holes in the Maddox to start the Vietnam War, and then you have a missile into the Stark to start the Persian Gulf War. It's not that hard to figure out. Attacking a boat is the usual way that they star wars in the United States if you think about it. They're not adverse to killing GI's and they train the terrorist groups around the world who set off these bombs at the embassies and they say, "Oh, it was our group, but we didn't know they were going to do that..."

Everyone says I'm paranoid. Oliver North built an 8-foot fence around his house with secret government funds to protect he and his 11-year-old daughter. He doesn't even go home for her birthday party but he's worried that Abu Nidal is going to come to his house. Well, Abu Nidal! Would come over for dinner! I have the article about North's ties to the terrorist group that Abu Nidal! Is supposedly part of!

They train the terrorists, they arm the terrorists, they set up the regimes, decide whether they're meant to oppose us, they insert new leaders when old fascists are going to fall, the up-front ones 'like Marcos or Pinochet. They insert the next level. 'You know, they'll bring in Cory Aquino and they'll give, her good press. They're jumping up and down, OH, Benigno Aquino was shot."

How many third world leaders and political activists have been shot that you've seen the U.S. press make such a fuss about? But with Aquino, it's "Oh he's shot, he's shot." You know who he was? He was the right hand to General Edwin Lansdale, one of the top psychological warfare experts and assassin experts for the CIA for many years. He worked with him against the Huks in the Philippines, he went to Vietnam with Lansdale, and was a right-hand to him there in the counter-insurgency and psychological operations. These are the inserts, the people that they place when the openly fascist regime falls so that a real democratic government can't get in.

That's why they're so infuriated with Nicaragua. Or were so infuriated with Vietnam. Because it didn't follow the pattern, they weren't able to inject the phony leadership in time. They weren't able to see the things coming. If they can, then they orchestrate it. They knew that the embassy was going to be taken over in Iran. They had the warnings. They knew if they brought the Shah here the student group would go in. They knew weeks and weeks in advance. And now we have 'North whining, "OH, we looked at those horrible pictures of Mr. Buckley... sob, sob, sob."

Well, the question is not what did Buckley tell them; the question is why did they leave Buckley behind? They took 150 personnel out of the embassy why was he expendable? So didn't he know enough? Was he instructed to give them false testimony and they told him they'd get him out in time? Who knows, you know, but he was left. He was somebody's enemy. He did something wrong to be left in such a position. And now we're supposed to believe that they had to change the whole of U.S. foreign policy because they were up at night crying over this guy getting tortured by the Iranians. They could care less about one or ten or ten thousand of our deaths, our torture, and us! How many people do they subsidize and train and pay for to carry out torture worldwide.

We're supposed to look at the guy with the popgun in the plane or a couple people take over a ship, and that's terrorism. I live my whole life under a threat of nuclear weapons and with the dangers of toxins and radiation in the atmosphere and women live day in and day out with constant fear of going on the street or battery at home and rape and the level of violence that's inherent in this society and we talk about kids with pop-guns as terrorism? The machinery that this country commands, the military and other machinery of death that it commands and uses abroad, and here at home. I mean it makes the Nazi Hohenzollern machine look like a rubber band affair compared to what we have.

We're 40 years down the technological pike and two years down the pike away from fascism. We brought the fascists here; it's their mentality, it's their plan. They went into the Pentagon. They went into the CIA and formed the Operations

Division. They headed up NASA. They formed the aerospace and munitions industries that became the military industrial complex. Hundreds of them, thousands if you count the families that came in, to do these special in the technological field and they didn't leave their fascism, their racism, their anti-Semitism and their genocidal ideas behind! They brought them along. They infiltrated and infested what happened over the ensuing years in this country.

What November 22 1963 represented in my research after I was done with it was the culmination of their rise to power. They snuffed Kennedy out in a public square with impunity, giving us the message over the years, "Yes, we killed him, what do you want to do about it?" And that's the message they want us to have, that there is nothing we can do about it, that we have no power. They spent the time in the intermitting years confusing us, dividing us one against another, making us feel that we have no way to change things when, in fact, we are the ones that have the power. We have so much power that we're the only enemy left.

They're not afraid of the Third World countries in terms of the long-term planning; those people in their worldview are part of the half of the world population that the RAND Corporation in 1968 said had to go! The Soviet Union is not their first concern, either, because they have long been well ahead of the Soviet Union in terms of any kind of aggressive military technology development. They like to point out how big the Soviet army is.

Well, how big is the Soviet Union? How many defensible borders does the United States have and how many does the Soviet Union have? The Soviet military is also the Soviet police. If you put all the police into our military, how big would it be, you see? They also like to point out how many tanks they have.

But you know they don't have a rapid deployment force in the Soviet Union. They can't move 10,000 Soviet troops anywhere in the world in a couple hours. They don't have a capacity anything like that. I think Reagan was just getting upset because they had their first aircraft carrier this year! They say, "OH, the tanks are going to come down into the arc of crisis..." (Remember the arc of crisis? Carter?) Somebody forgot there's this mountain range there, the highest one in the world just about, and no roads through for all these tanks, but we're supposed to think the Soviet Union is just going to jump right in and come across and grab all this oil. Well, it's us who has grabbed the oil. So it's not the Soviets that they're afraid of. The Soviets have a defense capability and they 're chary of it, but they're doing whatever they can to outstrip it to get to the point where they can overcome it in their terms even if that means limited nuclear war in their scenario.

But the people that they're afraid of, in the last analysis, are just us. Because if we get the point, if we unravel the lie and we take it apart and we claim democracy and liberation and we claim our own destiny, then that's it. That's the end of the game. And that's what the whole national security and secrecy concept is about. They're not lying to our supposed enemies. I mean, they come on the Contragate testimony and they say that the Soviets knew, the Cubans knew, the Nicaraguans knew. It was only the Americans that aren't allowed to know. Americans aren't supposed to get the information. Attempts to bring that information in are blocked. The press is controlled' and the lies go on and on.

They plan ahead, they plan generations ahead. Not everything works. They had a wider war planned into Cambodia, into Laos, into Thailand, the whole Southeast Asian sector that they had to abandon because of the GI movement, because of the struggle of the Vietnamese, because of the anti-war movement back home. They had to abandon an even wider war, so not every plan goes through. But don't think that they sit and wait or respond the next day to something in the news. They create the scandal. They create the crisis. They create the phony terrorism so that they can go and bomb Libya. They bombed the only disco in Beirut that allows Black service members to be in a bar with white women in Germany. A Black NCO was murdered in the bombing. They sent a form letter from the White House, a telegram without a signature from Reagan to the family. You know how Reagan likes to mug and cry, he loves to go to funerals, it's a favorite thing with him, he hugs everybody, and it's the only physical contact they get probably. He doesn't go near, I mean, they just send this form letter, "Sorry about that," but it's enough of a reason for national policy to go and bomb Libya.

A few weeks later we found out it wasn't Libya after all, it was some section of the PLO that happened to be connected to the CIA, but that's all right, we almost got him anyway.

It wasn't any different in 1939 at the Polish border when the Nazi troops went up and shot the Polish border guards dead and took their uniforms off and dressed them in the German uniforms and dragged the bodies back across into Germany and then said that the Polish guards had killed the German guards and then went to war with Poland. That's Operation Canned Meat, 1939.

"The first casualty of war is the truth." That's Aeschylus the Greek, 2,000 years ago. It's not that hard to figure out. You can't start a war any other way except with a lie. So they're going to give you one.

The second outline of this has to do with U.S. overthrow and U.S. intervention in many countries, the lies that allow us to go in and mess with the politics in Chile or Honduras, or Nicaragua or El Salvador or South Africa, Rhodesia, Zimbabwe or Zaire or wherever it is that we're sticking the CIA in these interventions and backgrounders or using surrogate troops. That's the second level.

Ollie North is not in the NSC anymore, but it was in the society page what his job is now, he's in the Marine Corps Plans and Mobilization Division at the Pentagon. He's in charge of mobilizing Marines everywhere in the world. He's going to make the decision if there's a Marine intervention. Problematic to building a war at this point is the history of Vietnam that they haven't been able to erase, even for the current generation.

They failed in Grenada, that's why they wouldn't let the press in. They didn't know if U.S. troops, primarily Black troops, the 82nd 101st Airborne crack units, would be able to be sent successfully against English speaking Blacks in Grenada. A six-hour invasion took three days because they refused on the field as they had in Vietnam. They were not given court martials because they didn't want it in the press. They were given bad discharges. We talked to the AWOL's coming back from 'Grenada of instances all across the island, so after that the Rapid Deployment Force Plans were dropped for the 82nd 101st. They tried to switch over to primarily white units in Texas.

That plane that went down in Greenland, Arrow, the defective plane that tailed out twice at the two airports and then went down in Greenland, and killed about 180 Black U.S. troops? Those were the troops from Fort Campbell, from the 101st Airborne that had refused in Grenada. It was those troops. And they replaced the troops in the unit after that. *[John refers here to the December 12, 1985 crash in which 248 servicemen died. A nine-person safety panel said (5 out of 9) that ice on the ings caused the crash, but the minority report (4 out of 9) suggested an onboard explosion. – Editor's Note]* But they weren't able to carry it out successfully because they had opposition within the ranks. So they're afraid. They're afraid of what's going to happen here. What you see in the newspapers, if you did see it on the 5th in the Mercury or the Miami Herald, about Oliver North's martial law plans and Federal Emergency Management Agency and the DOD coming in and ordered to set up martial law. The trigger was either nuclear war (or it could be nuclear terrorism), or it was military mobilization in the United States or an "insurrection" here at home. So, the first plan is to round up the Central American refugees, 400,000 of them. The second level is to round up the civilian dissidents because they have to increase the domestic repression in order to be able to start into a full scale war in the Third World.

The third level, that's the on-going secret government, the continuation of the financing with guns and drugs which are the only two commodities worth anything now, much more than gold or silver or the printed money. Guns and drugs are the means of exchange at the international level. They finance all of this, the ongoing assassinations and murders and the level of the orchestrated scandal, and that's what I'll try to finish with, and it's sort of the core of what I tried to talk about the other day on Barry's show. Then we can have some questions.

How this scandal, which feeds into all of those overall plans and backs them up, is really orchestrated, I believe, as a surgical incision to remove Reagan and the forces loyal to Reagan, as would have been done March 31, 1981 had the flechette not struck the seventh rib and ended up a quarter inch from the aorta, Reagan would have been on the ground. Instead, the Secret Service involved were screaming into the microphones, "Rawhide is okay," and pushed him into the car because he wasn't dead already and tried to take him to Bethesda hospital to finish the job and have the Navy do the same autopsy on him as they did on John F. Kennedy.

They would have done it that day with Bush out in Dallas on Air Force One. But they missed by an inch and Hinckley took the rap. Hinckley's family lived in Dallas on the same street and made all their social arrangements with another Dallas oil magnate named George Bush.

It's this same George Bush who's moving Oliver North and Poindexter and the secret team brought in by William Clark into the National Security Council from the Pentagon for the military coup d'état that they'd achieved and they're moving in this testimony to take Reagan out and set Bush up as the incumbent and to move Bush from that position probably into a position where he'll take on someone like Haig as a vice presidential candidate or one of the other fascists - Kemp, who relates to the Friends of the Anti-Bolshevik Nations and the World Anti-Communist League openly or the other ones that are running on those tickets out there, and continue to eliminate the democratic opposition if it gets in the way so that they can put Bush into office at this point.

That's the same way Nixon was moved out by Watergate. The purpose of Watergate was not to... I mean, so what, they broke into a room! I mean that's a national scandal? They broke into a room and tried to steal some secrets from Larry O'Brien, you know, what are the democrats doing for the election? They stole the debate books from Carter, that didn't take Reagan out of office. We weren't all scandalized enough to call off the election for that.

So why was it a scandal the first time? It's because Nixon had to be moved out so that we got the appointed Ford and Rockefeller. Well, Haig really comes in. I always refer to him as ex-president Haig. He ran the White House. I mean he surrounded Nixon. He threw out everybody that was loyal to him; they all had to-go stay over at the Watergate. He brought in the Ft. Devens psychological warfare team from the military to surround Nixon day in and day out. Kissinger's in there in case he starts crying to feed him a little bourbon. And Kissinger is the pal of these people too. And who comes out on the steps to say we've found the smoking gun? Haig and Jaworski. "We found this tape... and we told the president that if you won't reveal it, we have to reveal it... sob sob." It's bye bye Ronnie too! Now, he's fighting back.

That's what happened to Bill Casey, you know. What happened to Bill Casey? I'm in the cab and it says on the radio, "Bill Casey decided to resign today. White House spokesman said it was his decision." I said to the cabbie, "I didn't think he had ideas anymore." I mean, they mistook his frontal lobe for a tumor somewhere in there and who is in the room with him to help him write the two sentence resignation? Anyone remember? Meese! Ed Meese was sitting in the room.

So what we have... I brought these sections and I'll just try to go through them real quickly. These are some of the more important parts of my Contragate file. I'm not going to go into these articles. This is the overview and, as I say, these other committees are going to be very important because it is possible with public pressure to try to get the history of the drugs and the narcotics that's involved with this... and that could, actually, catch Bush by the tail.

Oliver North, you know, was the one that edited with Poindexter the Kirkpatrick Doctrine. Do you remember the Kirkpatrick Doctrine? Jeanne Kirkpatrick. It said the essence of the rapid deployment force is to take immediate action in the event of an oil embargo, rebellion, or revolution, or an outbreak of local conflicts between them. They want to establish what they call "political dominance over key strategic zones," that's what they talk about. So that's the oil. They have an article for the decoders and what country it is. Country 1 is Israel. I guess U.S. isn't number one anymore. Country 2, Saudi Arabia, you know. And you have the little codes.

But the basis of it all is just this Saudi money comes in. It starts to roll with the policy and people say well, what is Contragate, what's going on? Bud McFarlane comes up and he says, "I was afraid Jeanne Kirkpatrick would call me a commie." It's like if you tried to listen to it and figure out what on earth they were talking about, you couldn't possibly get to it. They go back and forth and the main issue is "Did Reagan know or didn't Reagan know and when did he know."

They had this great cartoon. Baker's in the White House and he's asking Reagan, "What did you know and did you ever know that you knew it?" (Laughter) It's all in the cartoons. You don't have to read the whole paper.

This is 'Oliver North: "I didn't engage in the fantasy that I was the president, or the vice president or a cabinet member or even director of the NSC. I've already got Mr. Reagan, Mr. Bush, and others engaged in that fantasy." (Laughter)

So he was doing it for the president but the president didn't know and they thought it was better not to tell him. And Ollie North comes out; I mean they had one good picture, its North in the Chronicle standing next to all these documents. He's got his jacket off and he doesn't have the boy scout grin and he's got a 5 o'clock shadow, and he really looks like North, the slimy little assassin from Vietnam and Operation Phoenix, the dirty killer and drug runner and covert operator, a racist dog... I can't say enough... that he is. (Applause) This is a real picture. I mean this is Ollie North. Not that little grinning Catholic, "Oh, hi sister!" that he learned when he was in grade school, but the real fellow here at the office. Every secretary's dream, Fawn Hall, ten years with classified documents! Now, she's only 27!

She said, "I've been handling documents for ten years." Not a one of them says, "Jeez, how did you get in that position when you were seventeen? (Laughter).

I came in the Pentagon at 15. I could have gone to work at 15 into the Pentagon library. My parents would have gotten me a job. I didn't want to work for them. I got in trouble at ten because I wouldn't hide under the desk for the atom bomb. I got kicked out of the room and sent to the principal's office. I asked him what the bomb did and I knew the desk wouldn't protect me. I wasn't going to sit under there like a doll. Then I wanted to know why they used things like that, you know.

So, I didn't want a job, but Fawn got one. Her mother got her the job with all the documents and her mother was the personal secretary to whom? To Henry Kissinger for years and years in the NSC. So they're not separate. Fawn knew Donna Rice. They had the same modeling agent. Alright... I mean, the 'connections... don't get me going. Everyone's connected to everybody... probably someone in this room... (Laughter).

This one says: "Bad news, Mr. President Poindexter's been granted immunity." He replies: Oh, that's okay, I've been granted amnesia." (Laughter)

My answer is that it doesn't matter. I think Reagan's not lying. I know it's a terrible thing to say because we all like to think presidents lie. I don't think he knew. And the reason I don't think he knew was when the Tower Commission Report came out, and once they made their statements, they named a day. And they said on this day, Reagan approved the Finding for the arms to go.

I have a chronological file on Reagan so I went back to my clippings for that day because I had a suspicion it was the day I remembered slightly wondering about George Bush. That was the day in the Tower Commission Report that Reagan was in prostate surgery. There was even an article the next day saying well maybe he was sedated and they had him sign it sedated and he doesn't remember because he was kind of groggy from the surgery. But that day there was an article in the Washington Post, maybe it didn't get out here to the West Coast that said that they didn't want a crisis to develop and they'd have a crisis management problem because what if Reagan died? So they made George Bush acting president for eight hours that day. So Bush was president the day that everybody says it was approved. So I think Bush approved it and Reagan's like: (Said dopily) "Could I have approved that?"

So they've got us going back and forth on whether or not he knew. Let it go. Bush knew that's enough. That's what you need to know. Then, the next thing they want us to believe is that it was all Casey because Casey's dead and he can't say anything. The dead are the best ones to blame it on, you know. So Casey's out of the way ergo Casey did it all and he had all this money and he was going to set up this secret CIA, but nobody is asking yet where is that money? Reagan's the only one I saw say it. They had a quote where he said, "I still don't know where all that money went." Do you really believe if you put $1000 in the bank in the wrong account, would you let it go seven months? And you put it in there and you said, "Well, I was going to put it in there and somebody was going to transfer it over here" and you ask everybody but the bank where the money went? "Did you get it yet?" "No...." (Laughter)

But it's $10 million, for Christ's sake! $10 million! They have this one cartoon, these two old people. The guy opens up a letter from his bank and he says, "Oh, that dumb Ollie North. My bank statement shows another $10 million deposited by mistake!" How dumb can they be? I mean it's like McCord and the second piece of tape in Watergate. When you put a piece of tape to keep the door open for the operation and you come back down and Frank Wills, the guard, has taken it off and the door is locked and you open the door back up, what do you do? You run upstairs and you say, "It's cut." I mean, the operation is known. There's danger we have to get out. What does McCord do? What's the name of his book? A Second Piece of Tape, he puts the tape back on! So then when Frank Wills comes around again and he finds it, so he has to call the cops. It's not like tape left over from last night's burglary, you know, it's like today's. So he had to call the police.

Then, across the street is McCord's guy Baldwin. And North's in the same position to set this thing up in charge of National Crisis. That's what McCord did. Sixteen man committee in the White House Office of Emergency Preparedness. He had control of all mail and media in the United States in time of national emergency. That's who McCord was. That's a high office. All right? All mail and all media he would have controlled, militarily, when they took over.

He's not some bumbling guy who doesn't know how to put a piece of tape on. He's a 20-year mechanic. He knows what he's doing. So you don't, you know, get compromised. Anyhow, he's got Baldwin over there with a walkie-talkie and he's watching and the lights go on the first floor and the second floor and the third floor and they're up on seven. And they've got to be searching. Baldwin can see them come in and out of each room and they turn off the lights as they go.

Does he pick up the walkie-talkie and say, "Cheez-it, it's the cops? No! He lets them get right to the seventh floor and arrest them. Then you start the scandal in the same way that you can orchestrate this one.

The other fascinating thing to me - well, they don't know where the money went and they're going to blame it all on Casey because Casey's not talking, but the other thing I found very interesting was that they all are up there testifying and they say, "Well, the Boland Amendment didn't apply to us." You start thinking the Boland Amendment was only passed to apply to Boland. But the real point is that it didn't, because you don't understand what the NSC is. It was put in there in 1947. It was Herbert Hoover's idea; he's the one that raised all the money internationally to finance the re-armament of Germany from 1918 to 1936. Herbert Hoover. He was with the industrialists and the monarchists and they wanted to get the Bolshevik revolution out. He raised money and they pumped it in and they rearmed Germany and they set up Hitler to go back and take the mother country, get Russia, and get the resources. He's the one that thought up the NSC. It's in there to not be the Congress, not be the legislature, not even be the intelligence agencies it's extra-legal, extra-governmental, and so it doesn't apply.

That's what nobody's getting. That's why they all come up there and say, "Well, yeah, if it had been the CIA it would have applied." And it really was pieces, sure. Dewey Claridge is CIA. He was intimately involved. You can link it that way. But the real nature of the NSC is that it's not in the real government, it's in the shadow government. It's there behind the lines. It's the government that operates in secret.

When Haig jumps up and Reagan's shot and Bush is out of town and somebody's got to take charge and there's a big fight, William French Smith and Haig and everybody's fighting down in the Situation Room and Haig comes up and he says, "Gentlemen, I'm in charge here until the vice president returns." Everybody said, "Gee, he doesn't remember the 25th Amendment.' These guys, they don't even read the Constitution.

The Iran-contra hearing is the first time in history that they ever took the Fifth! An officer took the fifth! I say if the officer can take the Fifth, the enlisted can take the First.

They don't know what the Constitution says. There's this great cartoon of Poindexter and North and they're shredding the Constitution in the NSC and the little pieces are on the floor. North's down on his knees and he says, "I found it, the Fifth Amendment!" It's the only one that counts.

But they tell you it didn't apply and everybody smirks and says, "Oh, you think it didn't apply, it really did." The 25th Amendment doesn't apply. What applies are Executive Orders, secret Military Succession orders, Federal Emergency Management Agency takeover, regional control, National Guard takeovers of state and local government. There are secret succession orders for crisis management. What's crisis management? It used to be called... emergency preparedness."

Well, it goes back to the McCarran act in the 50's, in times of national war, declared war, attack on the United States or its territories or possessions. (Truman declared war at the time of Korea, it wasn't revoked until Kennedy; Kennedy declared war for the Cuban missile crisis, it wasn't revoked until Nixon; Nixon put one in for Vietnam. There were other ones later on. It's still in effect. If they want to implement the rest they can, legally, but they have to have an excuse that someone's going to buy, okay they have to come up with some reason to go to the martial law. But two days before Reagan was shot in March of '81, there was a switchover between Haig and Bush as to whom was going to head Crisis Management. It was a phony feud, actually, but they pretend they were fighting over it and then Reagan chose Bush over Haig. Then, two days before the Reagan hit, someone asked Bush at a press conference, "What is a crisis? You 're just chosen to head crisis management, what is a crisis." Bush said, this is a quote: "The president will know it when he sees it."

That's the answer. You'll know it when you see it if you look.

"Army Spy Unit Lacked Controls." Let's suppose that it wasn't the C-I-A, but the D-I-A. Ever heard of them? Defense Intelligence Agency? National Security Agency, the largest 'spy network in the United States, DISC (Defense Industries Security Command, the largest internal police force in the United States), the branch intelligences, a budget, a personnel ten times as large? And secret organizations like the NRO, it's classified to even mention the initials. National Reconnaissance Organization, the satellite intelligence - every electronic communication in the United States gets monitored. They declassify so much paper every day at the NSA that they take it to the basement and burn it in the furnace to heat the rest of the building. This is a spy agency and they talk in this article about a secret, ultra-secret Army intelligence group, Intelligence Support Activity, "Yellow Fruit" which Oliver North is involved with. "When a military order may be disobeyed" In a separate, command perhaps, a counterterrorism unit a Policy And Operations of the NSC. "Secord Led Secret Counterterrorism Unit, Retired Air Force Officer Bypassed Controls."

When two people come from the Pentagon into the NSC and they don't have to tell the president what's going on, they figure not to let him know, and they begin to make the domestic and foreign policy decisions on martial law, on relations with Iran - that's military coup d'état. When everybody breathes a sigh of relief, "Oh, Reagan didn't know." Reagan didn't know? Reagan wasn't even on "Need to know!" Reagan just wears your boots; go out with Nancy, what's the difference. What's the difference? He doesn't need to know except what they tell him so who's in charge? Someone else. They come in and who opposes him? Who's the only one who opposes him in the NSC at the beginning? Not McFarlane or Schultz (Schultz comes in to replace Haig, remember) when he gets dumped out after the little brouhaha in March of '81 and he's the loyalist now, you know, Schultz defends Reagan blah 'blah 'blah). He's the other side. It was Richard Allen. Now what happened to Richard Allen? Because he and William Clark were the ones who first invited North and Poindexter in, there was a scandal. Do you remember there was Japanese money in a safe and they'd given it to Nancy for a visit with Nancy and he'd put it in a safe and if you listen to Robert Owen's testimony, he said, "Ollie and I used to joke about it because the money for Ollie used for the Contras, we kept it in Richard Allen's safe." That same safe, ha ha ha ha. I went back to the Richard Allen stories in my clip file. Who was it in the NSC that discovered the scandal money in the safe? Oliver North. Took him out, and began to make the decisions at the top.

So look to military intelligence. The CIA is fairly lame at this point. You can put William Webster in, you know, switch him over from the FBI, and what did this team do, once they were in? "Reagan Aids in the Secret Government" this is the Miami Herald. An absolutely important piece, not all of it got into the version in the San Jose Mercury out here. A very important paragraph didn't get in. I'll read it to you. About North's first duties when he came into the NSC. "About this same time 1981 I North completed his transfer to the NSC from the Marine Corps. Those who worked with North in 1981 remember his first assignments as routine, though not unimportant. North, they recalled, was briefly assigned to carry the football, the briefcase carrying the secret contingency plans for fighting nuclear war, which is taken everywhere the president goes. North later widened his assignment to cover national crisis contingency planning.

In that capacity he be came involved with the controversial plan drafted by the Federal Emergency Management Agency the martial law plan.

The football disappeared in Dallas for three hours after John Kennedy was shot while they planted the Oswald Red story in the press lest anyone not on "need to know" in the military over-react and begin an attack on the Soviet Union. Not only was the football missing and, lest somebody like Kennedy survive and respond in that fashion, not only was the football missing but every SAC bomber in the air, as well as Air Force Two bringing the cabinet back from the Philippines, were missing the military intelligence code books inside the secret locker on each plane necessary to decode the Fail Safe messages from the president or anyone else in the command and control modules. I talked to pilots who told me every book was gone from every bomber in the air and it's in Pierre Salinger that it was gone from there. The box disappears March 31 when Reagan was shot. A fellow named Morales is in the films that you saw on TV. He hits the deck in military uniform. He jumps back up when the shooting is done and he runs away from the limousine. He's gone for about three or four hours. He shows back up without the box to collect the magnetic card from Reagan's wallet, stripped from him as he went into the trauma room by the FBI. The FBI has the card; it's like a little magnetic tape to stick into the book to give the orders to identify you as the president. The FBI is holding it. The Secret Service shows us along with Morales how to get it back. The FBI call headquarters, 'headquarters calls Webster. 'Webster' in the situation room. Webster says, "Hold on to it. Who's in charge of the command and control communications center at the White House Situation Room at that hour if the box and the card had been reunited? Helena Von Damm, sitting at the control! Helena Von Damm, the personal secretary to Otto Albrecht Von Bolschwing - Otto Albrecht Von Bolschwing, the direct superior to Adolf Eichmann in the *Einsatzgruppen*, the "Kill Teams," the "Mobile Teams" in Europe. His personal translator in the 1950's when he came to the United States.

She and Von Bolschwing are the key founders of the corporate front for the CIA in southern California, called TCI, Trans-national Computer Investments. TCI employed Edwin Wilson, the arms dealer tied in with the current Contragate people, and much of the arms movement of the CIA. TCI sold its largest subsidiary, International Imaging Systems, to Albert Hakim and Richard Secord. They renamed it as Stanford Trading Group, International the "Enterprise" of Oliver North's Contragate scandal.

POOLSIDE WITH JOHN JUDGE

PWR Interview John Judge 10/14/1990

PWR: *John, I wanted to ask you a few things. It seems to me that the general consensus is that Bush is doing okay, he's fighting this war on drugs and I seem to have a hard time relating to friends and people that it's basically a 180 scam, that most everything he says in terms of the drug policies, it's actually exactly the opposite. I was wondering if you could elaborate a little bit and discuss Bush, his history, his roles back to the late 50's and early 60's and also perhaps a little bit of history on Bush and Reagan and why it makes sense that Bush would either want to get rid of Reagan or control him for those two terms.*

John Judge: George Bush comes from a ruling class family that's been instrumental in dominating American politics from the period of the late 1800's up into the· current century. That family is part of what would be considered the "old money" Eastern establishment. It's not the entirety of the ruling class, but it's the more established capital of the east coast, the banking capital. Bush is somewhat of a crossover phenomenon which began to happen in the post World War era because he speculates in oil in the southwest. But his financial roots and ties, his political loyalties, are still basically with the east coast establishment- the Rockefeller and other circles.

Prescott Bush Sr., Bush's father, graduated from Yale, and was one of the 15 people that are tapped each year by the secret society at Yale known as Skull & Bones, which is basically a ticket for life in terms of placement, job security, and being put in positions of control. He was tapped in a year that was dominated by people from the Brown Brothers and Harriman circles, financial investment people that helped to finance Hitler into power in the 1920's and 1930's. His father had close financial ties with those circles and many of those people fed into positions in the State Department. George Bush is a member of Skull & Bones and was tapped in his graduating class at Yale. This isn't just a simple ruling class fraternity. It's a rather ghoulish organization that is called Skull & Bones because part of the initiation rite is that members are required to go and dig up the skull and bones of a famous revolutionary personality, someone who opposed the established order and in that sense insult the remains of anyone who stood up against privilege. The current understanding is that Prescott Bush Sr. dug up the bones of Geronimo and there was an attempt recently by the Apache elders to get the bones back. There were some offers back and forth but I don't know what the eventual outcome was, but there were some reports in '89 in the newspapers about that.

The scuttlebutt has it that George himself dug up Emma Goldman. I hope that that's not true or if it is true I hope she bit him. But I think that it's possible. The rituals are you know, they sleep all night in a coffin with the bones and they have different kinds of strange rituals that are part of the initiation into this fraternity. But the initial thing is commission of a crime. I think like most powerful secret societies the initiation rites include participation in a group or individual criminal activity that then marks the person for blackmail and scandal for the rest of their life. So they have ongoing control over the person and that is part of the cost of entry into this insider's club. Prescott Bush Jr., George's brother, is also a member of a very powerful secret society within the Roman Catholic Church known as the Knights of Malta. To outline a whole history of the Knights and who's in them would be exhausting, but I think it's enough to say that the highest order of merit ever offered by the Knights of Malta was given to General Reinhardt Gehlen, the head of Hitler's spy service who eventually formed our CIA. Another high-ranking and well-honored member of the Knights was Allen Dulles who engineered the movement of the Nazi spy infrastructure into the American CIA after the end of World War two.

Bush is part of a circle of fascists and neo-Nazi elements within the American government. I believe his direct line of command goes up through Henry Kissinger to Fritz Gustav Anton Kraemer who Mae Brussell believed was one and the same Fritz Kraemer who was arrested for the Malmedy Massacre after World War two, American POWs that were murdered. This Fritz Kraemer in the Pentagon Plans Department was the mentor for both Henry Kissinger and Alexander Haig. In my analysis, Haig has served two terms in the White House and Bush has served three and those are the presidents that we've had since the beginning of the Watergate era. This was an attempt, I believe, by the eastern establishment forces to put themselves back in a relative position of power following the coup d'état of 1963 by the military-industrial complex in the southern rim economy. I believe that this was an attempt in the

70's to reassert the hegemony of the old banking interests against the new entrepreneurial money of the southern rim which was basically oil, munitions, aerospace, land speculation money, in a boom that led to a power shift to the southern rim in the economy.

Haig was powerful enough that he was jumped over 236 generals in the military pecking order to come in as White House Chief of Staff in the middle of the Watergate crisis. He came in with Leon Jaworski who had been instrumental in pardoning and undermining the prosecution of key Nazis at Nuremberg, who worked for 20 years with the J.M. Anderson Fund, which was a CIA conduit in Texas. Jaworski had also been instrumental in the Red Cross's International Rescue Division operations at the end of World War II, which included giving fake glosenpieler (?) or plastic ID cards to the Nazi criminals so they could move internationally through the refugee camps and escape prosecution.

Jaworski was the liaison appointed by the Warren Commission between their investigation and that of the state and local police in Texas to cover that up and then Jaworski shows up later in the middle of the Watergate scandal where he was called the "most trusted man in America." But at the key point when no one knew which way it would go in terms of Nixon staying in office after this attempt to force him out through the Watergate scandal which I believe was a created scandal in the same way that Contragate was in order to compromise Reagan and earlier, Nixon-because these two people represent the other end of the money and really have their roots much more in the southern rim Mafia and oil and munitions speculation end of the money. So I think that Reagan and Bush represent sparring ends of the class.

If you remember, when they didn't know which way the vote would go in the Judiciary Committee and it was down to the wire but there was no final evidence on Nixon's involvement and everybody was asking "What did the president know and when did he know it," this was the point at which Haig and Jaworski held a press conference on the White House steps like little innocent lambs saying, "Well, we found this tape and we asked Mr. Nixon to make it public but we told him even if he didn't make it public we felt that we had to make it public ... " and this tape just happened to be the smoking gun tape where Nixon is heard saying to make the payoff and do the cover-up.

Following the release of that tape and its contents, then the vote went against Nixon and he resigned rather than to be fully impeached. They effectively drove him out. They had control of the whole White House. When Haig came in he moved all of Nixon's loyalists out of the White House and no one was physically allowed in the White House except Haig, Kissinger, Jaworski, Nixon, and this special psychological warfare team from Fort Devens, called the "Fort Devens Eight" out of Massachusetts. They were brought in, I believe, for psychological control and manipulation. But Nixon's team was basically shunted out to the Watergate complex, Rosemary Woods and some of the others.

A number of other Nixon cronies and key people had been killed during the scandal including Murray Chotiner, so I think it's also important to realize that Bush had a role in that scandal, the development of that scandal, working on the Republican National Committee he had ties to CREEP (Committee to Re-Elect the President) and other people who helped to set Nixon up in that period and was part of the orchestration of the scandal and the cover-up of the reality of the scandal at that time. Bush was also apparently interviewed in relation to the Kennedy assassination at the time it happened as an acting operative of the CIA. Following his military career he went into these speculative ventures with oil, eventually forming Zapata Offshore Oil and making illegal deals to set up oil companies in Mexico with the Mexican nationals involved being merely fronts for Bush's investments rather than being indigenous oil operations which is part of what the Mexican government law tries to avoid. In the course of that speculation he made some of his fortune off of the oil and then he moved eventually into government positions including being ambassador to China at a key time in the development of the politics of China in the post-Mao period and helped, I believe, to put President Deng in power the person who's in there now- and the reactionary forces in China and to manipulate the situation there. Bush was then openly made Director of the Central Intelligence Agency but I think he had ties to the CIA going back into the 1950's and the early Zapata Oil stuff.

Zapata Oil in the 1960's also financially bailed out Vanderbilt Oil, the company owned by John W. Hinckley Sr. and there were ongoing social and financial relationships between Bush's family and the Hinckley family. They lived on the same street in Dallas for a number of years and Bush's daughter made all the dating arrangements for Scott Hinckley, the elder son in the Hinckley family. In fact, Neil Bush, who is currently caught up in the S & L scandal with Silverado, was to have dinner with Scott Hinckley (who works for Standard Oil) the night of the March 31, 1981 shooting of Ronald Reagan. They cancelled the dinner engagement, but news of it hit the press briefly and then disappeared.

There was a long-standing connection between the Bush and Hinckley families. Reagan when he came to in the hospital and realized what had happened to him, the first thing he said to the Secret Service was "Get me the demographics on that kid." Meaning, find out who he is, what his background is, etc. And I'm sure once he looked he realized that it was in fact George Bush who had engineered his demise. Fortunately for Reagan the tiny flechette that was shot into his arm bounced off the seventh rib and missed his aorta by a quarter of an inch and went into his lung instead.

Also, fortunately for Reagan, some of his loyal aides argued in the Situation Room to take him to GWU instead of up to Bethesda where the phony Kennedy autopsy was done and where Navy Intelligence would have finished the job of killing him, I believe. But I believe from that point on, Haig, who had been running the White House since he chased Nixon out, and Bush took over. We had a short period of appointed presidents with Rockefeller and Ford, the Warren Commission member and Rockefeller, who himself had a Jong history of intelligence relations to bringing the Nazis into the United States and working with C.J. Jackson and Nixon in that regard. Rockefeller was also a top-ranking Naval intelligence mind control expert Nelson Rockefeller, and had worked with General Edward Lansdale and others in the development in the late 40's of the whole mind control concept that the CIA and Defense Intelligence developed.

These people dominated after the Watergate period and then once Reagan got in, representing a push to the top by the other end of the class, the other end of the money, he surrounded himself with his own security and refused to cooperate with what I believe he was supposed to go along with. Haig, if you'll remember, was put in as head of the State Department briefly in the beginning of the Reagan administration, but the papers in Washington said it was the craziest appointment they had ever seen because the entire department was already fully formed, all the hiring had been finished and Haig had to report on everything he did and get cleared whether he would work or not or quit or not through the White House aides, Deaver and the others, and so it was basically only an appointment in name, a figurehead appointment to the State Department which he was angered about.

If you'll remember after the shooting, Bush was still in Texas flying around in Air Force I on a jaunt through Dallas and at first when he got the news the reports were that he was nonchalant. He didn't have any emotional reaction to the fact that Reagan had been shot. He considered whether he would bother coming back to Washington. But this huge fight in the White House Situation Room between the Reagan loyalists and the Bush forces, presided over, I believe, by Helene Von Damm, the Reagan private secretary who was down there at the time according to the Washington Post. That fight led eventually to Haig emerging in front of the press, visibly shaken, and saying as you may remember, "Gentlemen, I am in control until the vice president returns." To me that basically was the reassertion of the Haig and Bush lineage, their presidency, and the Kissinger element. Kissinger, too visible in his position as Secretary of State, instead was put into the president's Foreign Intelligence Advisory Board.

There was a tremendous shift of that kind of power the day that Larry McDonald supposedly died in the 007 crash and the Soviets supposedly shot down this American plane all of which was a cover, l believe, to test the Stealth bomber, for Oliver North to build this huge propaganda campaign with Jeanne Kirkpatrick about the "evil empire" and to preserve the cold war strategy for another period, to reverse attempts at that time to end the nerve gas stocks and experimentation with nerve gas, to get rid of the plans for Star Wars and for the B2 bomber, all of that was up for grabs in Congress right as this...

PWR: *Wasn't there a 30% cut in defense planned as well?*

John Judge: Yes, a huge cut in defense and, you know, a number of things were just about to go and get the ax in Congress when suddenly the "evil empire" of the Soviet Union was said to have shot down this American plane. I believe that we flummoxed Soviet defenses, lit them up, watched them from satellite's, saw how they responded, sent the Stealth bomber through. The Soviet pilots fired at what they thought was the target, which was not, and simultaneously the U.S. intelligence forces blew up the commercial plane which was still en route over the Kiral Trench.

North was in a position in the White House that included positioning the key spy satellites that went over the Soviet Union, the geophysically positioned satellites all around the world were under his command. Also, he was the one that physically worked on the tapes of the Soviet pilot announcements and other things that were presented in an edited version by Jeanne Kirkpatrick- carefully edited and so the whole thing was orchestrated very carefully.

It was written up, actually, in a book that l discovered about a year before, by one of the top aviation writers called, I believe, *Flight 709 is Down.* It's exactly that scenario, where a Stealth bomber is put through and the civilian plane is blown up and a key congressman is supposedly killed on the flight and the defense budget and the other contracting things for these defense contractors are preserved. But also immediately after that announcement of the 007 disappearance of McDonald, McDonald's position at Western Goals was filled by Carl Spitz Channel, who was a fundraiser for Oliver North. Scoop Jackson who paralleled the character in the book that was written a year before as the congressman that died on the fictional plane, died of a heart attack the day of the 007 incident. His top aide a right-winger, moved into a position in the government. Henry Kissinger replaced Jackson on the Foreign intelligence Advisory Board and the Central American Task Force to develop the bloodbath that we 're seeing carried out now in Central America. Scoop Jackson was taken off the board of Boeing and replaced by Alexander Haig that day, so it was clearly power shifts that went on during this period which is the purpose, I think, of these scandals.

I think in any other country people would understand what it meant when the head of the intelligence agency became the president of the country. Here we seem to shrug our shoulders and think it's meaningless. Mae Brussell called George Bush "Killer Bush" and she did that because he had a long history of involvement in the CIA genocidal operations, also because she believed his involvement went back to the time of the John F. Kennedy assassination when he was debriefed about that at the time and because she felt he was exposed as responsible for the bombing of Orlando Letelier because he knew that the anti-Castro Cubans were coming into the country and knew the threats to Letelier's life and did nothing to stop the momentum of this operation if, in fact, not being part of the planning of the operation to set a bomb off in the United States to kill a progressive person. His role in that is exposed in Don Freed's book Death in Washington about the Letelier born Bing. They attempted through lawsuits to stop the book from coming out, but it's an important piece of the evidence.

So Mae called him "Killer Bush" and she went to the republican convention to try to stop his rise into power. But I think from March 31, 1981 he was effectively president of the United

States. I think he pushed Reagan out to Camp David to watch old movies and wave at the press. I said in my talks about Contragate that I believe it was Bush, not Reagan who signed the order for the shipment of the arms to Iran because the day that Reagan was in for prostate surgery is the day that all the witnesses say that the presidential finding was signed and that was the day that Bush was legally president for a period of eight hours.

Jack Anderson, an old hand at cover-up and government propaganda, says that Bush played tennis that day and fell on his head and spent the day in bed, but I think he had better things to do than play tennis when he got a chance legally to be president and sign executive orders for that period. And I think Reagan didn't know, I don't think they would have put him in a position to know what was happening until it was too late when they could use it as a scandal against him to push him out in the same way that these forces under Bush orchestrated the desert invasion plan in Iran to free the hostages that was set up to fail to embarrass Carter and orchestrated the October Surprise payoffs so that the Iranian hostages would be kept until after the elections. The things that Barbara Honegger has exposed, Bush is part and parcel to almost every key covert operation and political assassination and especially the movement of drugs.

Bush was "drug czar" at the time that the amount of drugs increased coming into the country and so there's just no way to separate Bush and the operatives that deal exclusively in guns and drugs for their covert missions. To take Bush out of that and to suggest that because he puts on a public relations campaign of just say no that he's concerned about drug use totally belies the fascist nature of Mr. William Bennett, a racist to the core, who was soundly criticized for his role as Secretary of Education earlier and the policies that he wanted to put in that were racist, white-centered and dominant. During that period he was recommended to Reagan by the entire religious right as the choice to take over the position of Secretary of Education in the Reagan Administration.

After showing his true colors there, Bennett was put into this position as the "drug czar." In fact, all he's done is make moves to take civil liberties away from people in almost every aspect of the society from workers who have to take mandatory urine tests now to people on the street who can be and people living in HUD housing that are being kicked out on the mere suspicion of drugs. It's almost as if Bennett was put in to help solve the HUD housing scandal by emptying the houses of the people that were in them.

If he didn't do it, Jack Kemp, another neo-fascist and connected very clearly to the republican Heritage Council and the Nazis there, was moved in to take care of the poor people and so black youth are the victims of the drug war of George Bush, but George Bush was director of CIA in '76, I mean there's no way that he was not cognizant that the world heroin and world cocaine trafficking was being run by the same coalition of Nazis and CIA elements that have dominated covert operations and government policies in this country for all these years.

They don't put someone in as director of Central Intelligence Agency who is just a naive bumbling nice guy to see what happens. They put someone in who's going to carry out the interests and the policies. Bush is cleverer than Reagan, he's better at PR, he'll have you believe that, he'll even put out a campaign that he's a wimp so that you won't understand how truly dangerous the man is, what a lying slime and killer that he actually is. So he has this nice appearance with his wife Barbara and his grandchildren, as he so racist put it, the "little brown ones." But he doesn't care about black or brown or people of color. His policies are killing those people every day in the streets and the crack and other cocaine that comes into this country comes in because of the operations that the CIA and others have initiated around the world.

Those cocaine fields are controlled by CIA, as were the heroin fields for many years in Southeast Asia and since. So, it's not separate. People in this country live in a state of total denial. They want to pretend that their leaders are beneficent and innocent people who mean well and if anything happens it's just an aberration in policy, it's just a mistake that's been made. But the reality is that we live under fascism and we live under the control of the policies that were developed by Hitler and the Nazis in the period of the 1930's and 1940s and those policies have been embraced under the aegis of anti-Communism and the cold war since the 1940s and Bush has been part and parcel of carrying those policies out and we live in a genocidal society that is responsible for the deaths of many more people than the Nazi *Hohenzollern* machine killed during the holocaust just in the years since.

Even John Stockwell, an ex-CIA agent, admits to the CIA being directly responsible for 10 million deaths around the world and I'm sure the real figure is higher. If you took the covert operations and the created disasters because they're capable of using natural disasters as weapons, famines that they've created and encouraged elsewhere in the world. Bush shows disrespect every moment that he's in office for the life of people here in the United States not only just the quality of life but life itself for the homeless, for the blacks, for the poor, for unemployed people in this society.

Bush takes care of his rich, white, male, slimy, republican, fascist friends and that's whom he takes care of. He could care less about the people who are starving in the street. His attitude is, I am sure, that of most of the people in his class that they should die and get out of his way and not be an eyesore in his rich fantasy of America as the ruler of the world. He has the gall to go into the Arab states now and threaten the lives of millions of people there with all of his weapons because of a border dispute that's lasted since the time the British falsely set up the Kuwaiti borders years ago.

He can go on all he wants about "madman Hitler" Hussein, but the reality of the situation is that we are the ones... I mean, people think that this isn't fascism because they don't see the person with the storm trooper swastika on and they don't feel threatened. But they don't have to threaten them in the way that totalitarian fascism did because they have methods and means of propaganda that are much more effective. Hitler was developing those means, the Nazis had television at the end of the 40's, and they were beginning to use it. Goebbels knew how to use the radio, Speer knew how to build the buildings and flash the lights around for psychological manipulation. The fruits of that are our modern advertising and what passes as media in this country and the manipulation of all information and education so that it's nothing more than propaganda and lies to prop up a decadent system that keeps concentrating the wealth in fewer and fewer hands. I mean, a lot of people feel that they have some stake in this society because they can live on credit and they can have a car and a house and some appliances on credit, but hardly anyone besides the very 'very rich, owns anything. And the ability to produce anything is rapidly deteriorating because there is no connection between culture and agriculture, there is no connection between production and credit.

The whole economy is just an inflated balloon of paper and when it begins to collapse as it's doing in this S & L scandal, the reality comes out and what we see underneath all the time is the manipulations and machinations of the CIA and these intelligence agencies that Bush is connected to. Silverado S & L will eventually, when the truth comes out, be seen to be another conduit of funds to the CIA through Neil Bush. Neil Bush also should be called "Killer Bush," I believe, because of his role in the assassination of Bob Marley, the rock star, among others. He visited Marley in Jamaica after Seaga's men, who were CIA financed tried to shoot Marley at a rock concert. Marley went to hide in a mountain retreat and Neil Bush, posing as a reporter for Rolling Stone magazine came into the house and was close to him in the days before he suddenly left ill for England and found that he had a brain tumor and died. I believe that Neil Bush placed that brain tumor.

It was Neil Bush in this little arrangement with the Hinckley's to take care of Ronald Reagan. These people come off as if they're innocent little good boys and maybe that's what Barbara believes of them, but I think George and Neil and Jeb (who hangs around with the contras and the cigarette boat drug dealers and the others and has his hands in the dirty operations) at least know the score. It's exactly what George Bush said on the night of the last debate that he had with Dukakis. He said, "I've unleashed the Bush family on America." And that's what he has done, the dogs of the Bush family are unleashed and they're biting anywhere and everywhere that they can and they're taking whatever chunks they can and thank God there's a few people looking at them to catch them at a few things, but there's a whole other element of Bush, a mountain of information that this is only the tip of, that may never come out, that we'll never be able to get to the bottom of, so you can see the little pieces of it. People can live in denial and they can believe that George Bush is just a nice fellow who shrugs his shoulders and says, "Aw, gee, I'm just trying to run the government." But if people want to live in reality, they're going to have to realize that this is not a democracy, it's a fascist state and Bush is the puppet-master. It's about time that they woke up to that.

PWR: *A good example of that is that some women went into Skull & Bones and found a Nazi shrine, old bones and skulls and...*

John Judge: Well, I know a whole section of the Skull & Bones is called the "Wolfs Division" which is the Death's Head SS division. They called themselves the SS Wolves, so there's a Death Head Division and a Wolf Division - it's just the old Nazi structure, Skull & Bones, and the fascism goes on. I'm sure that it's there under the cover behind the closet door, the skeleton of fascism, that's what's in Bush's closet and the rest of them.

I mean, if you understand the nature of the Central Intelligence Agency and what it's done in reality, you can't be anything but totally naive to believe that they would put in as director of the CIA a nice know-nothing who might stumble across what they were doing and freak out and say something. You've got to put in somebody that's part of the team and that's what George Bush is. There's just no two ways about it. You can't believe that somebody's both a nice guy and the head of the most genocidal agency on earth unless you just want to be a "good German" and think, "Heil Hitler" no matter what. But it's easier for people to think that their leaders are benign and nothing's really wrong and even if something comes out that's wrong, it must have been a mistake, it must have been an error, rather than understand that this is policy, this is part and parcel of what goes on and it serves only the interests of the rich few, and there are fewer and fewer all the time and they're richer and richer all the time and more powerful and they could care less for the rest of the earth.

They want to get their hands on the damned oil in the Middle East and they don't care who they have to kill to do it or what kind of games they have to play to do it. They're going to control the Gulf, they're going to control the oil there, they're going to control uranium and gold and diamonds, bauxite and manganese and rubber all over the world. They're going to try and keep this country at a tremendously distorted consumption level where it's tremendously wasteful, no conservatism, when people could use intermediate technology and a reasonable level ...of consumption of energy. The money that's wasted in the defense department, one half of it could give adequate living and food and clothing to everyone in the United States.

You could take the technology right now and turn it towards meeting basic human needs and people would work two weeks a year and live in a paradise, but instead they've hidden the surplus of this huge industrial wealth under their war machine and under their lies and propaganda. And they have us scrounging as wage slaves 40 hours a week doing menial, meaningless jobs for nothing, with no purpose to our lives and totally alienated from everything except the joy of being a consumer in their society and buying their products which are linked to our psychological needs that they create. They give us tension about having a headache so we get a headache and then we need their aspirin to take care of it. It's just that kind of a cycle that they want everyone to live on. And then, as my friend Loris Button said, "Keep quiet, consume, and die." That's our role in society.

But some people don't want to be just consumers and don't want to be just objects of the system. Some people want to live and· they want to have control over their lives and they want to say what should happen and instead of this national security and secrecy state, .to have an open democracy, instead of being the damned bully of the world that kills millions of people a day through starvation that we would become a friend of the world and help people live and eat and survive and make the world a livable place for not only ourselves but other species and do the things that come naturally to people. But that all has to be distorted and bent around and hidden from us totally in order to make us into the little robots that go along with the scientific slave state of Nazi Bush and his minions.

If you want to, you can believe that he's the duly elected president of the United States, but I've been reading some historical analysis of Thomas Jefferson, whose ideas are always touted by those who say they believe in this country. They say that Jefferson was such a great man and he thought of such a flawless system. Well, Jefferson 'himself knew that systems and people and history change and he said that all Constitutions and all positive laws and all public debts should end entirely every 19 years and be renewed. We can't even begin to understand how we could end them in a few hundred years, but when you leave something in place for 200 years it goes rotten and that's what this has done, without any thought to what the technology is or what the changes in the society are. Because it maintains the privilege of the few, they teach us that it's the best possible system on earth.

But the best possible system on earth is the one that serves all the people and all the interests of all the people and serves people's humanity and takes care of the earth for future generations. That's not what our system is. This system is rapacious, it's eroding the land, and its desertifying sections of the earth at a higher rate than all the rest of history before humans came here. It's polluting the air and fouling the whole system, making it unlivable. It's creating weapons that threaten the existence of everything on the planet. It's recklessly using nuclear energy with no thought for how they're going to get rid of the waste and toxins. So people just go on moving back into smaller and smaller little safe hole spaces where there isn't a Love Canal or there isn't a this or a that, but there isn't that much space left before we're going to have to face reality and look at the end of the long spoon and see what the hell we're being fed for lunch.

It's not anything pleasant, you know. You can go stick your head in the TV, in the movie and entertain yourself, but at some point it's going to come knocking at your back door and you 're going to have to deal with it and most people have had to. But they're so deadened and they're so freaked out and they're so compliant that they would rather have the government come and take their sons and daughters off to die killing people in some other country than to stand up and say "Wait a minute, I own my life and these are people that I've invested 20 years of my life instead, they pat them on the back and say, "Go do your duty, boy" and off they go and we see what happens, how they come back even if they survive the war because it's a genocidal war.

You know, 153,000 veterans dead from suicide after the Vietnam War, and that figure dates back to 1981 - ten years ago there were 153,000 so it's probably over 200,000 now, which is four times as many as died in the war. There's just nobody dealing with that still. Looking at the war, letting a Vet understand what they were asked to do that it was genocide, they're just told to wrap a flag around themselves, say "I'd do it again," and they get their pension money or a little bit of help about their Agent Orange disease and then that's it. It's a foul lie and it's a rotten way to live and people can sit there and say, "Well, I'll do it because otherwise I won't be able to wear my air pump shoes or my Gucci dress, if 8 million people have to die to put me here, that's okay."

Those aren't my instincts, they aren't the instincts of people that I know or would care to know. I think that the people that would live that way, having gotten the information and being able to make the choice, are so few in number that there's no way they should be determining what happens in this country. 'Its just time for us to stop waiting for leaders to take care of us, if a leader was going to take care of our real interests, they'd blow his head off, and they've shown us that, so what's the point? It's got to be that we have to take democracy back into our own hands and demand that we control the decisions about our lives - nationally, internationally, and locally. And the decisions that affect us directly must become decentralized when we have direct participation and democratic control. There's no other solution that I can see to democracy.

The point of democracy it seems to me is to always increase the likelihood that decisions that affect people are going to be made by the people that are affected. How can you have an all-male Supreme Court, or one woman on the Supreme Court, how can you have them decide anything about abortion? How can you have men decide anything about abortion? But that's the situation. You have Bush getting up and talking about abortion! I mean, let him get pregnant and then talk about abortion. Or let him keep it in his pants. What have men got to say about that? That's women's bodies. What would men think if women had a vote about castration? But nobody is dealing with the power relationships; everybody just wants to make decisions. "I feel this is right, so I'll impose it on somebody else."

To me, that's where the seed of the fascism lies, in the ability to divide people and to make people insensitive to other people around them. To commoditize those people is one of the ways to do it, to make it a marketing economy so that you 're just an object of my desire to exploit someone, you serve some need or some purpose in my plan or my scheme so I use you, 'you are a commodity to me. I used to say to people if you think you 're getting all you can out of this system, then it's getting all it can out of you.

PWR: *Look at Arlen Specter. Specter covered up in the Warren Commission where he was a staff attorney and then he was paid off by, getting political power, but then he's used again to pry drug money out by agreeing with Bennett's Nazi policies. Or Gerald Ford who was another conspirator in the Warren Commission cover-up and later covered for Nixon... Speaking of Ford, who was trying to shoot him?*

John Judge: Well, there were other elements that wanted the southern rim money wanted him out because they knew this was Rockefeller and Ford basically appointed as President so they were setting up the assassination attempts. Squeaky Fromme from the Manson family was programmed and put up to the shooting, as was Sara Jane Moore. Both had connections with FBI and military intelligence background and were put up as the assassins. Which of the attempts was the most serious, I don't know. Ford was also supposed to do a presentation to the Legionnaires in the Belleview Stratford Hotel, which he cancelled, but that was the day that all the Legionnaires' disease broke out in the hotel there in Philadelphia.

PWR: *How about Charles Manson? Was there any government involvement in that or was it real?*

John Judge: The Manson family didn't come out of nowhere. Charlie Manson was a long time racist and pimp and inhabitant of juvenile criminal facilities. His mother was a prostitute. In fact, she was close friends with another prostitute who was the mother of Sara Jane Moore, someone that Manson played with, a kid that was part of another conspiracy... he grew up with one of the key figures in another operation. That's the way they get a lot of them, early on, but he was down in Cincinnati and then he was in the prisons and they just let him out. They just paroled him and let him go and he was able to get cars and trucks and credit cards and everything. But when he was arrested, strangely enough, nobody came forward and said, "That's the guy that stole my truck," or "Where's my credit card?" or brought any charges against him.

All these things were, I believe, just part of favors they were doing him to let him roam around and pretend to be the hippie king and recruit these women. The women came from top-ranking military intelligence families - they weren't little girls off the street with no money. They came from families with a lot of bucks and with ties into the Pentagon. Once the scenario was set up they gave him MKULTRA drugs, the mind control drugs, to give to the women. They gave him complete control over the women so that he had this... he'd make the Masonic hand signals and they'd do sexual favors for him or his biker friends. They let him think he was king out there in the desert in his little shack and beefed him up with the idea that there was going to be a race war and he was going to survive and all this crazy stuff. After he was rearrested and dragged back in, Manson said, "I want to know who was peeing on my leash." Because he understood that he was let out a certain amount and then dragged back in, pulled back with a collar before he could bite. So he understands enough to know that he was manipulated. No pleasant fellow. I mean, not somebody you'd want to spend a lot of time with, but not him the real mover and shaker of the situation.

The killer was Tex Watson, whose family is in the sheriff's office in Dallas and was at the time of the Kennedy assassination. The Watsons are the dominant family there who ran the turf for the sheriff's office under Captain Fritz. Tex Watson was well connected enough that they couldn't even extradite him to California for trial. Vincent Bugliosi said they had to go down and try him in Texas. In Texas he gave a completely different trial if you get that transcript. He didn't say that Manson ran Watson and controlled him by mind control and hardcore charisma and all the nonsense that he pushed up in California. He said that Watson did the killings, and Watson made the decisions and that was the case. Watson took the girls with him Charlie wasn't there. Watson went into the house, and this was an all American boy, a football star, born again Christian, no one could understand why or how he became a hippie convert.

I don't think he was. I think the drugs at the ranch were supplied by military intelligence. The ranch itself had been the scene of many of the western movies that were made by Howard Hughes in the '50's, the Spahn Movie Ranch, where they had their operations. Jane Russell was out there and *The Outlaw* was made there. The owner of the ranch next door, who eventually bought out the Spahn ranch after the Manson family scandal was over and is turning it into a Bavarian beer garden operation is the Krupp family, the munitions and arms provisioned for Nazi Germany. Not the sort of folks who'd have just a bunch of scrounger neighbors without commenting on it. So I think the whole thing was a setup to discredit hippies and the counter-culture and the left. After that period, you never saw any positive images of counter-culture people on the media.

All you saw was Manson and the idea that if you didn't go along with the society, dropped out, or lived communally or took drugs that you'd turn into this raging beast and stab people in the stomach. In the same way Altamont, I believe, was set up by military intelligence to discredit Woodstock and to be the dark side of the coin with the Rolling Stones and Melvin Belli. But there were deeper connections behind who Manson was and whom he knew. He was a Rosicrucian in the prisons and Sirhan had ties with the Rosicrucian church. He came out and for a while did recruiting for Scientology, he learned the Masonic secret signals from Alvin "Creepy" Carpis, the old mobster that challenged Hoover in the 30's and who was in prison with Manson in the California system for a while. He would attend house parties he knew the Beach Boys, he knew Dennis Wilson, he played music and cut a record with one of them. He also attended parties regularly at the Tate mansion where Tate and Polanski had these wild sex and drug parties up there and Manson would go. So would Sirhan. Whether they were there at the same time I don't know, but Ed Sanders in his book *The Family* revealed some of this in one of the chapters and then, took a lot of it out of the paperbound edition after some of the churches threatened to sue Scientology and others said they'd sue him for putting the information in. But I don't think it was bad information, I think that they actually knew each other.

Robert Kennedy ate dinner at the Tate house the night before he went to the Ambassador and was shot, and so I think there is a link between the Robert Kennedy assassination and this circle. I think it's basically a Pentagon Hollywood Axis, as Mae Brussell called it. Key people who hung around the Tate house were part of that drug circle that was fairly sadistic. They'd take young kids in off the street and rape them, black magic nonsense, there were tapes of that the police found in the house. There were also clues that didn't match such as a pair of glasses that dido 't belong to any of the family members, the bodies seemed to have been repositioned after the time of the murder, maybe evidence removed. If you will remember, the pair of glasses was the key clue in the movie *Chinatown* by Polanski that was added to the script by Polanski because there was this extra pair of glasses left on the porch of the house afterwards.

I don't think you control people with acid, I don't think that it's a control drug. It makes you slightly suggestible, but I don't think you give somebody acid and then start ordering 'them around. I think that the acid they are referring to is MKULTRA, an acid derivative or psilocybin derivative that was used for mind control by the CIA and defense intelligence. I think it's the same "acid" that's talked about by David Berkowitz' best friend in Korea in the Army who was quoted in the Philadelphia Inquirer saying that when they were stationed in Korea and Berkowitz was a file clerk, that he applied as a conscientious objector for a discharge and he said at that point that the "brass gave him acid."

Well, I don't think the brass gives you acid; I think they give you MKULTRA. I think they did and he became Son of Sam or, as Mae used to say, "Son of Uncle Sam", one of the programmed killers that they were able to manipulate and use. Of course, who knows what they make them believe that the devil's talking to them or a black dog or a man from outer space whatever paradigm they use for the control system, but the reality is that the CIA is training the assassins. So I think Manson was basically just set up to take this fall. He's not beyond killing somebody, but I don't think that he did the actual Tate and LaBianca murders. Those people were also dealers. Voytek Frykowski was a big dealer of MDA and Mr. La' Bianca was a coke and smack dealer for the Toronto syndicate, the drugs that were coming down through Toronto after the Cuban connection and the Marseilles connection had been cut off. A lot of drugs came through Seattle and down the coast into San Francisco and the Bay Area. So these people were major dealers and I think they pulled a burn and they got paid back as pan of this scenario because when you do these things at the orchestrated level they usually are "bonus operations" you get several things done at once. That's how you peg it, you know, we're going to do a killing, let's make the killing count, accomplish as many things as they could.

PWR: *Can you tell me about - You said at one point yesterday that Patty Hearst stayed at Bill Walton's house.*

John Judge: Well, when she was on the run they said that Bill Walton - that's a sports character, right, was putting her up. He was talking to the press about that himself. But the whole SLA operation was a CIA front and Patty was kept in CIA safe houses so anybody that harbored her, to me, has to be suspect of some ties. There was Walton and a guy from the University of Cincinnati, I believe is where he originally played ball, and the, was it UCLA? Okay, well there was some other guy that maybe Walton knew, but I think this guy was the coach at the University of Cincinnati. He put her up for a period of time - then he was involved in some scandal about racism in the picking of players down there at the school. But neither of these guys seemed openly politically progressive at the time, so it didn't make sense, why were they harboring this SLA fugitive from the "revolution?"

There were also a lot of funny things going on in Ohio at the time. There were people hiding Patty there seemed to be Patty doubles, there was a pickup of somebody who said that she wasn't Patty Hearst but she looked exactly like her and she had gone to school up in Cleveland, a cop picked her up and she had a scar in the same place and everything was identical but she wasn't Patty Hearst. Then an FBI agent supposedly came into the scene and said that if she ever got picked up again all she had to do was tell them to call this FBI agent and he would clear her, so it was a perfect way for Patty to move if there was an accidental pickup, they had created a phony double.

I went through the yearbooks in Cleveland high schools where they said this girl went and there was no pictures of her, no name, no record of this person's existence who was supposedly the perfect double for Patty Hearst. They were raiding women's organizations and bashing the doors down on the entire lesbian and progressive women's groups, witch hunting, supposedly looking for an underground "lesbian railroad" that was hiding Patty. I think also there was somebody's brother that was involved! I think it was this coach's brother was an FBI guy who began to speak out about it and he was put into an alcohol ward and he said that the FBI knew where she was and this was a government plot. But the whole thing was orchestrated. It was orchestrated to discredit the left.

PWR: *Why Patty Hearst, of all people?*

John Judge: That's a long-standing feud between the Rockefeller and the Hearst money so I think this was an attempt to get back at the Hearst's and target them. E. Howard Hunt, I believe, is the author of a porno novel called *Black Abductors* that was written in 1972, two years before the kidnapping and it describes a radical biracial group that kidnaps the daughter of a west coast publishing figure and rapes her into submission because in the porno novel she likes the sex so well she decides to stay with the revolutionaries even though she's been raped. But I think that those kinds of scenarios are put out. The publishing company and the author didn't really exist, but the book was out there and it described this scenario.

Milton Caniff, who used to draw Steve Canyon, l used to follow that because he used to always put Steve Canyon in the country that we were about to go into with a covert operation or something and he'd make Dragon Lady there, or whatever the hell was supposed to go on. He came from Dayton, Ohio and l was there one summer and the local newspapers liked to interview him. He'd come home summers to visit his family and they interviewed him to see what was going on and he said in the course; of his interview that for the first time in his career he' had actually cancelled a story, had decided' not to, draw a whole strip. Apparently they draw these strips months in advance so that they have week after week ready to go way before they actually hit the papers so when he decided to cancel this story he was stuck: and he had to come up with another whole tale very quickly m get it in and meet the deadlines. So they asked him, "What was it and why did you cancel it," and he said it was spooky, he said it paralleled the Patty Hearst kidnapping and he didn't want to embarrass the family so he just didn't put it in.

Well, I think it wasn't so spooky except in the sense of the intelligence spook. I think that he would come back to Wright Pat and visit his military intelligence friends and they would give him the inside scoop on what they were doing and he would whether he was conscious of it or not he'd write it up as ideas in his comics and the comics would become a trial balloon or a pre-conditioned acceptance operation for the propaganda. You know, Steve Canyon's there and that's why he's there and that's why we've got to go into Thailand or whatever else the boys are going to do. So I think this was a military intelligence operation, a fight between the Hearst's and the Rockefeller end of the CIA and that's why Hearst was targeted.

There's more about it in the book *Glass House Tapes* by Louis Tackwood, an undercover agent that was central to some of these operations. But the Symbionese Liberation Army was a fiction, I mean, there was no such revolutionary group. It's just like now every time there's one of these bombings or assassinations, the group that takes credit for it, no one's ever heard of them, they've never been in the news before, and you never hear of them again. They're phony CIA constructs that do the terrorism in order to create the backlash and frighten people but they don't exist. Or they exist as CIA infiltrated and dominated or created groups that you have heard of. The George Habash section of the PLO is entirely a CIA creation and does much of this the Black September operation came out of them and much of the violence comes directly from the CIA as provocateurs.

No one on the left ever heard of the SLA or Donald De'Freeze or Colston Westbrook who started the group out of what he called the "Peking House," and went into the prisons with the Unity program and was able to talk politics to blacks which you're not allowed to do in prison. Colston Westbrook came out 'of a Pacific Engineering Company in Vietnam which was part of Pacific Corporation, the largest CIA subsidiary in the world. He was a photographer there and he comes over and he gets a job teaching "Black Lexicon" at UCLA Berkeley and he has this "Peking House" and to that house come all these what Mae Brussell called 'migratory birds.'

The Harris's, William and Emily Harris, had no radical background. They worked at the University of Indiana, Bloomington, which is a recruiting school for the CIA and, you know, people don't go from a change in political consciousness to armed revolutionaries in a matter of days or weeks! It takes years for somebody to develop to that level and most people don't, in this country, do that as a rational exercise. People see other options in this country, so these were not people that spent their lives being oppressed and suddenly decided, "Let's take up the arms." They didn't work with any other groups except that DeFreeze went around and spooked everybody out when he was first released from prison' He wasn't released, he was let go, he was sent on a trustee job when he had no such parole status and was left without guards all night long and showed up a few hours later (he obviously had a car and a clothing change) in the city. He went to Venceremos Brigade and the VVAW (Vietnam Vets Against the War) and offered his services as a hit man. They threw him out the door because they know that's exactly how the police operate. So failing to infiltrate the existing groups, Westbrook and these others then formed his phony Symbionese

Liberation Army.

None of the people in it were radicals except at the very end I believe maybe Camilla Hall and Patty Solystik were sucked in, and I don't even know if they joined they were just said to have joined. Their death certificates list their death at another location than the SLA burned out house and their bodies weren't found in the rubble for three days. I think they killed them someplace else and moved them in and then said that they were part of it just so they could have a few real radicals in the SLA. Thero Wheeler had no background; DeFreeze had a long background as a police informant, intelligence agent and provocateur in Cleveland and on the West Coast. The gun that he was using in the bank robberies was from the police, it was supposed to be a police confiscated gun, but somehow he had it back out in his hands from the LAPD. This is the kind of stuff that is revealed in Glass House Tapes, that these were operations by people who are still around, Darryl Gates and these other slimy fascists that run the so-called "police departments" in Los Angeles. The same people covered up the Robert Kennedy assassination and many other operations.

PWR: *Mae Brussell had brought up some information about the Red Brigade in Italy and how that was a fascist group...*

John Judge: I think the Red Brigades in Italy, were infiltrated from the beginning, by the CIA and run by them. I think that things were done in their name after they killed the radical leadership in the prisons. There were interlinks between the Red Brigades and the Bader Meinhof group and some of the Bader Meinhof were taken into prison and given "heart attacks."

I think the so-called kidnapping of General Dozier was an entirely created incident to beef up the security forces and other things. I think the Red Brigades were part of what was used as the "strategy of tension" which is a political theory that the right uses in Europe to create social tensions, posing as the left and doing provocateur actions like the train bombing at Bologna. First they blow up the thing and kill people, blame it on the left, and then later it eventually comes out that it was the right wing that did it and the fascist 'Stefano Delle Chiaie' is the mastermind of this kind of stuff. Mae recognized certain groups like the Bosch section of the PLO, the Red Brigades, and others as operating with CIA money and CIA background and connections. In some cases, like the bombing of the U.S. Embassy in Beirut, the group that took credit turned out to have worked with the CIA at some point. When this came out, the CIA said, "Well, we never had any idea that they'd do something like this!" It's just all denial and nonsense. These people are put up to these jobs by the government or, if they're not, they're so out of touch with the people that they're acting out an operation that has. No relation to human values.

PWR: *With regard to the Beirut killings 'the Mossad actually knew a week in advance do you know about that?*

John Judge: Oh, I'm sure the intelligence agencies know ahead of time, if not plan it ahead of time. They can both stand by and let it go if it's real or they can manipulate it if it isn't. You don't hide in a modern society, in a technological age. You don't go underground; you don't move weapons and explosives without being seen. Usually these groups are set up with the help of the government. The government sends an agent in, gives the group access to all of these things and tries to provoke them into the action because the government loves terrorism. They love an excuse to be more repressive and they can use it against everyone. That's why I think people who want to act in the best interests of people don't take those kinds of actions except in the extreme situation where you have a long history of struggle like in South Africa or in Central America, like in El Salvador where the popular organizations build and they try nonviolence but all they get is Death Squad activity and murders and disappearances for years and years and finally an armed force develops to protect the people. And that armed force defends the people. But that's a much different situation, you know, than some group coming out of nowhere with no popular backing and no connection with any of the broad-based movement organizations and claiming a vanguard or a revolutionary right to go in and start blowing things up.

PWR: *It 's sort of like the "lone nut" assassin theories where a lot of these men are put up to a killing and then everyone scatters away and leaves one or two patsies to hang. Maybe you can touch a bit about you know, you mention to people that Lennon was knocked off and Marley was knocked off and they think you 're nuts, but then when you look at Marley's lyrics you hear him say, "I'm ambushed in the night, they come hunting after me" and then the next thing you know he's one of the youngest men to die of cancer on the island. Then you have Chapman maybe you can go into a little more about Chapman, I don't really know that much.*

John Judge: Well what I think would be revealing for people is to get the history of the years prior to the rise of Hitler, from '28 to '32 in the Weimar Republic in Germany. There's a film out if you can get to see it by Ingmar Bergmann called *The Serpent's Egg* that depicts those years and what was happening, It' not perfectly clear from the film, but there are a series of political assassinations going on and they were being carried out by a group called the *Freikorps*. Which was a reactionary right wing veteran group from World War I who felt that they'd been betrayed by the communists and the elements back at home in the war so they became a paramilitary reactionary force. They began to knock off progressive journalists and professors and musicians and labor leaders and people who could organize or speak to or sing the truth to the people. It's not coincidence that Victor Jara winds up in the stadium in Santiago, Chile when the fascists take over because he's a popular singer and he gives voice to the aspirations of the people and the rights of people and their true liberation. So all these things are up for grabs.

There was an increasingly open society in Germany in the end of the Weimar years. There was a lot of art and there was sexual expression and freedom was opening up and all of that was pan of what went under in terms of the reaction. The gay people were persecuted in Nazi Germany, the people in the mental institutions were the first to be killed, the gays and the radicals were locked up with pink and red badges, black for the anarchists, and then the yellow stars for the Jews. Then the Gypsies had to be rounded up because they didn't fit into the society.

People that don't fit, that go against the program under fascism, are expendable. Think about how they spent the time and the money that they did in Vietnam, the billions of dollars to carry on a war there or what they're doing right now in Saudi Arabia. Or consider what they've done in Eastern Europe or in Panama or other places in our own lifetime. Think about the amount of money it cost to do that and the amount of time and the lives that it took, and they made that investment to make sun that some little country didn't get a leader that they didn't want because it had some resource or geographical position. So what the hell do you think its worth to them to determine who the leader is in the country where it really matters, in the one that's going to run the world?

I mean if they're going to go to that extent to decide whether or not Mossedegh is going to be in or the shah of Iran is going to come in, whether it's going to be British or American petroleum interests, if there going to make sure that there can't be a people's alterative in Nicaragua, anything that looks like a democratic model anywhere in the world, they go in and destroy it. Rather than let the Vietnamese pull out from under colonial rule and live under the Declaration of Independence and the U.S. Constitution, instead we backed the French.

Of course they're going to control the elections here! There's too much at stake not to do it. So what is it to them the death of a labor leader who's threatening us? We all know the history if anybody wants to take a moment to look at it, of what happened to people that organized slave revolts. If the system could get their hands on them, of course they murdered them. The history of the Pinkertons that went in and murdered the labor leaders, the way the Wobbley's were treated and dragged out and the leadership killed and beaten.

People that work for change in a closed society are up for grabs. To think that they wouldn't kill somebody because you like their music doesn't mean a thing. If their music doesn't say anything political, if their music just soothes you back into your dream world, then they can stay there, you can live in a world where the people who sing to you are fascists like Frank Sinatra old' blue eyes. And you can get your humor from fascists like Bob Hope. But if you want your humor from somebody real like Lenny Bruce, he's going to end up with a needle in his arm in a toilet when he doesn't even shoot dope! If you want your humor from John Belushi, who's going to make fun of Henry Kissinger, act like he's a Nazi in the bunker and going to put out a movie about the DEA dealing drugs, "Moon Over Miami," then he's going to end up with a highball even though his wife said he didn't like needles.

If the lyrics of the people that are singing to you are going to motivate you politically like the Big Sur pop stars and carry on the culture, then Janis Joplin and Jimmy Hendrix and Jim Croce and the rest of them are going to have to die. And they'll say it was a drug overdose or it was a this or a that and if you don't take the time to look at the statistics and to look at the record of what drugs they were using and what happened and take a glance at the autopsy report, then you can go on dreaming that it's just a kind of sad natural tragic end to things.

So we just passed this weekend now where everybody is celebrating the life of John Lennon. I celebrate his life. But I think I'd celebrate it more if l worked on his death and who killed him so that the next person whose life I might celebrate can't be wiped out. We live in a world where in the Christian model it's more important for us to see Christ dead on the cross which doesn't make anybody nervous because we not only got the little bastard, we pinned him up and we shut him up!

Christ is fine when he's silent and dead and hanging on the cross, but when he's alive and talking and challenging the system and making people change, then he's trouble. But that's not what we're depicted, so you know, Martin Luther King... I mean, George Bush can go out and put his arms around Coretta Scott King and sing "We Shall Overcome" because they did overcome! They killed him! And they took his movement away and they knocked him down and so they "overcame." And Coretta is dumb enough to sit there with the fascists of the world and think that that's what non-violence means-linking arms with the people that are going to kill her family and kill the hope for black survival in America.

Well, she can be a member of the black bourgeoisie and do that, but the reality is something else. People have to understand that it's the first lesson the government kills people. And it kills people for a reason. And that reason is a political reason and it's to preserve privilege, preserve economic power and keep the truth from keeping out. A hundred and seventy five people were killed who were key witnesses in the Kennedy assassination or people who got hold of the information later like Dorothy Kilgallen and others, there were probably 80 murders in Martin Luther King's and Robert Kennedy's assassinations and 30 Watergate deaths that Mae

Brussell tracked and hundreds and hundreds of deaths. There were 400 political murders laid out by Mr. Gumbel in his book "Four Years of War Murders" in the Weimar Republic and there are probably 4,000 murders here in the United States to keep this rotten system in power.

A human life means almost nothing to them if it's in the way. You're allowed to survive and live in this society as long as you play by its rules and you don't open your mouth and you don't get in the way. But when you become an effective organizer. John Lennon could move a million people into the street overnight if he wanted to. They were able to shut him up and string him out on heroin for years, but he had finally gotten over that and had established his family and was going to start singing again. And the minute the new album came out, Reagan was just about to start the military buildup, double the huge military budget in a number of years, and Lennon had to be shut up. He had to be killed because he would have been in the way. It's a voice like Marley's, it's too political, it's too real, and so they don't want you to listen to it. So the counterculture people and the others are all dead and the people who don't sing about anything, that give you bubble gum and love songs and nonsense, they can go on. Or, if they sing politically but they're willing to change their tune, I think that they can go on. But to think that nobody ever gets killed for a political reason, that the government just wouldn't do that, I think its hopelessly naive and it's just not the way that the world operates. They can't afford not to operate the other way. Do you think they could afford to try to maintain the privilege and then let you have any spokesman you want with as much airtime as you want? They have to control the airwaves, they have to control what comes on and what doesn't come on and what's said and what's meant and the propaganda because otherwise we'll wake up. And when we wake up, we'll say,

"This isn't my game, it's yours, and I'm not interested in playing it anymore."

PWR: *You said you thought Yoko Ono had some hand in John's death and that her father was a fascist...*

John Judge: I don't know if she had a direct hand in his death, but you know Yoko Ono is one of the richest people in the world and her father was one of the major financial officers of the Sumitomo Bank in Japan which was one of the Axis banks during the war, one of the key institutions. In fact, when the Vatican Bank went broke, Sumitomo came in and bailed them out recently and the Vatican has long ties to the fascist regime. So she came out of a very fascist family. Her father, even though he was Japanese, was allowed in and out of the United States all through World War II. Other people, Japanese Americans, were put in concentration camps and treated as persona non grata. He was connected to the real money and the real money talks moves where it's going to just the same way that the American corporate ties to the Nazis all through the war.

I believe that most people that have analyzed the 'Beatles, their analysis is that she was central to the break in the group and a number of the books 1 have seen suggested that she was responsible for introducing him to the heroin that strung him out. He was gelling very political at the end he worked with the White Panthers, started doing socialist music and albums that were totally political. I don't think that they were able to control him any longer except through drugs. To what extent she's conscious about that, 1 don't know, but I haven't seen her do too much to challenge her level of privilege, to speak out politically about what's happening in the world, which I think is her moral responsibility. She certainly hasn't done too much to solve his death, which I think she ought to be busy doing.

She should be asking whom Mark David Chapman is, not living in some little dream world where she hides off with Sean and sings a song and lights a candle.

I don't have a lot of respect for the people who say that they loved John Lennon and then they come out with a candle on his birthday or they go down to Strawberry Fields and they cry over them, but they won't pick up one newspaper article, they won't read anything about who Mark David Chapman was. They won't try to find out what was World Vision or the people that he worked for or where he came from and they don't care. Because what good does it do you to have a John Lennon and then cry over him unless you just want to live in some kind of tragic soap opera where you can convince yourself there's nothing you can do because your heroes are killed, that it's a kind of self-fulfilling prophecy of tragedy, that you just can't get out of the cycle.

But I say you can get out of it. You can solve murders, and that's your responsibility in a society, in a democracy if you want to live some other way. You don't just boo-hoo and take out the handkerchief and cry about it, you try and figure it out. Figure out who's doing it and put the finger on them and expose them at least. If not put them in jail, at least know who you 're dealing with and get people to be conscious of it and realize that they're taking chance when they're political. It's telling because people who don't have any political analysis and understanding of the history back themselves into corners. Martin Luther King gets a birthday and the first time It's celebrated, Reishi Sasakawa, who describes himself in the press as 'the richest fascist in the World' because he's a philanthropist and backs the Center on non-Violence financially, is invited to be keynote speaker at Martin Luther King's birthday.

King would roll in his grave if he knew who this guy was! He's got connections to the worst money and the worst fascists and brags about it, but he's invited there and the people who did the Live AID to raise money, a portion of that fund was distributed through World Vision! They hand the money over to World Vision and have them give it out in the camps. So if you don't have any political consciousness, you're going to end up paying your enemy to strangle you and not understand what you're doing. It's just impossible, it seems to me, to exist in the modern world at the level of money they have and to be politically naive except that I think that the only other explanation is that they're just deathly afraid and they're afraid that if they learn what the World is they'll have to act on it. If they act like they don't know, no one will hurt them, they won't be the 'target, and so they just hide.

Sylvia Meagher, in her book *Accessories After the Fact*, on the Kennedy assassination, said that you don't weigh the evidence in the light of the Kennedys' acquiescence, you weigh their acquiescence in light of the evidence." Why does the solution of the Kennedy assassination have to rest on me? I wouldn't have even voted for John F. Kennedy. I think he did some good things, but I'm not politically aligned with the Democratic Party in the United States, why does it have to rest on me to bring it up? Where are his children? Where is his family? Where are his friends? Did he have a friend who has the courage, the gall to stand up and say, "My friend was murdered and I want to know why?" Leo Ryan had a friend like Holsinger, it didn't do him any good in terms of his vision of the world to speak out, but he spoke out and he said, "The CIA was involved in killing my friend and I want to get to the bottom of it."

But the Kennedys, it's better for them to keep quiet, keep their own family dirt in the home, go on about their business, live out their money and live out their privilege. Well, they can afford to do that, but the rest of us have to live in a world where democracy is just mocked right in front of our faces. The President was gunned down like a dog in an open street and we're told that there's nothing we can do about it. Maybe if you're rich enough that doesn't bother you, but I think people that are less powerful in society understand that it means that any option for change is taken away from us.

PWR: *In terms of the control of the media...*

John Judge: The main electronic media, television, was owned all three major networks, owned through stock front manipulation and corporate fronts by the Rockefellers from the 1940's on. This was exposed in 1974 in a major congressional investigation on corporate disclosure that was done by one of the sub committees. I have the reports on that. There have been other books since then about who owns the media and how it's controlled. There 've been some shifts in terms of the ownership of media. ABC was sold out to Capital Cities which William Casey was a major investor in and had CIA money behind it. NBC was sold to General Electric. It just says enough that the corporate entities in this country would own the media and the media is a corporate entity itself and it's little more than an extension of the business that their parent companies are about. So it can't be anything except a propaganda arm of theirs. It can't be what it should be - an effective tool for democratic participation and debate and open exposure of ideas and reality. Instead it's a controlled game show where a wheel spins and we wait to see what our fortune is. Whether it's in the Persian Gulf or we're trying to guess what the secret word is. The secret word is "FASCISM."

PWR: *Could you give us a bit more about World Vision and maybe some background on Mark David Chapman?*

John Judge: Chapman has an unusual history. He traveled around the world. He was in Beirut at a critical time when Wilson and Terpil were there training assassins and I believe they may have trained him in their school. He clearly had military training at the time he shot John Lennon. He took a military stance, feet apart, arms up and said, "Mr. Lennon," and then shot him in the back. But it was a military stance; he had been trained. I think it was more than just the rent-a-cop training he might have gotten in Hawaii. In Hawaii he worked guarding major military-industrial institutions. He was institutionalized for a while in Castle Memorial Institute which was the scene of some of the MKULTRA experimentation and some of the doctors there were directly involved in the mind-control operations of the CIA in Hawaii so I think that that might be where he got the final program to kill Lennon.

He's not the only people that I've got information on that were told to go around and try and get Lennon, but he's one of them. I think that, as usual, they would have had Team A team B kills Lennon in a different instance if he had not succeeded. Security wasn't particularly tight there. It's an open driveway entrance. There is a guard stand, but they were used to people coming around for autographs. A lot of famous people live in the building and generally Chapman was low-key enough. He had money unexplainably. He didn't have a huge salary. He had an Asian wife but he had no money to fly all the way to New York and to stay at the Waldorf Astoria and to hang around there which also seems similar to the case of people like Hinckley, just living on the street barely surviving- then suddenly he goes to D.C. and stays in the expensive hotel. The guy that shot George Wallace was the same way. He suddenly had the money to travel. All of them are like this, like James Earl Ray, he could travel internationally when he was a little two-time hood with

$38 in his pocket if he's lucky. Suddenly he's flying from country to country.

Somebody finances these people at the last moment and puts them in the position to do it and does the programming. A shrink named Rappaport, who was also a psychiatrist, programmed Hinckley, for his double that we located in Philadelphia who was stopped at the Port Authority and arrested. Hinckley's double's name was Richardson I believe, he was in Philadelphia, but he had been in Evergreen, Colorado and programmed by this same shrink that programmed Hinckley and put electrodes in his head and these other things just before I think Chapman was given military training in Beirut. He was also out at Fort Chaffee, Arkansas, part of the Thai refugee they had several places where they were putting refugees from other countries and all those programs were being run by World Vision, founded in the 1950's and headed by none other than John W. Hinckley an anti-communist alternative for people fleeing from the communist menace in these countries, in other words the reactionary elements in these countries would flee and they'd pick up these refugee populations. They're eminently manipulatable. They're without a country, they're without a job, they're without family ties, and so their history is severed so they're excellent recruiting grounds for intelligence operations, assassins, which is exactly what they were doing. I think that World Vision is the current version of the old John Howard Bowen Mexican assassin squads that were utilized in the Kennedy assassination and discussed in The Torbitt Document 'A breeding ground for assassins'.

MUSEUM OF HIDDEN HISTORY INTERVIEW

I got John to do an interview to support what had become his dream, the Hidden History Museum, around August of 2012, and it ran on the now-defunct Examiner.com website in September 2012. John sent me an email shortly thereafter saying how happy he was with the final product. This interview was also reprinted in my book Dissenting Views II. *The Hidden History Museum has since evolved into the Hidden History Center, thanks to the hard work of Marilyn Tenenhoff and Dave Ratcliffe. I subsequently joined the Board of Directors in late 2015.*

GREEN: *That's an intriguing name. Why the Museum of Hidden History?*

JOHN JUDGE: I think most of history, including our own, is hidden from us by various means. As a simple example, the history of the Europeans in America is not the same history as the indigenous people who were nearly eliminated in the process of "civilization" and occupation. History is often intentionally destroyed by conquering cultures and colonizers.

The history we are taught in school is from one perspective, the dominant paradigm of the culture, and omits many other aspects, perspectives and facts as less relevant. Mahatma Gandhi said that history is usually told as the history of war, conflict and military victories, but that the real history of humanity is one of cooperation, which in fact is why the species has survived, but rarely mentioned.

President Truman one said that the only new thing in the world is the history we do not know. The National Archives uses the slogan, "The Past is Prologue," pointing to the fact that our history is important to our present and our possible future.

Especially in the modern era, since the start of WWII, history has increasingly become a commodity of warring nations and their emerging security organizations. Winston Churchill noted that in wartime, "Truth must be surrounded by a bodyguard of lies." Secrecy became the norm with the Manhattan Project and the inception of the nuclear arms race and the Cold War. Since then, nearly one billion records have been classified and kept from public view relating to both military and civilian agencies and operations of the United States, both at home and abroad. Our history is literally buried in underground vaults controlled by undemocratic agencies for the assumed protection of the society and the democracy this thwarts.

Even recent history is being lost and distorted, and we are in danger of entering a post-historical consciousness because so little emphasis is put on history.

People are naturally curious about secrets, about what is hidden or untold. We want to use that curiosity to expose millions of visitors to Washington, DC to three types of history they are not likely to know. We define hidden history as:

History we don't see because of miseducation and assumptions; History we can't see because of our paradigms and lack of counter-narratives; and History we are not allowed to see because of the National Security State. Our core will be the history of America's recent past and the covert operations it has carried out against people around the world as well as its own citizens. But we will also present both national and local history from diverse perspectives, new investigations and released files, and fresh revisions based on unearthed facts.

GREEN: *Where would this be located? Why?*

JJ: The Museum of Hidden History will be located in Washington, D.C. It will focus on American history, so the nation's capital seems to be the right location for that. Washington is also host to tens of millions of visitors each year from around the world that we hope to introduce to the history Americans do not know, but many others in the world do. The Museum will combine a library, an archive and exhibits. We will locate the initial stage, a Hidden History Research Center, and eventually the Museum, near a Metro for public access, and in an area of community development to engage participation from local residents as well. In addition, we hope to have traveling exhibits displayed at other museums around the country, and possibly a mobile exhibit van that would include examples of local hidden history wherever it stopped, creating an exhibit in D.C. that would highlight those aspects from many different cities and states.

GREEN: *D.C. is of course the heart of our national security state in many ways. Why is it important to have an alternative voice in our nation's capital?*

JJ: The history presented by the Smithsonian, while often including other perspectives, is still told in the framework of assumptions that distort real or deep historical realities. Much of our buried history resides in the National Archives and Records Administration facilities in and around Washington, and we will promote further transparency and declassification instead. The local International Spy Museum works from a perspective of defending our cover operations and our national security apparatus. The recent creation of museums about Native Americans and African- Americans are welcome new perspectives on the dominant stories. We hope to include even more voices and perspectives including diverse immigrant communities, women, and others. We want to present "people's history," as Howard Zinn put it, the untold story of struggles for civil liberties, civil rights, peace, economic justice and democratic society as well as the government and corporate operations that were created to oppose them. The need to both preserve alternative history and to present it arises from centuries of distortion and decades of miseducation that have made our world so confusing to all but the victims.

Thomas Jefferson once said that, given the choice between a government without a newspaper and a newspaper without a government, he would always choose the latter. He understood that the flow of information and knowledge was more central to a democratic society than the government machinery that functioned to carry it out. Similarly, Jefferson believed that there was no safe repository for the powers of a society but in the people themselves. He knew that if one believed these people "unable to exercise their discretion in a wholesome fashion", the remedy was not to "take the power from them, but to inform their discretion". That is what we hope the museum will help to do.

GREEN: *Why is so much of our history hidden? What does that say about the place we live in?*

JJ: History carries both lessons and self-identity and realization. Cultures and societies build on and rely on their histories. Oral traditions carried these for many people in pre-literate societies, but we are now entering a post- literate era that threatens the loss of even written history for the current generations. George Orwell's theme in his dystopian future novel, 1984, was that, "Those who control the present control the past and those who control the past control the future." The job of Winston, his protagonist in the novel was to destroy historical records and photographs down the "Memory Hole", to rewrite the past newspapers to reflect the present, and to manipulate the historical reality of wars and state propaganda. His associate at the Ministry of Truth had the task of reducing the number of words in the dictionary so that concepts considered dangerous could be eliminated as well. It has always been in the interest of conquering cultures to destroy and distort the history of the vanquished and of those in power to control the history and image of their ascendency to power. Added to this trend, we now have the demands of the National Security State, which asserts that some concepts are classified at birth, and that our history is better conducted in secret. "History," Henry Kissinger wrote, "to be successful, must be negotiated in absolute secrecy."

However, in a democracy, policies cannot be evaluated or changed without public scrutiny and open and transparent government operations. This commoditization of our history since WWII has put the decisions back into the hands of an elite which perpetuates its control through that secrecy. We are now approaching the event horizon of a black hole of classification, with 15.5 million new records classified each year, searches for one million declassified records to make them secret again since 9/11, and a petabyte of electronic records classified every 18 months. Human readers could not be hired in sufficient numbers to even view such volumes of information in the same time periods to review them for declassification. Meta-tags will now be used to mark the electronic files for classification and for declassification reviews by machines, not humans.

GREEN: *There are some fantastic names attached to the Museum. How did Howard Zinn, for example, come to know and support the idea?*

JJ: I approached Howard Zinn after a public talk in Washington, D.C. to introduce him to our idea for a Museum of Hidden History and he asked me to send more information. He agreed to sponsor the effort, sending a note before he passed on that he supported what we were planning to do. Other historians, investigative journalists, scientists and academics of note are also on our current sponsor list. We hope to have some of them, as well as others across diverse specialties, be part of an Advisory Committee that will evaluate proposed ideas for exhibits on hidden history, using the best practices of historical research, academic standards, journalistic rules, museum presentation and scientific methods to create thought-provoking exhibits using solid factual evidence. We hope to work closely with the Zinn Education Project, which continues to promote his writings and teaching in public schools, to present a People's History at our museum. We mourn the loss of his insights and historical research and his integrity, personal warmth and spirit.

GREEN: *You spoke at Zinn's memorial.*

JJ: The event, which was aired on C-SPAN, was held in Washington at the local Busboys & Poets restaurant, run by a progressive local activist who knows me personally. I was added to the agenda at the last minute to say a few words because he knew Zinn had sponsored our work. I took the opportunity to present the idea of the museum and to ask for interested people to contact me directly. Some of the early volunteers that helped to plan the museum's beginning stage were located through that broadcast.

GREEN: *Cynthia McKinney has also continued to support the Museum, is that right?*

JJ: Yes. Former Congresswoman Cynthia McKinney from Georgia, who spent six terms in Congress, is a sponsor as well. She has a continuing interest in the military-industrial-intelligence complex that came to power in the wake of the assassination of President Kennedy, and that President Eisenhower had warned about. She is also interested in many aspects of hidden history, including COINTELPRO and other operations against popular, democratic movements, as well as political assassinations. She introduced legislation to release tens of thousands of government records still classified regarding the murder of Dr. Martin Luther King, Jr.

GREEN: *In your mind, what would the Museum look like? What might a couple of the exhibits be?*

JJ: The Museum of Hidden History will combine a library of over 4,000 books, and thousands of articles, clippings, and audio and video recordings. Three libraries have been cataloged already on intelligence history and operations, major political assassinations, and the historical framework, events and response to the attacks of 9/11. These include many government investigations, reports, testimony and documents and related archives. These will form the basis for the first stage of the museum, a Hidden History Research Center. The traveling exhibits on such topics as the JFK assassination, the Pentagon Papers and whistleblowers, and intentional community experiments, will form the permanent exhibits that will highlight all three aspects of our hidden history, as well as local examples. The finished museum will include the research center and will host many public presentations of new books, released files, film documentaries and panel discussions on topics related to our theme.

One interesting thing that would come about as the result of such a Museum is that people would be given a deeper alternative to existing so-called "alternatives." To take an example, the Watergate is still poorly understood by most Americans, although it is often held up as a pillar of investigative journalism. In this case, however, even the "deeper" version is a mask covering the real machinations behind the events. Can you talk about this a little bit?

The day after the Watergate break-in I saw a small UPI article about the people who had been arrested in the local Dayton, Ohio newspaper. I recognized all of them from my research into the assassination of President Kennedy and the Bay of Pigs operation. Some had testified to the Warren Commission. I called my mother in Washington, D.C. and asked her to clip the newspapers there for any further articles about the arrest. It was significant they had been arrested. Her clipping mailings grew week by week over the next three years and they educated her to some of the hidden history and politics of our country. The true story of Watergate goes much deeper than the illegality of a burglary of the Democratic National Headquarters, and real purpose of the botched attempt was to corner, if not frame, President Nixon. The use of CIA operatives and their army of available covert operations "teams" dating back to the Bay of Pigs in a White House initiated crime reveals much about the government behind the one we see.

Nixon, who had a long history with both the intelligence agencies and organized crime, was intent on covering up parts of his own hidden history and stopping "leaks" with his team of "Plumbers". Deeper still were plans to implement martial law and "Continuity of Government" in a "national emergency" (arising presumably from the rise of powerful social movements for peace, civil rights and justice, movements for change that threatened and challenged an entrenched undemocratic elite in power), to be implemented by a team of 16 in the Office of Emergency Preparedness at the White House which included Watergate burglar and long-time CIA hand Bernard Barker, who placed the "second piece of tape" on the garage door, leading to the arrests. Perceptive investigative researcher Mae Brussell exposed much of what would only emerge in Congressional hearings years later in her article two weeks after the event, "Why Was Martha Mitchell Kidnapped?" in The Realist.

The lawyer who showed up to defend the Watergate burglars at their arraignment came without any of them making a call, Douglas Caddy, a member of William F. Buckley's Young Americans for Freedom, and who had worked with Tom Charles Houston, author of the infamous plan for martial law created by Nixon's teams. The portions of that plan that were revealed are instructive to the responses and destruction of civil rights and liberties that have followed 9/11. The current plans and protocols for an even more undemocratic Continuity of Government response, drafted after the Senator Frank Church hearings into intelligence community abuses that led to limits and reforms by bitter opponents at the Reagan White

House, Donald Rumsfeld and Richard Cheney, and later by Contragate operative Oliver North, were implemented in part on the day of September 11, 2001, creating a "Shadow Government Operating in Secret" according to the Washington Post headline a month later. The scope of these plans has resisted scrutiny by several Congressional investigations and by members of the oversight committees that approve the intelligence budgets devoted to such plans and their implementation come Code Red.

GREEN: *Fascinating information. I look forward to the day when I can buy a ticket to go in.*

GOOD AMERICANS
(1983)

Almost since its inception, the successful revolution in the Soviet Union in 1917 came under attack. (1) The Romanov family was spirited out of the country, along with the royal treasury. (2) The monarchists, the white Russian counter-revolutionaries, and the colonial powers of France, Germany, England, and even the United States saw the great wealth of Russia as a prize worth regaining or winning. From 1918 to 1932, that royal treasury, as well as funds from rich monarchist families, international investors, and U.S. investors led by President Herbert Hoover, poured into the secret plans for the military rearmament of Germany's (3) Monarchists from around the world, and White Russians began an international network of reaction known as the Solidarists. Inside the Vatican, relying on an alleged apparition of the Virgin Mary at Fatima who warned the Pope about the fall of the Tsar, powerful forces worked to assist in toppling the new Bolshevik rule.

A group of the most fanatically conservative elements of the Catholic Church, men who still supported the inquisition in Spain and who used flagellation as prayer, formed a lay order known as Opus Dei, the Works of God. (4) These were joined in rank by the ancient military order of the church, the secretive Knights Hospitallers, or the Knights of Malta. (5) Their ultimate objective was the downfall of the new Soviet government. No method or means was too extreme, so these forces backed and helped to create Franco in Spain, Mussolini in Italy, and Hitler in Germany. Some of the U.S. firms continued their financial trade and support of the fascists throughout all of World War II, with Russia as the target. (6)

But the fascist offensive failed at Stalingrad, though the cost had been enormous, with 22 million Soviet citizens dead. At this crucial turning point, they retreated and retrenched, adding to their ranks under the evil genius of Allen 'cold warriors' and Klansmen of America, and even worse elements. From 1943 forward, plans began to escalate the 'cold war' of propaganda and paramilitary spying into the nuclear exchange of World War III. (7) Still, no other goal was so important as the fascist hands. But now they had also added the perspective of the eugenicists and the 'scientific' racists of the Third Reich, who saw most of the non-white world as expendable. (8) The term 'useless eaters' was applied by the Nazi doctors to their concentration camp victims, and later by former CIA director William Colby to the peoples of Mexico.

Add to this international fascist cabal the following sources of power: *Kameradenwerk, Die Spinne* and Odessa, the secret webs of Nazi SS men and mass murderers who escaped justice after the war and found a home in Europe, South America and the obliging United States. (9)

Project Paperclip. A successful American operation, which brought to the U.S. literally hundreds of top aerospace and munitions experts from Nazi Germany to form the corporate leadership and the expertise behind the technological and military advances of a growing military-industrial complex. (10)

Belarus Brigade -The dreaded combined forces of Nazi and White Russian troops in Byelorussia during World War II, a counter-revolutionary stronghold since World War I and a Nazi-infested army against Russia. The top government officials, nearly 300 of them, were brought to the United States and given important government and intelligence jobs by our thankful CIA and OSS. (11)

Dictatorships - Arisen in South America and throughout the world whose fascist rhetoric and genocidal direction come directly from Nazi collusion and training, not historical chance. (12)

The Gehlen Network - A black orchestra of spies whose infamous dealings during World War II, had put the Nazi spies in bed with every major intelligence network in the world from British MI5 and MI6, to the American OSS and the heavily the embittered revanchists of Eastern Europe, the infiltrated KGB. (13) Under the evil genius of Allen Dulles, whose espionage attacks on the Soviet Union date back to the 1920's, $200 million in Rockefeller and Mellon funds was directed into the hands of Hitler's spymaster Reinhardt Gehlen and his 350 Nazi spies, who formed and founded our Central Intelligence Agency in 1947. (14) Later, these same forces created post war European intelligence, our Defense Intelligence Agency, our National Security Agency, and covert groupings here and abroad whose very initials are considered classified information. (15)

Assassins - An international fascist network of terror, congealed in the grey underworld of Mafia murders, drug trafficking, gun smuggling and political murders worldwide (16) These mercenary armies still draw their ranks from the refugees encamped everywhere, still operate with names like Alpha 66 and Omega 7, (17) AAA or DINA, the Kuomintang of Chiang Kai Shek, the Somocistas along the Honduran border now, the Hmong peoples of Laos and the reactionary ranks of the Vietnamese, the Phalangists in Lebanon, and even the Grey Wolves of Turkey whose members include Mehmet Ali Agca, the attempted assassin of the Pope now so falsely accused of working with the Soviet KGB. (18)

Interpol - An international police intelligence agency begun at the end of World War II in collaboration with Nazi war criminals and our own J. Edgar Hoover of FBI fame. (19)

These elements meet internationally under the aegis of organizations like the World Union of National Socialists, the Asian People's Anti-Communist League, and the World Anti-Communist League. 'Journalists' like Claire Sterling provide their cover, (20) and Marvin Kalb of Opus Dei. (21)

Their legitimacy and recruiting is aided by evangelical fronts like 'World Vision,' which runs many of the refugee camps and includes John W. Hinckley, Sr. (22) They draw their funds from the illicit and profitable world heroin and cocaine trade, (23) and their training from CIA experts like Mitch WerBell, Edwin Wilson, Frank Terpil and unreconstructed Nazi torturers who provide 'techniques.' (24) their weapons come from an equally lucrative gun smuggling trade, assisted by intelligence agencies. (25)

This is the real historical framework of current events that follow from 'cold war' to 'COINTELPRO' and 'CHAOS (26) from the framing of the Rosenberg's to 'Operation Garden Plot,' (27) from Alger.Hiss to the 'Houston Plan,' (28) from McCarthy to 'MK-ULTRA,' (29) from the Third Reich to the Fourth. What the demon Dulles brothers engineered, (30) the massive cold-war lies (31) that justified any excess in the direction of fascism, is the root of Malcolm X's statement on Vietnam, that 'the chickens are going to come home to roost. Under the current rubric of the World Anti-Communist League (32) the Solidarists, the Nazis and other fascists, the reactionary forces in every part of the globe unit to bring us a legacy of deception and murder, of war profits and starvation, of open dictatorial rule. Their now three-quarter-century-old goal of crushing the Soviet revolution has brought us to both financial and physical ruin, and to the brink of World War III. (33) To attain that goal, fascism has come home to roost. (34)

During World War II, the Nazis in France gained collaboration and capitulation by going first to the task of corrupting the courts, compromising the judges, and turning the slim hope of judicial justice into a political weapon. (35) In our own country, the most respected Justice of the Supreme Court was unable to solve the obvious case of conspiracy in the assassination of President John F. Kennedy. The primary role of the state police has become spying and suppression of legitimate attempts to challenge the undemocratic and secret rule of the national security state. (36) The purpose of the law now is to put the protection of profits above people at all costs, even to the point of police destruction of the evidence necessary to reconstruct the crime. (37) Do you think we are in some better or more holy condition in our own courts today? What special sort of American chauvinism leads us to blindly assert, 'it can't happen here?' For it has.

In a recent editorial in the Boston Globe, dated February 12, 1983, we can see the delayed reaction of the established press shortly after the extradition of Klaus Barbie, (38) the Nazi 'Butcher of Lyons,' from Bolivia to France:

Barbie is only one of many notorious Nazi leaders who were welcomed like prodigal sons into service with Western intelligence agencies after the war. Their unspeakable crimes against humanity were implicitly forgiven and conveniently forgotten. They were paid and protected so that they could return to active duty in the anti-Communist crusade, which their fuehrer, Adolf Hitler, had temporarily discredited with his extremism.

Their names compose a rogue's gallery of fascist thuggery. Hitler's master spy, Reinhardt Gehlen, was made chief of the Western German intelligence agency (BND) and shared his Nazi intelligence data with his protectors in the CIA. Otto Skorzeny, a Nazi specialist at organizing terror networks in occupied countries, was employed in the U.S. Army's historical division, which served as a way station for former Nazis who would go on to serve in the Gehlen CIA intelligence network. Skorzeny used his tacit immunity to shepherd old Nazi comrades out of Europe, working through cover organizations known as Odessa, Kamaradenwerk, and Die Spinne.

As the years went by, Gehlen, Skorzeny and their network of old-boy collaborators accumulated enormous influence both in Europe and Latin America. Skorzeny shuttled between Franco's Spain and Peron's Argentina where he served the Argentine dictator as a gray eminence. His goal was to foster the growth of a fascist Fourth Reich centered in Latin America.

He could count on such loyalist operatives as Josef Mengele in Paraguay, on Adolf Eichmann and Hans Ulrich Rudel in

Argentina; on Walter Rauff in Chile; and on Klaus Barbie in Bolivia. Rauff, who is charged with sending 97,000 Jews to their death, has served as a revered adviser to the fascist dictatorship imposed on Chile by Augusto Pinochet after the overthrow of Salvador Allende, and was instrumental in setting up the infamous Chilean secret police agency known as DINA. Barbie, in Bolivia, organized paramilitary death squads and drug smuggling networks for a succession of military regimes.

To grasp the full meaning of Barbie's belated appointment with justice, his career may be seen as an emblem of the unchecked metastasis of fascism. It is particularly mortifying for Americans to be reminded that our government put Barbie on its payroll a few years after he worked for Hitler.

Erhard Dabringhaus of U.S. Anny Intelligence sheltered this mass murderer, paid him $1700 a month to run a spy network in France, and helped him escape to South America. 'I am a good American of German extraction and I did my job,' he said recently from his position as a German history professor at Wayne State University. (39)

These people, and those who aided them, have names, addresses, and connections to the top levels of the United States government. They figure prominently in the hidden history of our police-intelligence state, and in the rash of political assassinations and other crimes that keep it in place. The names of the men most responsible for bringing them here read like a roll call of the world establishment, and those who collaborated with them fit together like pieces of a puzzle in decoding events since World War II. (40)

Allen Dulles - Who collaborated with Gehlen's spies, headed the CIA, and later sat on the Warren Commission investigation of J.F. Kennedy's death. (41)

John J. McCloy - A High Commissioner of Germany after the war who pardoned key Nazi criminals like Krupp, Abs, Dohrnberger, Schacht, and others. (42) His long career has made him a 'God- father of the American establishment.' He sat atop the World Bank, directed construction of the Pentagon, worked with Earl Warren to set up the Japanese concentration camps in America, and blocked any military attacks on the Nazi death camps as Assistant Secretary of War. He stopped the summary execution of Nazis in favor of the Nuremberg Trials, which he later thwarted, and also sat as a member of the Warren Commission. (43)

General Lucius Clay - The military commander of Germany at the end of the war, Clay helped undermine the prosecution of Otto Skorzeny, and later worked with Nazi generals at Oberammer-gau to train Eastern European revanchists, Nazis and American GI's into the 5,000-strong 'Special Forces' against communism. This team later became our Green Berets. (44)

Henry Kissinger - Worked with General Lucius Clay at Oberammergau, and then with key stateside Army Intelligence and CIA units responsible for bringing in the Nazi spies. (45) Kissinger, who came from Germany to join U.S. Anny Intelligence during World War II, had as his 'mentor' the mysterious Fritz Kraemer. (46) Kraemer's 30-year silent career in the Pentagon plans division includes the prepping of Alexander Haig. (47) It may also conceal his real identity, prisoner #33 in the dockets at Dachau the special Lieutenant to Hitler, Fritz Kraemer. (48) Mr. Kissinger still relies on his advice, and did so while Secretary of State.

C.D. Jackson - Joined Nelson Rockefeller and Richard Nixon in the scheme to bring the Byelorussian government here. He worked for the Henry Luce publishing empire, and for Life magazine when they published the doctored photos of Lee Harvey Oswald holding a rifle. Both Time and Life were owned by Luce, and were responsible for much of the cold-war propaganda that allowed the national security state and the Pentagon to grow untouched. (49)

Richard Milhous Nixon - Former President whose work with Navy Intelligence at the end of World War II included the importation of Nazi criminals through the Gould family estate on Long Island. Among them was Nicolae Malaxa, whose collaboration with Hermann Goering was apparently no problem for Nixon, who defended Malaxa's U.S. citizenship. (50) In fact, a special bill was introduced in Congress, to secure the citizenship by Senator Pat McCarran of Nevada. McCarran and Senator Joe McCarthy later introduced legislation to set up 'detention and internment camps' in the U.S. in times of war or national emergency for 'internal security. (51)

Other figures involved in this dirty little secret connect to the highest levels of our government and intelligence agencies. The solemn pledge to end the Nazi regime was completely betrayed. (52) Instead, the British and American spies saw a more important function, that of finding a new common enemy. The cohesiveness and control offered by this scenario seemed too urgent and so appealing that they even considered creating the illusion of an enemy from outer space. (53) For the less inventive, the communist revolution still served as sufficient scapegoat, and historical target.

Frank G. Wisner - An official of the OSS and a CIA veteran who brought the Byelorussian government here, the Latvian Thunder Cross, the Hungarian Arrow Cross, and the Rumanian Iron Guard among others. As many as 5,000 came to work at Radio Free Europe and Radio Liberty, the CIA, the Voice of America, the Defense Language Institute, 'for the United States in defense of liberty. (54) Allen Dulles said of Gehlen, 'He's on our side now.' Bobby Inman of the NSA and CIA networks today admitted recently that these fascists were 'the bedrock' of covert operations in Europe in the 40's and 50's by the CIA, and molded the anti-communist policy there. (55)

J. Peter Grace - A scion of the Grace fortunes, he is currently head of Reagan's commission to study domestic economic cuts (56) For 30 years his company employed Otto Ambrose, a Nazi war criminal from the German drug cartel I.G. Farben. Ambrose, a chemist, developed 'Zyklon B,' the actual gas used in the chambers to kill the Jews and others deemed 'inferior (57) The German steel group, Flick, which has extensive Nazi ties in the past and whose scandals are rocking German politics today, hold a controlling stock interest in the Grace Company. (58) The Grace family is intimately involved with the formation of the anti-Communist American Institute for Free Labor Development (AIFLD). (59) AIFLD played a key role in the Kissinger plan to overthrow Allende in Chile, and insert the ruling fascist Pinochet. (60) After the coup, which involved American Green Berets, (61) Kissinger sent a Mr. Rauff from the State Department to advise the newly formed Chilean secret police (DINA). Rauff had been in charge of the 'mobile ovens' used to kill Gypsies and Jews, homosexuals and Political dissidents in Eastern Europe for the Nazis. (62) These same forces were later involved in the assassination of Chilean diplomat Orlando Letelier in Washington, D.C. (63)

Helene von Damm - Personal White House appointment secretary and long-time personal secretary to Ronald Reagan, she stands to be appointed Ambassador to Vienna, and controls all cabinet level appointments in the Reagan administration. (64) She came to the United States in the 1950's in the company of Albrecht Otto von Bolschwing, and worked for him as a translator. (65) Von Bolschwing gave the direct orders to Adolph Eichmann in the dread Eisenstatz group, the SS killers. (66) Helene's husband, Christian von Damm, ran the Bank of America in La Paz, Bolivia, which defaulted on a huge U.S. loan. (67)

Errol Flynn - The famed actor, whose exploits included meetings with Nazi sympathizers, and the Duke and Duchess of Windsor, and Nazi spymasters during the late 30's His roommate and constant companion at the time was 'actor Ronald Reagan. (68)

Anna Chenault - A Nixon confidant, and head of the old 'China Lobby' that got us involved in both Korea and Vietnam. (69) Her husband, General Claire Chennault, formed the Flying Tigers in World War II, which later flew heroin for the CIA from Vietnam as 'Air America. (70) She sits on the board of 20th Century Fox with Henry Kissinger, William Rogers, Gerald Ford, and until recently, Princess Grace Kelly of Monaco. (71)

Evita Peron - Once a ruler in Argentina, Evita got her funds from the Nazi treasuries stolen by Martin Bormann at the end of the war, and put hundreds of millions in the 'Evita Peron Foundation' and Swiss bank accounts. This money aided war criminals like Josef Mengele, Heinrich Dorge, Hjalmar Schacht (who had worked under Herman Abs at the Reichsbank), Rudolf Freude, Dr. Fritz Thysseni Dr. Gustav Krupp, Otto Skorzeny, and others. (72)

Peter Drucker - Well-known industrialist who began the multinational corporation concept, he was responsible for bringing Nazi leader Fritz Kraemer from Frankfurt to the Pentagon. (73)

General George Patton - An American hero of World War II, whose credit for invading Sicily was later tarnished by the

Kefauver commission study suggesting that he traveled into friendly Mafioso villages as part of a secret deal between Navy Intelligence and mobster 'Lucky' Luciano. (74) In his assignment to construct a history of the war, Patton assembled Nazi Army officers and had 'admiration, affection and sympathy' for them. He picked the 'best brains,' Von Manteuffel, Brandenberger, Count von Schwerin and Fritz Kraemer. (75) After the war, Patton worked closely with John J. McCloy. In relation to Russia he said, 'anyone who says there won't be a future war is a goddamn fool.' (76)

George Bush - Former head of the CIA who employed, among others, U.S. Army officer, Capt. William Rhine of the Bay of Pigs operation. Rhine is really top SS spy Helmut Streicher, who worked directly with Hitler, Gehlen, Otto Skorzeny, and then U.S. Army Intelligence from October 1945 on. (77)

General Douglas MacArthur - Another World War II hero, he helped to cover up Japanese war crimes involving chemical and biological experiments on American prisoners so that we could use the secret results. (78) This operation and others directly involved MacArthur's chief of staff, Colonel Charles Willoughby, who is in reality a Nazi criminal, Kurt Weidenbach. (79)

J. Edgar Hoover - Who formed the FBI, and without whose help the Nazi criminals could never have entered the U.S., worked in Interpol with founder Reinhardt Heydrich, SS head of Nazi police from 1940 to 1942, and his successor, SS officer Ernst Kaltenbrunner, later hanged at Nuremberg. (80) Hoover's career involved extensive mob connections, (81) and his death 'has yet to be fully investigated. (82)

Thomas Dewey - The 'gangbuster' New York prosecutor who put Luciano in jail, and then later petitioned for his release and deportation to Italy in honor of his 'wartime services. (83) In 1948, Dewey ran for President in a close race with Harry Truman. Dewey's vice-presidential candidate was Earl Warren and his campaign manager was Allen Dulles. (84) Historically interconnected with the Solidarists and the fascists, powerful elements in the Vatican continued their work through high church officials, Opus Dei, and the Sovereign Military order of Malta, the Knights of Malta. (85)

Monsignor Montini - An OSS operative in Southeast Asia at the end of World War II, he was later appointed Pope Paul VI. He used Caritas Internationalis, a welfare organization, to provide refugee travel documents to such Nazis as euthanasia killer Hans Hefelman and Hitler's secretary, Martin Bormann, aiding in their escape to Argentina. (86)

Pope John Paul II - Worked at Auschwitz in a rubber plant run by Nazi financier Hermann Abs for Solvay Drugs of I.G. Farben. (87) Farben, which also employed Fritz Kraemer, has 750 subsidiaries worldwide, including U.S. firms. 88 In the wake of the recent Vatican Bank scandals, Pope John Paul II appointed a four-man committee to study and run Vatican finances, which included Hitler's personal banker and the pontiff's old boss, Hermann Abs. 89 Nazi hunter Simon Wiesenthal protested this recently. 90 The Pope also elevated Opus Dei, with 72,000 members in eighty countries, to the status of a religious order. (91)

Cardinal Spellman - Religious leader in New York, he was a protégé of Cardinal Pacelli, Poe *Pius XII, who is often accused of collaboration with the Nazis (92) Spellman is the U.S. spiritual leader of the Knights of Malta. (93) He is responsible for introducing Ngo Dinh Diem to Allen Dulles, and then proposing his residency of South Vietnam to President Kennedy. (94) When Diem resisted the introduction of

American troops into Vietnam, Dulles told General Westmoreland to ahead anyway, and our CIA helped to kill Diem. (95)

Father E. Walsh - His Georgetown University Center for International Affairs and Strategic Studies became the first major CIA training center. (96) This Jesuit priest was the motivating force behind Joe McCarthy's campaign against 'communism' in the 50's, and he is a long-time member of the Knights of Malta. (97) Avery Dulles - Son of John Foster Dulles, then Secretary of State, and a nephew to Allen Dulles, then CIA director. Avery worked with Martin Bormann to help his escape to Argentina, and is now working as an advisor at Georgetown University. He also is a member of the Knights of Malta. (98)

Roy Cohn - The key lawyer in the prosecution of the Rosenberg case, the alleged 'Atom Spies' executed in the 1950's, (99) he worked with Joe McCarthy and David Schine to spread the 'Communist Menace' lies. He currently sits on the board of the anti-communist Western Goals Foundation, and his law partner, Tom Bolan, is a member of the Sovereign Military Order of Malta (100)

Alexander Haig - A long-time protégée of the Pentagon 'Iron Mentor' Fritz Kraemer, (101) Haig extended favors and NATO links to the fascist cell in Italy known as P-2 or Propaganda Due, whose 'puppet master,' Licio Gelli, worked with Franco and Mussolini and shares dual citizenship in Italy and Argentina. (102) The involvement of high government officials in this secret order of Free-Masons scandalized and rocked the whole Italian government, and opened the ensuing scandal of Banco Ambrosiano and the Vatican Bank's missing billions. (103)

Many of the key figures are either imprisoned (Licio Gelli and Michele Sindona, former head of the Vatican Bank) or dead (Roberto Calvi, known as 'God's Banker,' found hanging beneath Blackfriar's Bridge in London.) (104) Haig has just been knighted into the secretive Knights of Malta, which includes his brother, and prestigious members like William Colby (CIA), William F. Buckley (CIA), J. Peter Grace, John McCone (CIA), General Vernon Walters (Reagan's 'roving - ambassador'), James Angleton (CIA), and others. (105)

Charles G. Bludhorn - The founder and chairman of Gulf and Western conglomerate, he came from Vienna in 1942. He worked closely with Michele Sindona and his boss, Licio Gelli, had secret dealings with Antonio Guzman of the Dominican Republic, and knew Vatican Bank scandal figure Archbishop Paul Marcinkus. (106) Bludhorn bought Music Corporation of America (which gave Reagan his start), Madison Square Garden, and much more. His financial manager, Kirk Kerkorian began with a $50,000,000 loan from West German banker Otto Schoeppler to buy MGM. Alexander Haig was soon on the board. (107)

Michele Ledeen - Reagan's appointed state department official is the unofficial source for the 'Bulgarian Connection' like about the KGB role in the shooting of the Pope. He is the major source on 'Soviet terrorism' misinformation to Claire Sterling, who deftly covers up fascist terrorism and state terrorism alike. (108) Ledeen has close ties to Alexander Haig, the Georgetown University grouping, Henry Kissinger, Licio Gelli, Opus Dei, and the P-2 Masonic Lodge scandal. (109) He is also close to Francesco Pazienza, suspected to have set up 'God's Banker' Roberto Calvi for murder. (110) At the time of his death, Calvi was director of Banco Ambrosiano, and his family members openly claim Opus Dei killed him. (111)

Joseph Lehman - A brother to John Lehman, currently Secretary of the Navy. John Lehman is involved in a growing scandal involving contracts between the Pentagon and the Abingdon firm (a front for Lockheed and Boeing), which employs Joseph, Christopher and other Lehman family members. (112) A cousin of the family, Princess Grace Kelly, was knighted into the Sovereign Military Order of Malta shortly before her death, and her home at Monaco was a center for fugitive Nazi activity for many years. (113)

The Lehman's have worked openly to curb the Catholic bishops who favor a nuclear freeze, scaring them with the 'KGB shot the Pope' nonsense. (114) In this effort, Christopher Lehman works closely with Senator John Tower of Texas. Senator Tower's brother-in-law is Samuel Cumming's, a CIA gun runner to international fascist terrorists, including 'Carlos,' Frank Terpil, Ed Wilson, Gregory Korkola, and others. (115)

Once the cast of characters is clear, the interconnections continue. One of the front companies used by Wilson and Terpil in California. Helene von Damm and Otto Albrecht von Bolschwing founded TCI. (116) The relative importance of von Bolschwing cannot be underestimated. He was placed in charge of the Gehlen-CIA network in the United States when Gehlen returned to Germany to set up their post-war intelligence agency. (117) Many of the people mentioned already have direct or indirect links to the assassination of John F. Kennedy, later political murders, and their cover-ups. (118) Others make the connections of the international fascist cabal very clear in the murder of John F. Kennedy and many more progressive leaders.

Werner von Braun - Whose infamous 'Rocket Team' developed the first intercontinental missiles at Peenemunde, and were then brought here to develop NASA rocketry, and the growing aerospace industry. (119) The NASA security teams are implicated in several sources in connection with the murder of John F. Kennedy. (120) The actual physical capture of von Braun, who had used slave labor to build the rockets, was done by American troops in Switzerland led by Clay Shaw, later charged by District Attorney Jim Garrison for his role in the Kennedy killing. (121)

General Walter Dohrnberger - A Nazi murderer convicted at Nuremberg for working with then 'Butcher of Auschwitz' to kill 6,000 Jews, 'he was scheduled to be hanged, according to British prosecutor Shawcross. (122) He had been a 'mentor' and friend to Von Braun throughout the war, getting materials and labor denied at times by Hitler for the rocket works. Von Braun refused to work on NASA rockets unless we intervened to save Dohrnberger. Of course, we did, and John J. McCloy arranged a full pardon. (123)

General Dohmberger came to the United States, worked at NASA briefly, and then became director of the Helicopter Division Bell Aerospace, in Dallas and Houston, Texas. (124) He still trains pilots abroad, working with dictators like the Shah of Iran. Dohrnberger employed top-ranking military intelligence agent Michele Paine, who housed Marina Oswald in his home in Irving, Texas. 125 Marina, who married Lee Harvey Oswald in Russia, lived in Minsk, Byelorussia, and was the niece of the top officer of the NKVD, the Soviet secret police. 126 Her family was openly anti-communist. (127)

George de Mohrenschildt - His whole family was Byelorussian, and rabidly anti-communist after their fortune was lost to the revolution at the Nobel family oil fields. They moved to Germany and worked with the Nazis during World War II. George was a spy, carrying papers from Nelson Rockefeller after the war, and his cousin Baron Meyerling was a Nazi film propagandist. His brother, Von, was put to work at the Pentagon after the war, and now sits on the CIA' s Tolstoy Foundation. His wife was related to CIA and OSS employees, and her father ran the railroads in China before Mao took power. George later lost another oil fortune of his own in Cuba following the ouster of Batista by Fidel Castro. (128)

He was the contact for the Oswald's to the White Russian Solidarists community in Dallas, and the CIA 'babysitter' and best friend to Lee Harvey Oswald. De Mohrenschildt introduced the Oswald's to the Paines, and it was Ruth Paine who got Oswald the job in the Texas School Book Depository, and lied to the Warren Commission about 'Oswald's rifle' and set him up as the patsy in the Kennedy assassination. (129)

Leon Jaworski - Considered by some to be 'the most trusted man in America' due to his role as special prosecutor in the Watergate and Koreagate scandals, he spent 20 years with the CIA's Kaplan Foundation in Houston, Texas. (130) A lawyer at the Nuremberg trials, Jaworski undermined prosecutions, then worked with the Red Cross international rescue division to move the Nazi Odessa network around the world. (131) He was later Special Liaison between the Dallas police and the Warren Commission. (132)

Otto Winnacker - The actual author of the Warren Commission Report, he was taken away from his job as an official Pentagon historian (recall that the U.S. Army historical division was the way station for the Gehlen operation), and he had come to the United States after years of faithful service as one of Hitler's official historians of the Reich. (133)

Believe it or not, these are only a few of the thousands of connections that history has hidden, only a few of the thousands of fascists brought to light, their worst crimes still unexposed. (134) This is the dirtiest secret of post-war America: our vast intelligence networks were a haven for, and eventually a tool in the hands of international fascism. The increasing challenge to simple Constitutional rights is a direct result of the legislative and political role, played behind the closed door of 'security' by these elements.

The growing threat to the already damaged economy by the military-industrial complex is out of control. All is geared to a new world war, a bloodbath in section of the Third World, a reduction of population worldwide. The attacks in Congress and the courts on rights are the prelude to open martial law and fascist rule in America, a new 'final solution. (135) 'When they came for the Jews, I did nothing for I am not a Jew... when they came for me, who was left to defend me?' asked Martin Niemoller of Germany in the 1940s.

The continuing murders of labor leaders, musicians, political dissidents, progressive thinkers, Black and Hispanic leaders, and others here in the United States parallels the hundreds of political murders in the late 20's and early 30's in Weimar Germany that preceded Hitler's rise to power. (136) When the came for the socialists and communists in the 1950's, the targets of the Smith Act and other repressive treatment, many of us did not act since we were not members of such organizations. Will be make the mistake twice? Hanging solemnly over the mass murder at Jonestown, Guyana, was the George Santayana quote 'those who do not remember the past are condemned to repeat it. (137) We are not far from the open collusion of the courts in all aspects of state repression. Recent events must be seen for what they are, an attack on us all, spearheaded by the very forces of reaction that threaten life and freedom world wide, hiding beneath the cloak of anti-communism. To sit back now will put us in a category akin to

Klaus Barbie's Army Intelligence contact, Ernst Dabringhaus. Will we be 'Good Germans of American extraction' and 'do our job,' or will we rise?

John Judge

(Based on my own research, that of Mae Brussell, (138) and the few researchers looking into the truth of what became of democracy in America.)

REFERENCES (for *Good Americans*)

1. On a Field of Red, Anthony Cave Brown; Donovan of OSS, Corey Ford; The Great Conspiracy, Sayers & Kahn.

2. The Rescue of the Romanovs, Richards; The File on the Tsar, (Anthony Sampson); The Conspirator Who Saved the Romanovs, Hull.

3. Donovan of OSS, Corey Ford; The Great Conspiracy, Sayers & Kahn; Trading with the Enemy, Charles Higham; Who Financed Hitler? Pool.

4. John Paul's Shock Troops, Time, 9/20/82 'Showdown for the Jesuits' NYT Magazine 2/14/82.

5. 'The Men Behind the Counter-reformation,' Para politics, #6, 3/31/82 The Knights Templar, Stephen Houston; Real Lace, Stephan Birmingham.

6. Trading With the Enemy, Charles Higham, Behind the Nylon Curtain, Zaeiff.

7. The Nazis Go Underground, Kurt Reiss; Germany Will Try It Again, Sigrid Schultz; The Plot Against the Peace, Sayers & Kahn.

8. The Legacy of Malthus, Allen Chase; From Genesis to Genocide, Stephan Chorover.

9. Aftermath. Ladislas Farrago; The Bormann Brotherhood, William Stephenson; Spiderweb, Joseph Persico; Skorzeny: Hitler's Command, Glen Infield~ Martin Bormann: Nazi in Exile, Paul Manning; Skorzeny, Charles Whiting; Hitler's Heirs, Paul Meskil; The Damned Engineers, Janice Giles; The Pledge Betrayed: Denazification of Post-War Germany, Bower; The Nazis Among Us, Charles Allen, Jr.

10. Project Paperclip, Lansby; Power Shift, Kirkpatrick Sale.

11. The Belarus Secret, John Loftus.

12. The Washington Connection & Third World Fascism, Herman, Chomsky, and Bitter Fruit: Untold

Story of American Coup in Guatemala, Schlesinger; An American Company, McCann; Missing, Powers; 'The Knights Who Fight Communism,' SF Chronicle, 12/19/74; 'The Nazi Legacy: Military Might in Latin America,' S.J. Mercury, 3/21/82.

13. Gehlen: Spy of the Century, E.H. Cookeridge; The Service, Reinhardt Gehlen; A Man Called Intrepid, William Stephenson; Armies of Ignorance, Corson.

14. The Yankee & Cowboy War, Oglesby.

15. 'CBS Reports Aid to Nazi Collaborators,' UPI, 5/13/82; they Call It Intelligence, Joachim

Joesten.

16. The Great Heroin Coup, Henrik Kruger; The Secret War Report of the OSS, Anthony Cave

Brown.

17. 'Omega 7' Gallery, 11/81

18. The International Fascist Network Today, Henrik Kruger; The War Conspiracy, Peter Dale

Scott; 'The KGB Plot to Assassinate the Pope: A Case Study in Free World Disinformation,' Covert Action, #19, Spring/Summer, 1983; 'Documents Undercut Case Against Bulgarian in Papal Plot,' LA Times, 3/30/83; 'Confessions of a Dangerous Man, PBS transcript.

19. The Interpol Connection, Meldahl, Young, et al; The Secret World of Interpol, Omar Garrison.

20. The Real Terror Network, Ed Herman (reply · to Sterling's Terror Network); 'The KGB Plot to Assassinate the Pope,' op. cit.

21. 'The Pope, Lumumba and the Kalb Connection' Village Voice, 1/4/83

22. 'In the Spirit of Jimmy Jones,' Akwesasne Notes, Winter, 1982.

23. The Politics of Heroin in Southeast Asia, McCoy; The Luciano Story, Feder & Joesten; The Luciano Project, Campbell; The Heroin Trail, Committee of Concerned Asian Scholars.

24. 'Confessions of a Dangerous Man,' op. cit.; 'Ex-CIA Agents' Associates,' NYT, 9/6/81; 'Capitalizing on the CIA,' NYT, 9/6/81; 'The Gadhafi Connection,' NYT Magazine, 6/14/81; 'Exposing the Libyan Link,' NYT Magazine, 6/21/81; '77 Shakeup Linked to Libyan Connections,

Washington Post, 9/17/81; 'Ed Wilson Arrested,' NYT, 6/16/82; Spooks, Jim Houghton; 'U.S. Terrorist Trainers,' NYT, 8/28/81; Hidden Terrors, Langguth; 'U.S. Books on Torture Reported,' SF Examiner 11/2/81.

25. 'World's #1 Dealer,' LA Times, 12/9/81 (Samuel Cummings, CIA)

26. Shattered Peace, Daniel Yergin; Origins of the Cold War, D.F. Fleming; The Free World Colossus, Horowitz; COINTELPRO, Pathfinder Press; The Age of Surveillance, Frank Donner; Spying on Americans, Theoharis; Un-American Activities, Rips.

27. The Judgment of Julius & Ethel Rosenberg, Wexler; Invitation to an Inquest, Walter & Miriam Schneer; The Great Fear, David Caute; Spying on Americans, Theoharis.

28. Friendship and Fratricide; Spying on Americans, op. cit.; 'Why Was Martha Mitchell Kidnapped?' by Mae Brussell, The Realist, August, 1972

29. The Haunted Fifties, I.F. Stone; The Nightmare Decade, Fred Cook; The Great Fear, op. cit.; Project MK-ULTRA: The CIA's Program Research in Behavior Modification, The Government Role in Individual Behavior Modification, Sen. Ervin's Constitutional Rights Subcommittee Report, 1974; Operation Mind Control, Bowart; Search/or the Manchurian Candidate, John Marks.

30. Dulles, Moseley; The Devil & John Foster Dulles, The Secret Surrender, Dulles.

31. Origins of the Cold War, op. cit.; The Politics of Lying, David Wise.

32. The Dallas Conspiracy, Peter Dale Scott (unpublished ms.); 'The World Anti-Communist League,' Public Eye, 1975.

33. The Plot Against the Peace, Sayers & Kahn; Bodyguard of Lies, Anthony Cave Brown; Global

Reach, Richard Barnet; The War Conspiracy, Peter Dale Scott; The CIA and the Cult of Intelligence, Marchetti & Marks, Trilateralism, Holly Sklar, Food First and Lappe et al.

34. Friendly Fascism, Bertram Gross; The American Police State, David Wise.

35. 'The Sorrow & the Pity,' film by Marcel Ophuls.

36. State Secrets: Police Surveillance in America, Nat Hentoff, et al. 'The Puzzle Palace. James Bamford.

37. Forgive My Grief (4 volumes), Penn Jones (JFK witness deaths); Accessories After the Fact,

Sylvia Meagher (destruction of evidence, JFK); Post-Mortem, Harold Weisberg (JFK cover-up);

The Assassination of Robert Kennedy, Turner & Christian (RFK cover-up), Frame-Up, Harold Weisberg (M.L. King cover-up).

38. NYT & WP, February, 1983 coverage of extradition; 'Barbie: If Germany Had Won the War...' Boston Globe. 2/14/83

39. Boston Globe, 2/14/83 (editorial) 'Barbie's Postwar Ties With U.S. Army Detailed,' Boston Globe, 2/14/83.

40. Wanted: The Search/or Nazis in Control of the World, Fletcher Prouty; The Pledge Betrayed, op cit., The Ominous Parallels: The End of Freedom in America, Peikoff; Friendly Fascism, op. cit.

41. Dulles, Moseley; Bay of Pigs, Peter Wyden; Great True Spy Stories, Dulles (for contrast); 'Nobody will read it anyway,' Allen Dulles to Earl Warren on JFK evidence.

42. 'Minister Without Portfolio,' Harpers, 2/83; 'Mass Killers Assisted CIA, Helpful Nazis Evaded

Justice.' WP 11/6/82. 'The Arms of Krupp William Manchester', 'The Crime and Punishment of I.G. Farben.' Joseph Borkin.

43. Minister Without Portfolio op. cit.

44. Gehlen: Spy of the Century op. cit. (Dr. Franz Six, Friedrich Buchardt); The Belarus Secret, op. cit. 'To Acquit a Nazi,' Springfield (MO), 11/82-2/83 (Skorzeny role); 'The Green Berets are Back,' Parade, 8/2/81; 'Ex-Green Beret Unfolds Secret Life,' NYT Magazine, 7/5/82 (Luke Thompson); 'CBS Reports Aid to Nazi Collaborators,' UPI, 6/13/82.

45. The Price of Power, Seymour Hersh

46. Kissinger: Uses of Power, David Landau; 'Kissinger,' NYT Magazine, 3/2/75; 'Fritz Kraemer, The Enemy of Publicity, NYT, 8/21/79; Henry Kissinger, Ralph Blumefeld (NOTE: There is growing evidence to suggest and earlier and more sinister role of Kissinger and Kraemer in the death of American troops at the massacre at Malmedy, see the following); Hitler's Last Gamble, Jacques Nobecourt; Eclipse, Alan Moorehead; Massacre at Malmedy, Charles Whiting.

47. 'The Iron Mentor of the Pentagon,' WP, 3/2/72

48. Pictorial History of the SS - 1923-1945, Mollo (Photo Kramer, Dachau trial, '46; 'World

Watcher's,' #593, side 2 (sheet accompanies taped broadcast by Mae Brussell), reprints photo from Defense Audiovisual Agency of Dr. Fritz G.A. Kraemer, Pentagon, 1970, for comparison; Hitler's Bodyguards. Allan Wykes, (Photo Fritz Kramer, #33, Malmedy trial) (NOTE: Dr. Fritz G.A. Kraemer currently with the Institute on Strategic Trade, 490 S. Capitol St., 404 A Washington, D.C. 20023, along with Ernest Lefever and Dr. Stefan Possony, members of the World Anti-Communist League).

49. Life, 11/64; Luce; The Belarus Secret, op. cit.

50. Wanted: The Search/or Nazis in America, op. cit. 'How Nixon Came to Power,' by Mae Brussell, Realist, August, 1972; (An article appeared in the NYT, 12/8/73, concerning a 20-year employee of the INS who quit over the Malaxa case and the Nixon connection.)

51. Spying on Americans, op cit.; 'Concentration Camps in America?' Look, 1968 (Charles Allen, Jr.).

52. The Pledge Betrayed, op. cit.

53. Messengers of Deception, Jacques Vallee.

54. The Belarus Secret, op. cit.

55. 'Bobby Inman, Smartest Spy,' Playboy, 5/82; Gehlen, Spy of the Century, op. cit.; Inman quote from appearance at University of Pennsylvania. 2/83.

56. 'Grace is Named to Lead U.S. Cost Control Survey,' NYT, 3/6/82.

57. 'Reagan Appointee J. Peter Grace Under Fire,' LA Times, 4/24/82; 'Reagan Choice's Link to War Criminal.' SF Chronicle 3/6/82 Crime and Punishment of G. Farben, Joseph Borkin.

58. 'German Politicians Implicated in Scam.' SF Chronicle. 11/29/82.

59. 'The Amazing Grace,' NACLA Latin America & Empire Report

60. CIA & American Labor: Subversion of the AFL-C/O's Foreign Policy, George Morris. 'The Murder of Allende,' Rojas Sandford

61. 'Ex-Green Beret Unfolds Secret Life.' NYT Magazine. 7/5/82.

62. 'How Nixon Came to Power.' Realist, August 1972 (Mae Brussell).

63. Assassination on Embassy Row, Landau & Dinges; Labyrinth, Propper & Branch; Death in

Washington. Freed & Landis, 'Letters Say Chile Aided Letelier Murder Figure,' WP, 2/23/82.

64. 'Politics, Ambassadorships.' NYT 11/16/82.

65. 'Ex-Nazi's Brilliant Career Strangled in a Web of Lies.' San Jose Mercury. 11/20/81.

66. The Order of the Death's Head, Heinz Hahne; 'The Dark Past He Couldn't Escape,' SF Chronicle,

11/21/82. 'Former Nazi Gives Up U.S. Citizenship,' Houston Post. 12/23/81.

67. 'Bolivia Pledges to Pay Foreign Debt.' SF Examiner. 9/9/82.

68. Errol Flynn: The Untold Story, Charles Higham (NOTE: Flynn's SS contact was Dr. Herman

Frederick Erban, who joined the Nazis in 1922, the Gestapo in 1930, and became a U.S. citizen)

69. The Hidden History of the Korean War. I.F. Stone; The War Conspiracy, Peter Dale Scott.

70. Politics of Heroin in Southeast Asia, op. cit.; Air America.

71. Indecent Exposure, David McClintick; 'Kissinger, E.B. Williams Named to Fox Board,' LA Times. 1/11/81.

72. Skorzeny: Hitler's Commando, op. cit. Martin Bormann: Nazi in Exile, op. cit.

73. Adventures of a Bystander, Peter Drucker.

74. Politics of Heroin in Southeast Asia, op. cit.; Luciano Project, Campbell; Luciano Story, Feder & Joesten.

75. The Last Days of Patton, Ladislas Farrago.

76. The Last Days of Patton, op. cit.

77. The CIA's Man for All Nations.' Gung-Ho, May 1982 (William Seymour).

78. The Devil's Gluttony, Seiichi Morimura (Japan, 1982); 'The Japanese Experiments,' 60 Minutes, CBS, 4/4/82; 'Germ Tests: Manchurian Mask Lifted,' LA Times, 12/9/82; 'A Hidden Chapter in History,' Bulletin of Atomic Scientists, 10/81; Japan Killed U.S. POW's in Experiments.' WP.

79. American Caesar. William Manchester.

80. The Interpol Connection, op cit.

81. John Edgar Hoover, Hank Messick.

82. 'The Senate Committee is Part of the Cover-up,' Mae Brussell Realist, August 1973.

83. Politics of Heroin in Southeast Asia, op. cit.

84. 30 Against the Mob, Dewey.

85. Inside the Vatican, Bulle; The Pontiff, The Final Conclave, Malachi Martin; The Rise & Fall of the Roman Catholic Church, Malachi Martin; 'Vatican Vortex,' Wall Street Journal, 7/2/82.

86. Martin Bormann: Nazi in Exile, op. cit.

87. 'Pope Once Slaved for Vatican Aide's Firm,' SF Chronicle, 1/12/83.

88. Crime & Punishment of I.G. Farben, op. cit.; Martin Bormann: Nazi in Exile, op. cit.; All Honorable Men, James Martin; (NOTE: Carl Duisberg, the founder of JG Farben, sent his son to the U.S. in 1933 to start LG. Farben in New Jersey. Herman Schmitz, head of the operation in Germany, worked with Otto Skorzeny. His brother, D.A. Schmitz, became a U.S. citizen and had a son here, Robert Schmitz. Robert, a nephew to the head of I.G. Farben, worked with Charles E. Wilson of General Electric, who openly favored the 'permanent war economy' we now suffer under. Wilson is famous for his quote: 'What's good for General Electric is good for the country.' G.E. was later to use Ronald Reagan for promotional efforts, and brought him national prominence.)

89. 'Ex-Reich Aide in Vatican Irks Jews.' Philadelphia Inquirer. 12/30/82.

90. Ibid'.

91 Opus Dei Strengthened.' SF Chronicle. 11/29/82.

92. The Deputy, Rolf Hochhuth.

93. 'The Men Behind the Counterreformation.' Parapolitics. #6 3/82

94. Why Vietnam. A. Paddi.

95. Final Report on Vietnam, General Westmoreland; Deadly Deceits, Frank McGhee.

96. Invisible Government, op. cit.

97. The Dollar & The Vatican, Avro Manhattan (London) The Answer to Tai/gunner Joe, Roy Cohn.

98. Tracing Martin Bormann, I. Bezymensky.

99. Invitation to an Inquest, op. cit.

100. 'Roy Cohn Joins Board of Anti-Communist Group.' NYT, 5/15/82; 'The Men Behind the Counterreformation.' Parapolitics. #6. 3/82.

101. 'The Iron Mentor: Fritz Kraemer,' Washington Post, 3/2/75; 'Haig's Campaign of Cunning,' Playboy, 8/82.

102. 'International Operation of P-2 Directed from U.S.' NYT. 5/31/81 'The Ledeen Connection.' 'In these Times' 9/8/82

103. The Vatican Connection, Richard Hammer, 'How the Vatican Bank Got Itself Implicated in the Ambrosiano Scandal,' Wall Street Journal, 11/23/82; 'Italian Authorities Find Possible Link Between Secret Lodge and Banco Ambrosiano,' Wall Street Journal, 9/15/82; 'Scandal Erupts Over Italian Masonic Lodge,' NYT, 5/26/81; 'Fraud, Fascism & the Vatican Connection,' Guardian, 1/19/83; 'P-2 Revelations are Startling,' In These Times, August 12/15, 1982.

104. 'Milan Mystery... A Murky Maze' Wall Street Journal, 8/30/82 'Convicted Italian Banker Found Hanged in London,' Houston Post, 6/20/82.

105. 'Wotta Knight.' 'NY Daily News' 1/9/83 (Alexander Haig and Rev. Francis Haig) (NOTE: Other Knights in key positions of power include the following: William Casey (CIA Director), Franklyn Nofziger (White House aide), Richard V. Allen (Nat. Security Advisor), James G. Watt (Sec. of Interior), D. Lowell Jensen (Asst. Sec. General), Raymond J. Donovan (Sec. of Labor), James Buckley (Under sec. of Security), Fred Fielding (Nixon Watergate counsel), E. Pendleton James (Watergate, Reagan), John D.J. Moore (Amb. Ireland, Grace Co.), Felix Larkin (Pentagon counsel, Grace Co.), Robert Millikan (Citibank, Grace Co.), Reinhardt Gehlen (Nazi, CIA, since 1948), Nicholas Brady (Spellman, Pacelli, Grace), Robert Abplanalp (Nixon confidant), Joseph Bettinger (Bilderberger, Bernhard), Wild Bill Donovan (OSS, Nazis), Peter Flanagan (Nixon, Grace), Barron Hilton (of the hotels), Lee Iacocca (Ford Motor Co.), Joseph Kennedy (father of JFK, RFK), James Ling (Ling, Tempco, Vogt), Michele Sindona (Vatican scandal, P-2), John Volpe (Amb. Italy, P-2). For more information, see article cited above, 'Men Behind the Counterrefonnation'.

106. 'Bludhorn Dies, Head of G & W Empire,' NYT, 2/21/83; 'Death of G & W Founder Stirs Wall Street Interest,' Houston Post, 3/15/83; 'G & W and Dominican Republic,' NYT, 8/21/79; 'Antonio Guzman, Dominican President Shot to Death,' 7 /5/82; (Marcinkus, Sindona, Gelli connection source?)

107. Kirk Kerkorian: American Success Story, Dial Torgerson; Indecent Exposure, 'op. cit. (Music Corporation of America source?)

108. 'The Ledeen Connection.' In These Times, 9/8/82; The Real Terror Network, op. cit.

109. The Ledeen Connection op. cit.

110. 'God's Banker.' Frontline show ABC, op. cit.

111. 'New Inquest Set in Calvi 's Death,' NYT, 3/30/83 Family Doubts Death... was Suicide,' Wall Street Journal, 8/19/82.

112. 'Navy Boss' Probe: Revolving Door or Defense Iron Triangle?' Chicago Tribune, 1/5/83; 'Shift of Funds to F-18 Production Riles Congress,' Wall Street Journal, 1/24/83; 'Lehman Denies Improper Ties to Finn,' DC Times, 12/28/82; 'Ethics Unit Probes Lehman', WP, 12/28/82

113. 'Why Grace was murdered', National Examiner, 11/2/82 (Linedecker and Brussell) 'A World Without Grace: 7 Unanswered Questions', Philadelphia, June 1983 The Fairytale Business. Forbes 10/11/82. 'A New Role for Princess Grace', NY Post. 9/7/82. American Swastika Charles Higham (Monaco Nazis)

114. 'NBC Says CIA Agents Under Investigation,' S.J. Mercury, 3/24/83; 'Documents Undercut Case Against Bulgarian Papal Plot,' LA Times, 3/30/83; The KGB Plot to Assassinate the Pope Disinformation, op. cit.

115. World's #1 Dealer. LA Times, 12/9/81 (Cummings) Arms & The Man. WP Magazine 10/19/81 Frank Terpil 60 Minutes, CBS 11/15/81 Confessions of a Dangerous Man. PBS,' op. cit.

116. 'Ex-Nazi's Brilliant U.S. Career Strangled in a Web of Lies.' San Jose Mercury. 11/20/81.

117. Ibid. The Secret History of SS Glenn Infield

118. Nomenclature of an Assassination Cabal, William Torbitt; The Dallas Conspiracy, Peter Dale Scott (unpublished ms.); The Kennedy Conspiracy, Paris Flammonde; The Secret Team, Fletcher Prouty, 'They've Killed the

President' Robert Sam Anson; Assassinations: Dallas & Beyond, Scott, et al.; Coup d'état in America, Webberman & Canfield; Treason for my Daily Bread, Mikhail Lebedev; Eagle Times, June 1982 (Vatican, Permindex links).

119. Dora: Nazi Concentration Camp Where Space Technology was Born, Michel; The Rocket

Team Ordway et al'

120. Nomenclature of an Assassination Cabal, op. cit.

121. Ibid.

122. Inside the Third Reich, Albert Speer; Project Paperclip, op. cit.

123. Secret Agents, Hurt; Project Paperclip, op cit.

124. Coup d'état in America, op. cit.

125. Ibid.

126. Marina & Lee, Priscilla Johnson McMillan; Coup d'état in America, op. cit.

127. Marina & Lee, op. cit.

128. The Kennedy Conspiracy, op. cit. Coup d'état in America, op cit.; Who Killed Kennedy? Buchanan.

129. Coup d'état in America, op cit.

130. Boston Globe, 2/14/83 (Editorial quoted in text).

130. Ibid.

131. The Killing of Corporal Kunze, Wilma Parrell.

132. Warren Commission Report.

133. (NOTE: The interconnections multiply, and the Joe McCarthy story is but one indication. Fr. Walsh, his 'mentor,' worked with the Papal Relief Mission in the 1920's, along with Herbert Hoover, as a cover to rearm the monarchists. McCarthy was supported directly by Nazis here in the U.S., including Frank Seusenbrenner, then President of the Board of the University of Wisconsin, and Walter Harnishfeger. In turn, McCarthy took over the Senate hearings on the Massacre at Malmedy to cover the Nazi criminals. Other examples of interlinks abound:

134. **Charles Willoughby** really Weidenbach, helped found Young Americans for Freedom in Dallas in 1963, which had a role in the JFK

assassination. Also involved there was Robert Morris, a Navy intelligence Psych-war expert in World War II, who chaired the Committee to Restore Internal Security, assisted in the McCarthy purges, and linked to the Dallas YAF plot. Fr. Walsh himself had ties with a Nazi Major General, Karl Houshofer.

Sven Kraemer the son of the notorious Fritz Kraemer, links closely with Rev. Moon, the World Anti-Communist League, and the Pentagon.

Mike Burke of G & W's Madison Square Garden had CIA connections, worked in an early plot to overthrow Albania, and links to Sonny Werblin at the Garden, an early Hollywood publicity agent for Reagan. (NYT, 4/17/82)

Banco Ambrosiano is now further scandalized by the recent discovery of guns and drugs at their Milan headquarters, part of an international traffic that ties to Nazi smuggling operations and CIA plots. (LA. Herald 11/26/83).

Nugan Hand Bank, formed with the heroin profits of Southeast Asian CIA drug operations, and tied to various covert operations, ended in scandal and suicide. The story makes many more connections in this web. See 'Australian Mystery,' WSJ, 8/24-25-26, 1982.)

135. The Secret History of the SS, Infield; Friendly Fascism, Bertram Gross; 'U.S. Needs Military Coup,' UPI 10/21/81 (Sen. John Schmitz. CA).

136. The Ominous Parallels: The Endo/Freedom in America, Peikoff; Four Years of War Murders, Gum bell; Forgive My Grief (Vols. 1-4) Penn Jones, Jr. (JFK witness deaths); '30 Key Watergate Witnesses Met Violent Deaths,' (Brussell), Midnight Globe, 7/12/76; 'The Serpent's Egg,' film by Bergman.

137. 'In the Spirit of Jimmy Jones,' Akwesasne Notes, Winter 1982 (photo of quote).

138. 'World Watcher's International,' weekly cassettes, Mae Brussell; 'Aries Research,' P.O. Box 1107, Aptos, CA 95003, $1.00 for a book catalog; The Continuing Inquiry, Penn Jones, Jr., Rt. 3, Box 356, Waxahachie, TX 76165; Para politics, Jonathan Marshall, 311 E. Reed St. #7, San Jose, CA 95112; Covert Action information Bulletin, P.O. Box 50272, Washington, DC 20004; Counterspy, P.O. Box 647, Ben Franklin Station, Washington, DC 20044; Grassy Knoll Gazette, P.O. Box 1465, Manchester, MA 01944; Organizing Notes, Campaign for Political Rights, 201 Mass. Ave.' NE, Washington, DC 20002; Overthrow, P.O. Box 392, Canal St. Station, New York, NY 10013; Suppressed Facts Quarterly, c/o FAIRCO, P.O. Box 448, Shreveport, LA 71161; Cassettes, Ted Gondolfo, 1214 First Ave., New York,

NY 10021 (broadcasts, . etc.); Cover-ups, Gary Mack, 4620 Brandingshire Place, Fort Worth, TX 76133; 'CIA & the Nazis,' cassette of Charles Allen, Jr., Jeff McConnell, Dept. of Linguistics, MIT, Cambridge, MA 02139; Hearings on Nazi War Criminals, Subcommittee on Immigration, Refugees & International Law, 21-37 Rayburn HOB, Washington, DC 20515 (recent), and CONSPIRACY!, John Judge, P.O. Box 7147 Washington, DC 20044.

THE BLACK HOLE OF GUYANA

The Untold Story of the Jonestown Massacre (1985)

Somewhere in the concrete canyons of New York City a recently formed rock group is using the name Jim Jones and the Suicides. Irreverent and disarming, the name reflects the new trend in punk rock, to take social issues head on. Cynicism about the Jonestown deaths and its social parallels abound in the lyrics of today's music. The messages are clear because we all know the story. In fact, people today recognize the name 'Jonestown' more than any other event, a full 98% of the population. 1 'The television and printed media were filled with the news for more than a year, even though the tale read like something from the National Enquirer tabloid. But despite all the coverage, the reality of Jonestown and the reasons behind the bizarre events remain a mystery. The details have faded from memory for most of us since November 18 1978, but not the outlines. Think back a moment and you'll remember.

You Know the Official Version

A fanatic religious leader in California led a multiracial community into the jungles of remote Guyana to establish a socialist utopia. The People's Temple, his church, was in the heart of San Francisco and drew poor people, social activists, Blacks and Hispanics, young and old. The message was racial harmony and justice, and criticism of the hypocrisy of the world around his followers. 2

The Temple rose in a vacuum of leadership at the end of an era. The political confrontations of the 60's were almost over, and religious cults and 'personal transformation' were on the rise. Those who had preached a similar message on the political soapbox were gone, burnt out, discredited, or dead. The counter-culture had apparently degenerated into drugs and violence. Charlie Manson was the only visible image of the period. Suddenly, religion seemed to offer a last hope. 3

Even before they left for the Jonestown site, the People's Temple members were subjects of local scandal in the news. 4 Jim Jones claimed these exposes were attacks on their newly-found religion, and used them as an excuse to move most of the members to Guyana. 5 But disturbing reports continued to surround Jones, and soon came to the attention of congressional members like Leo Ryan. Stories of beatings, kidnapping, sexual abuse and mysterious deaths leaked out in the press. 6 Ryan decided to go to Guyana and investigate the situation for himself. The nightmare began.

Isolated on the tiny airstrip at Pon Kaituma, 7 Ryan and several reporters in his group were murdered. Then came the almost unbelievable 'White Night,' a mass suicide pact of the Jonestown camp. A community made up mostly of Blacks and women drank cyanide from paper cups of Kool-Aid, adults and children alike died and fell around the main pavilion. Jones himself was shot in the head, an apparent suicide. For days, the body count mounted, from 400 to nearly 1,000. The bodies were flown to the United States and later cremated or buried in mass graves. 8

'Temple member Larry Layton is still facing charges of conspiracy in Ryan's murder. Ryan was recently awarded a posthumous Medal of Honor, and was the first Congress member to die in the line of duty. 9

Pete Hamill called the corpses 'all the loose change of the sixties. 10 The effect was electric. Any alternative to the current system was seen as futile, if not deadly. Protest only led to police riots and political assassination. Alternative life styles and drugs led to 'creepy-crawly' communes and violent murders, 11 'and religious experiments led to cults and suicide. Social utopias were dreams that turned into nightmares. The television urged us to go back to 'The Happy Days' of the apolitical 50's. The message was, get a job, and go back to church, 12 'the unyielding nuclear threat generated only nihilism and hopelessness. There was no answer but death, no exit from the grisly future. The new ethic was personal success, aerobics, material consumption, a return to 'American values,' and the 'moral majority' white Christian world. The official message was clear.

But Just Suppose It Didn't Happen That Way...

The headlines the day of the massacre read: 'Cult Dies in South American Jungle: 400 Die in Mass Suicide, 700 Flee into Jungle.' 13 By all accounts in the press, as well as People's Temple statements 14 there were at least 1, 100 people at Jonestown. There were 809 adult passports found there, and reports of 300 children (276 found among the dead, and 210 never identified). The headline figures from the first day add to the same number: 1,100.15 The original body count done by the Guyanese, 16 which was the final count, was given almost a week later by American military authorities as 913. 17 A total of 16 survivors were reported to have returned to the United States 18

Where were the others? At their first press conference, the Americans claimed that the Guyanese 'could not count.' These local people had carried out the gruesome job of counting the bodies, and later assisted American troops in the process of poking holes in the flesh lest they explode from the gasses of decay 19 Then the Americans proposed another theory they had missed seeing a pile of bodies at the back of the pavilion. The structure was the size of a small house, and they had been at the scene for days. Finally, we were given the official reason for the discrepancy, bodies had fallen on top of other bodies, adults covering children. 20 It was a simple, if morbid, arithmetic that led to the first suspicions. The 408 bodies discovered at first count would have to be able to cover 505 bodies for a total of 913. In addition, those who first worked on the bodies would have been unlikely to miss bodies lying beneath each other since each body had to be punctured. Eighty-two of the bodies first found were those of children, reducing the number that could have been hidden below others. 21 A search of nearly 150 photographs, aerial and G1 close-up, fails to show even one body lying under another, much less 500. 22

It seemed the first reports were true, 400 had died, and 700 had fled to the jungle. The American authorities claimed to have searched for people who had escaped, but found no evidence of any in the surrounding area. 23 At least a hundred Guyanese troops were among the first to arrive, and they were ordered to search the jungle for survivors. 24 In the area, at the same time, British Black Watch troops were on 'training exercises,' with nearly 600 of their best-trained commandos. Soon, American Green Berets were on site as well. 25 The presence of these soldiers, specially trained in covert killing operations, may explain the increasing numbers of bodies that appeared.

Most of the photographs show the bodies in neat rows, face down. There are few exceptions. Close shots indicate drag marks, as though someone positioned the bodies after death. 26 Is it possible that the 700 who fled were rounded up by these troops, brought back to Jonestown and added to the body count? If so, the bodies would indicate the cause of death. 27 The media coined a new word, 'suicide-murder.' But which was it? 28 Autopsies and forensic science are a developing art. The detectives of death use a variety of scientific methods and clues to determine how people die, when they expire, and the specific cause of death. Dr. Mootoo, the top Guyanese pathologist, was at Jonestown within hours after the massacre. Refusing the assistance of U.S. pathologists, he accompanied the teams that counted the dead, examined the bodies, and worked to identify the deceased. While the American press screamed about the 'Kool-Aid Suicides,' Dr. Mootoo was reaching a much different opinion. 29

There are certain signs that show the types of poisons that lead to the end of life. Cyanide blocks the messages from the brain to the muscles by changing body chemistry in the central nervous system. Even the 'involuntary' functions like breathing and heartbeat get mixed neural signals. It is a painful death, breath coming in spurts. The other muscles spasm, limbs twist and contort. The facial muscles draw back into a deadly grin, called 'cyanide rictus. 30 All these telling signs were absent in the Jonestown dead. Limbs were limp and relaxed, and the few visible faces showed no sign of distortion. 31

Instead, Dr. Mootoo found fresh needle marks at the back of the left shoulder blades of 80-90% of the victims. 32 Others had been shot or strangled. One survivor reported that armed guards forced those who resisted. 33 The gun that reportedly shot Jim Jones was lying nearly 200 feet from his body, not a likely suicide weapon. 34 As Chief Medical Examiner, Mootoo's testimony to the Guyanese grand jury investigating Jonestown led to their conclusion that 'persons unknown' murdered all but three of the people only two had committed suicide they said. 35 Several pictures show the gunshot wounds on the bodies as well. 36 The U.S. Army spokesman, Lt. Col. Schuler, said, "No autopsies are needed. The cause of death is not an issue here." The forensic doctors who later did autopsies at Dover, Delaware were never made aware of Dr. Mootoo's findings. 37

There are other indications that the Guyanese government participated with American authorities in a cover-up of the real story, despite their own findings. One good example was Guyanese Police Chief Lloyd Barker, who interfered with investigations, helped "recover" 2.5 million for the Guyanese government, and was often the first to officially announce the cover stories relating to suicide body 38 ' J counts and survivors. Among the first to the scene were the wife of Guyanese Prime Minister Forbes Burnham and his Deputy Prime Minister, Ptolemy Reid. They returned from the massacre site with nearly $1 million in cash, gold and jewelry taken from the buildings and from the dead. Inexplicably, one of Burnham 's political party secretaries had visited the site of the massacre only hours before it occurred. 39 When Shirley Field Ridley, Guyanese Minister of Information, announced the change in the body count to the shocked Guyanese parliament, she refused to answer further questions. Other representatives began to point a finger of shame at Ridley and the Burnham government, 40 and the local press dubbed the scandal "Template," all accused them of taking a ghoulish payoff.

Perhaps more significantly, the Americans brought in 16 huge C-131 cargo planes, but claimed they could only carry 36 caskets in each one. These aircraft can carry tanks, trucks, troops and ammunition all in one load. 41 At the scene, bodies were stripped of identification, including the medical wrist tags visible in many early photos. 42 Dust-off operations during-Vietnam clearly demonstrated that the military is capable of moving hundreds of bodies in a short period. 43 Instead, they took nearly a week to bring back the Jonestown dead, bringing in the majority at the end of the period. 44 The corpses, rotting in the heat, made autopsy impossible. 45 At one point, the remains of 183 people arrived in 82 caskets. Although the Guyanese had identified 174 bodies at the site, only 17 (later 46) were tentatively identified at the massive military mortuary in Dover, Delaware. 46

Isolated there, hundreds of miles from their families who might have visited the bodies at a similar mortuary in Oakland that was used during Vietnam; many of the dead were eventually cremated. 47 Press was excluded, and even family members had difficulty getting access to the remains 48 Officials in New Jersey began to complain that state coroners were excluded, and that the military coroners appointed were illegally performing cremations. 49 One of the top forensic body identification experts, who later were brought in to work on the Iranian raid casualties, was denied repeated requests to assist. 50 In December, the President of the National Association of Medical Examiners complained in an open letter to the U.S. military that they "badly botched" procedures, and that a simple fluid autopsy was never performed at the point of discovery. Decomposition, embalming and cremation made further forensic work impossible. 51 The unorthodox method of identification attempted, to remove the skin from the fingertip and slip it over a gloved finger, would not have stood up in court. 52 The long delay made it impossible to reconstruct the event. As noted, these military doctors were unaware of Dr. Mootoo's conclusions. Several civilian pathology experts said they "shuddered at the ineptness" of the military, and that their autopsy method was "doing it backwards." But in official statements, the U.S. attempted to discredit the Guyanese grand jury findings, saying they had uncovered "few facts." 53

Guyanese troops, and police who had arrived with American Embassy official Richard Dwyer, also failed to defend Congressman Leo Ryan and others · who came to Guyana with him when they were shot down in cold blood at the Port Kaituma airstrip, even though the troops were nearby with machine guns at the ready. 54 Although Temple member Larry Layton has been charged with the murders of Congressman Ryan, Temple defector Patricia Parks, and press reporters Greg Robinson, Don Harris and Bob Brown, he was not in a position to shoot them. 55 Blocked from boarding Ryan's twin engine Otter, he had entered another plane nearby. Once inside, he pulled out a gun and wounded two Temple followers, before being disarmed. 56 The others were clearly killed by armed men who descended from a tractor-trailer at the scene, after opening fire. Witnesses described them as "zombies," walking mechanically, without emotion, and "looking through you, not at you" as they were murdered. 57 Only certain people were killed, and the selection was clearly planned. Certain wounded people, like Ryan's aide Jackie Speer's, were not banned further, but the killers made sure that Ryan and the newsmen were dead. In some cases they shot people, already wounded, directly in the head. 58 These gunmen were never finally identified, and may have been under Layton's command. They may not have been among the Jonestown dead. 59

At the Jonestown site, survivors described a special group of Jones' followers who were allowed to carry weapons and money, and to come and go from the camp. 60 These people were· all white, mostly males. They ate better and worked less than the others, and they served as an armed guard to enforce discipline, control labor and restrict movement. 61 Among them were Jones' top lieutenants, including George Phillip Blakey. Blakey and others regularly visited Georgetown, Guyana and made trips in their sea-going boat, 'the Cudjoe'. He was privileged to be aboard the boat when the murders occurred. 62 This special armed guard survived the massacre. Many were trained and programmed killers, like the "zombies" who attacked Ryan. Some were used as mercenaries in Africa, and elsewhere. 63 The dead were 90% women, and 80% Blacks. 64 It is unlikely that men armed with guns and modern crossbows would give up control and willingly be injected with poisons. It is much more likely that they forced nearly 400 people to die by injection, and then assisted in the murder of 500 more who attempted to escape. One survivor clearly heard people cheering 45 minutes after the massacre. Despite government claims, they are not accounted for, nor are their location known. 65

Back in California, People's Temple members openly admitted that they feared they were targeted by a "hit squad," and the Temple was surrounded for some time by local police forces. 66 During that period, two members of the elite guard from Jonestown returned and were allowed into the Temple by police. 67 The survivors who rode to Port Kaituma with Leo Ryan complained when Larry Layton boarded the truck, "He's not one of us." 68 Rumors also persisted that a "death list" of U.S. officials existed, and some survivors verified in testimony to the San Francisco grand jury. 69 A congressional aide was quoted in the AP wires on May 19, 1979, "There are 120 white, brainwashed assassins out from Jonestown awaiting the trigger word to pick up their hit. 70

Other survivors included Mark Lane and Charles Garry, lawyers for People's Temple who managed to escape the massacre somehow. 71 In addition to the 16 who officially returned with the Ryan party, others managed to reach Georgetown and come back home. 72 However, there have been continuing suspicious murders of those people here. Jeannie and Al Mills, who intended to write a book about Jones, were murdered at home, bound and shot. 73 Some evidence indicates a connection between the Jonestown operation and the murders of Mayor Moscone and Harvey Milk by police agent Dan White. 74 Unidentified killers shot another

Jonestown survivor near his home in Detroit, 75 and yet another was involved in a mass murder of school children in Los Angeles. 76 Anyone who survived such massive slaughter must be somewhat suspect. The fact that the press never even spoke about nearly 200 survivors raises serious doubts.

Who Was Jim Jones?

In order to understand the strange events surrounding Jonestown, we must begin with a history of the people involved. The official story of a religious fanatic and his idealist followers doesn't make sense in light of the evidence of murders, armed killers and autopsy cover-ups. If it happened the way we were told, there should be no reason to try to hide the facts from the public, and full investigation into the deaths at Jonestown, and the murder of Leo Ryan would have been welcomed. What did happen is something else again.

Jim Jones grew up in Lynn, in southern Indiana. His father was an active member of the local Ku Klux Klan that infests that area. 77 His friends found him a little strange, and he was interested in preaching the Bible and religious rituals 78 Perhaps more important was his boyhood friendship with Dan Mitrione, confirmed by local residents. 79 In the early 50's, Jones set out to be a religious minister, and was ordained at one point by a Christian denomination in Indianapolis. 80 It was during this period that he met and married his lifelong mate, Marceline. 81 He also had a small business, selling monkeys, purchased from the research department at Indiana State University in Bloomington. 82

A Bible-thumper and faith healer, Jones put on revivalist tent shows in the area, and worked close to Richmond, Indiana. Mitrione, his friend, worked as chief of police there, and kept him from being arrested or run out of town 83 According to those close to him, he used wet chicken livers as evidence of "cancers" he was removing by "divine powers. "84 His landlady called him "a gangster who used a Bible instead of a gun 85 His church followers included Charles Beikman, a Green Beret who was to stay with him to the end 86 Beikman was later charged with the murders of several Temple members in Georgetown, following the massacre. 87

Dan Mitrione, Jones' friend, moved on to the CIA-financed International Police Academy, where police were trained in counter-insurgence and torture techniques from around the world. 88 Jones, a poor, itinerant preacher, suddenly had money in 1961 for a trip to "minister" in Brazil, and he took his family with him. 89 By this time, he had "adopted" Beikman, and eight children, both Black and white 90 His neighbors in Brazil distrusted him. He told them he worked with U.S. Navy Intelligence. His transportation and groceries were being provided by, the U.S. Embassy as was the large house he lived in. 91 His son, Stephan, commented that he made regular trips to Belo Horizonte, site of the CIA headquarters in Brazil. 92 An American police advisor, working closely with the CIA at that point, Dan Mitrione was there as well. 93 Mitrione had risen in the ranks quickly, and was busy training foreign police in torture and assassination methods. He was later kidnapped by Tupermaro guerillas in Uruguay, interrogated and murdered. 94 Costa Gavras made a film about his death titled State of Siege. 95 Jones returned to the United States in 1963, with $10,000 in his pocket. 96 Recent articles indicate that Catholic clergy are complaining about CIA funding of other denominations for "ministry' in Brazil; perhaps Jones was an early example. 97

With his new wealth, Jones was able to travel to California and establish the first People's Temple in Ukiah, California, in 1965. Guarded by dogs, electric fences and guard towers, he set up Happy Havens Rest Home. 98 Despite a lack of trained personnel, or proper licensing, Jones drew in many people at the camp. He had elderly, prisoners, people from psychiatric institutions, and 150 foster children, often transferred to care at Happy Havens by court orders. 99 He was contacted there by Christian missionaries from World Vision, an international evangelical order that had done espionage work for the CIA in Southeast Asia 100 He met "influential" members of the community and was befriended by Walter Heady, the head of the local chapter of the John Birch Society. 101 He used the members of his "church" to organize local voting drives for Richard Nixon's election and worked closely with the Republican Party 102 He was even appointed chairman of the county grand jury 103

"The Messiah from Ukiah," as he was known then, met and recruited Timothy Stoen, a Stanford graduate ·and member of the city DA 's office, and his wife Grace. 104 During this time, the Layton family, Terri Buford and George Phillip Blakey' and other important members joined the Temple. 105 The camp "doctor," Larry Schacht, claims Jones got him off drugs and into medical school during this period 106 these were not just street urchins. Buford's father was a Commander for the fleet at the Philadelphia Navy Base for years. 107 The Laytons were a well-heeled, aristocratic family. Dr. Layton donated at least a quarter-million dollars to Jones. His wife son and daughter were all members of the Temple 108 George Blakey, who married Debbie Layton, was from a wealthy British family. He donated $60,000 to pat the lease on the 27,000-acre Guyana site in 1974. 109 Lisa Philips Layton had come to the U.S. from a rich Hamburg banking family in Germany. 110 Most of the top lieutenants around Jones were from wealthy, educated backgrounds, many with connections to the military or intelligence agencies. These were the people who would set up the bank accounts, complex legal actions, and financial records that put people under the Temple's control. 111

Stoen was able to set up important contacts for Jones as Assistant DA in San Francisco. 112 Jones changed his image to that of a liberal. 113 He had spent time studying the preaching methods of Fr. Divine in Philadelphia, and attempted to use them in a manipulative way on the streets of San Francisco. Fr. Divine ran a religious and charitable operation among Philadelphia's poor Black community. 114 Jones was able to use his followers in an election once again, this time for Mayor Moscone. Moscone responded in 1976, putting Jones in charge of the city Housing Commission. 115 In addition, many of his key followers got jobs with the city Welfare Department and much of the recruitment to the Temple in San Francisco came from the ranks of these unemployed and dispossessed people. 116 Jones was introduced to many influential liberal and radical people there, and entertained or greeted people ranging from Roslyn Carter to Angela Davis 117

The period when Jones began the Temple there marked the end of an important political decade. Nixon's election had ushered in a domestic intelligence dead set against the movements for peace, civil rights and social justice. Names like COINTELPRO, CHAOS, and OPERATION GARDEN PLOT, or the HOUSTON PLAN made the news following in the wake of Watergate revelations. 118 Senator Ervin called the White House plans against dissent "fascistic. 119 These operations involved the highest levels of military and civilian intelligence and all levels of police agencies in a full-scale attempt to discredit, disrupt and destroy the movements that sprang up in the 1960's. There are indications that these plans, or the mood they created, led to the assassinations of Martin Luther King and Malcolm X, as unacceptable "Black Messiahs." 120

One of the architects under then Governor Reagan in California was now-Attorney General Edwin Meese. He coordinated "Operation Garden Plot" for military intelligence and all police operations and intelligence in a period that was plagued with violations of civil and constitutional rights. 121 Perhaps you recall the police attacks on People's Park, the murder of many Black Panthers and activists, the infiltration of the Free Speech Movement and antiwar activity, and the experimentation on prisoners at Vacaville, or the shooting of George Jackson. 122

Meese later bragged that this activity had damaged or destroyed the people he called "revolutionaries." 123 It was into this situation Jones came to usurp leadership 124

After his arrival in Ukiah, his methods were visible to those who took the time to investigate. 125 His armed guards wore black uniforms and leather jackboots. His approach was one of deception, and if that wore off, then manipulation and threats. Loyalty to his church included signing blank sheets of paper, later filled in with "confessions' and used for blackmail purposes, or to extort funds. 126 Yet the vast membership he was extorting often owned little, and he tried to milk them for everything, from personal funds to land deeds. 127 illegal activities were regularly reported during this period, but either not investigated or unresolved. He clearly had the cooperation of local police. Years later, evidence would come out of charges of sexual solicitation, mysteriously dropped. 128

Those who sought to leave were prevented and rebuked. Local journalist Kathy Hunter wrote in the Ukiah press about "Seven Mysterious Deaths" of the Temple members who had argued with Jones and attempted to leave. One of these was Maxine Swaney 129 Jones openly hinted to other members that he had arranged for them to die, threatening a similar fate to others who would be disloyal. 130 Kathy Hunter later tried to visit Jonestown, only to be forcibly drugged by Temple guards, and deported to Georgetown. She later charged that Mark Lane approached her, falsely identifying himself as a reporter for Esquire, rather than as an attorney for Jim Jones. He led her to believe he was seeking information on Jones for an expose in the magazine, and asked to see her evidence.

The pattern was to continue in San Francisco. In addition, Jones required that members practice for the mysterious "White Night," 131 a mass suicide ritual that would protect them from murder at the hands of their enemies. 132 Although the new Temple had no guards or fences to restrict members, few had other places to live, and many had given over all they owned to Jones. They felt trapped inside this community that preached love, but practiced hatred. 133

Following press exposure, and a critical article in New West magazine, Jones became very agitated, and the number of suicide drills increased. 134 Complaints about mistreatment by current and ex-members began to appear in the media and reach the ears of congressional representatives. Sam Houston, an old friend of Leo Ryan, came to him with questions about the untimely death of his son following his departure from the Temple 135 Later, Timothy and Grace Stoen would complain to Ryan about custody of their young son, who was living with Jones, and urge him to visit the commune 136 Against advice of friends and staff members, Ryan decided to take a team of journalists to Guyana and seek the truth of the situation 137 Some feel that Ryan's journey there was planned and expected, and used as a convenient excuse to set up his murder. Others feel that this unexpected violation of secrecy around Jonestown set off the spark that led to the mass murder. In either case, it marked the beginning of the end for Ryan and Jones. 138

At one point, to show his powers, Jones arranged to be shot in the heart in front of the congregation. Dragged to a back room, apparently wounded and bleeding, he returned a moment later alive and well. While this may have been more of his stage antics to prompt believers' faith, it may also have marked the end of Jim Jones. 139 For undisclosed reasons, Jones had and used doubles. 140 This is very unusual for a religious leader, but quite common in intelligence operations. 141

Even the death and identification of Jim Jones were peculiar. He was apparently shot by another person at the camp 142 Photos of his body do not show identifying tattoos on his chest. The body and face are not clearly recognizable due to bloating and discoloration 143 The FBI reportedly checked his fingerprints twice, a seemingly futile gesture since it is a precise operation. A more logical route would have been to check dental records. 144 Several researchers familiar with the case feel that the body may not have been Jones. Even if the person at the site was one of the "doubles," it does not mean Jones is still alive. He may have been killed at an earlier point.

What Was Jonestown?

According to one story, Jones was seeking a place on earth that would survive the effects of nuclear war, relying only on an article in Esquire magazine for his list. 145 The real reason for his locations in Brazil, California, Guyana and elsewhere deserve more scrutiny. 146 At one point Jones wanted to set up in Grenada, and he invited then Prime Minister Sir Eric Gairy to visit the Temple in San Francisco. 147 He invested $200,000 in the Grenada National Bank in 1977 to pave the way, and some $76,000:' was still there after the massacre. 148

His final choice, the Matthew's Bridge section in Guyana is an interesting one. It was originally the site of a Union Carbide bauxite and manganese mine, and Jones used the dock they left behind. 149 At an earlier point, it had been one of seven possible sites chosen for the relocation of the Jews after World War II. 150 Plans to inhabit the jungles of Guyana's interior with cheap labor date back to 1919. 151 Resources buried there are among the richest in the world, and include manganese, diamonds, gold, bauxite and uranium. 152 Forbes Burnham, the Prime Minister, had participated in a scheme to repatriate Blacks from the UK to work in the area. Like all earlier attempts, it failed. 153 Once chosen, the site was leased and worked on by a select crew of Temple members in preparation for the arrival of the body of the church. The work was done in cooperation with Burnham and the U.S. Embassy there. 154 But if these were idealists seeking a better life, their arrival in "Utopia" was a strange welcome. Piled into busses in San Francisco, they had driven to Florida. From there, Pan American charter planes delivered them to Guyana. 155 When they arrived at the airport, the Blacks were taken off the plane, bound and gagged. 156 The deception had finally been stripped bare of all pretenses. The Blacks were so isolated and controlled those neighbors as close as five miles from the site did not know that Blacks lived at Jonestown. The only Public representatives seen in Guyana were white. 157 Guyanese children were "bought" also. 158

According to survivors' reports, they entered a virtual slave labor camp. Worked for 16 to 18 hours daily, they were forced to live in cramped quarters on minimum rations, usually rice, bread and sometimes, rancid meat. Kept on a schedule of physical and mental exhaustion, they were also forced to stay awake at night and listen to lectures by Jones. Threats and abuse became more common. 159 The camp medical staff under Dr. Lawrence Schacht was known to perform painful suturing without anesthetic. They administered drugs, and kept daily medical records 160 Infractions of the rules or disloyalty led to increasingly harsh punishments, including forced drugging, sensory isolation in an underground box, physical torture and public sexual rape and humiliation. Beatings and verbal abuse were commonplace. Only the special guards were treated humanely and fed decently. 161 People with serious injuries were flown out, but few ever returned 162 Perhaps the motto at Jonestown should have been the same as the one at Auschwitz, developed by Larry Schacht's namesake, Dr. Hjalmar Schacht, the Nazi minister of economics, "Arheit Macht Frei," or "Work Will Make You Free." Guyana even considered setting up an Auschwitz-like museum" at the site, but abandoned the idea. 163

By this point, Jones had amassed incredible wealth. Press estimates ranged from $26 million to $2 billion, including bank accounts, foreign investments and real estate. Key members set up accounts worldwide, often in the personal name of certain people in the Temple. 164 Much of this money, listed publicly after the massacre, disappeared mysteriously. It was a fortune far too large to have come from membership alone. The receivership set up by the government settled on a total of $10 million. Of special interest were the Swiss bank accounts opened in Panama, the money taken from the camp, and the extensive the extensive investments in Barclay's Bank 165 Other sources of income included the German banking family of Lisa Philips Layton, Larry's mother. 166 Also, close to $65,000 a month income was claimed to come from welfare and social security checks for 199 members, sent to the Temple followers and signed over to Jones. 167 In addition, there are indications that Blakey and other members were supplementing the Temple funds with international smuggling of guns and drugs 168 at one point, Charles Garry noted that Jones and his community were "literally sitting on a gold mine." Mineral distribution maps of Guyana suggest he was right. 169

To comprehend this well-financed, sinister operation, we must abandon the myth that this was a religious commune and study instead the history that led to its formation. Jonestown was an experiment, part of a 30-year program called MK-ULTRA, the CIA and military intelligence code name for mind control. 170 A close study of Senator Ervin's 1974 report, Individual Rights and the Government's Role in Behavior Modification shows that these agencies had certain "target populations" in mind, for both individual and mass control. Blacks, women, prisoners, the elderly, the young, and inmates of psychiatric wards were selected as "potentially violent. 171 There were plans in California at the time for a Center for the Study and Reduction of Violence, expanding on the horrific work of Dr. Jose Delgado, Drs. Mark and Ervin, and Dr. Jolly West, experts in implantation, psychosurgery, and tranquilizers. The guinea pigs were to be drawn from the ranks of the "target populations," and taken to an isolated military missile base in California. 172 In that same period, Jones began to move his Temple members to Jonestown. They were the exact population selected for such tests. 173

The meticulous daily notes and drug records kept by Larry Schacht disappeared, but evidence did not. 174 The history of MK-ULTRA and its sister programs (MK-DELTA, ARTICHOKE, BLUEBIRD, etc.) records a combination of drugs, drug mixtures, electroshock and torture as methods for control. The desired results ranged from temporary and permanent amnesia, uninhibited confessions, and creation of second personalities, to programmed assassins and preconditioned suicidal urges. One goal was the ability to control mass populations, especially for cheap labor. 175 Dr. Delgado told Congress that he hoped for a future where a technology would control workers in the field and troops at war with electronic remote signals. He found it hard to understand why people would complain about electrodes implanted in their brains to make them "both happy and productive. 176

On the scene at Jonestown, Guyanese troops discovered a large cache of drugs, enough to drug the entire population of Georgetown, Guyana (well over 200,000) 177 for more than a year. According to survivors, these were being used regularly "to control" a population of only 1,100 people. 178 One footlocker contained 11,000 doses of Thorazine, a dangerous tranquilizer. Drugs used in the testing for MK-ULTRA were found in abundance, including sodium pentothal (a truth serum), chloral hydrate (a hypnotic), Demerol thallium (confuses thinking), and many others. 179 Schacht had supplies of haliopareael and largatil, two other major tranquilizers as well. 180 The actual description of life at Jonestown is that of a tightly run concentration camp, complete with medical and psychiatric experimentation. The stresses and isolation of the victims is typical of sophisticated brainwashing techniques. The drugs and special tortures add an additional experimental aspect to the horror. 181 This more clearly explains the medical tags on the bodies, and why they had to be removed. It also suggests an additional motive for frustrating any chemical autopsies, since these drugs would have been found in the system of the dead.

Full Gospel Christian Businessman's Association including Lionel Luckhoo, a Temple lawyer in Guyana. 182 This same group, based in California, also reportedly converted Guatemalan dictator Rios Montt prior to his massacres there and they were in touch with Jim Jones in Ukiah. 183 They currently conduct the White House prayer breakfasts for Mr. Reagan. 184 With Ryan on his way to Jonestown, the seal of secrecy was broken. In a desperate attempt to test their conditioning methods, the Jonestown elite apparently tried to implement a real suicide drill. 185 Clearly, it led to a revolt, and the majority of people fled, unaware that there were people waiting to catch them.

One Too Many Jonestown's

Author Don Freed, an associate of Mark Lane, said that Martin Luther King, "if he could see Johnstown would recognize it as the next step in his agenda, and he would say, one, two, three, many more Jonestown's. 186 Strangely enough, almost every map of Guyana in the major press located Jonestown at a different place following the killings. One map even shows a second site in the area called "Johnstown. 187 Perhaps there were multiple camps and Leo Ryan was only shown the one they hoped he would see. In any case, the Jonestown model survives, and similar camps, and their sinister designs, show up in many places.

Inside Guyana itself, approximately 25 miles to the south of Matthews Ridge, is a community called Hilltown, named after religious leader Rabbi Hill. Hill has used the names Abraham Israel and Rabbi Emmanuel Washington. Hilltown, set up about the same time as Jonestown, followed the departure of David Hill, who was known in Cleveland, a fugitive of the U.S. courts. Hill rules with an "iron fist" over some 8,000 Black people from Guyana and America who believe they are the Lost Tribe of Israel and the real Hebrews of Biblical prophecy. 188 Used as strong arm troops, and "internal mercenaries" to insure Burnham's election, as were Jonestown members, the Hilltown people were allowed to clear the Jonestown site of shoes and unused weapons, both in short supply in Guyana. 189 Hill says his followers would gladly kill themselves at his command, but he would survive since, unlike Jones, he is "in control." 190

Similar camps were reported at the time in the Philippines. Perhaps the best-known example is the fascist torture camp in Chile known as Colonia Dignidad. Also a religious cult built around a single individual, this one came from Germany to Chile in 1961. In both cases, the camp was their" Agricultural Experiment." Sealed and protected by the dreaded Chilean DINA police, Colonia Dignidad serves as a torture chamber for political dissidents. To the Jonestown monstrosities, they have added dogs specially trained to attack human genitals. 191 The operations there have included the heavy hand of decapitation specialist Michael Townley Welch, an American CIA agent, as well as reported visits by Nazi war criminals Dr. Josef Mengele and Martin Bormann. Currently, another such campsite exists as Pisagua, Chile. 192 Temple member Jeannie Mills, now dead, reported having seen actual films of a Chilean torture camp while at Jonestown. The only source possible at the time was the Chilean fascists themselves. 193

In the current period, Jonestown is being "repopulated" with 100,000 Laotian Hmong people. Many of them grew opium for CIA money in Southeast Asia. Over 1,000 reside there already under a scheme designed by Billy Graham's nephew Ernest, and members of the Federation of Evangelical Ministries Association in Wheaton, Illinois (World Vision, World Medical Relief, Samaritan's Purse, and Carl McIntyre's International Council of Christian Churches). 194 Similar plans devised by the Peace Corps included moving inner city Blacks from American to Jamaica, and other Third World countries. And World Relief attempted to move the population of the Island of Dominica to Jonestown. 195 It is only a matter of time before another Jonestown will be exposed, perhaps leading again to massive slaughter.

The Links to U.S. Intelligence Agencies

Our story so far has hinted at connections to U.S. intelligence, such as the long-term friendship of Jones and CIA associate Dan Mitrione, but the ties are much more direct when a full picture of the operation is revealed. To start with, the history of Forbes Burnham 's rise to power in Guyana is fraught with the clear implication of a CIA coup d'état to oust troublesome independent leader Cheddi Jagan. 196 In addition, the press and other evidence indicated the presence of a CIA agent on the scene at the time of the massacre. This man, Richard Dwyer, was working as Deputy Chief of Mission for the U.S. Embassy in Guyana. 197 Identified in Who's Who in the CIA, he has been involved since 1959, and was last stationed in Martinique. 198 Present at the campsite and the airport strip, his accounts were used by the State Department to confirm the death of Leo Ryan. At the massacre, Jones said, "Get Dwyer out of here" just before the killings began. 199

Other Embassy personnel, who knew the situation at Jonestown well, were also connected to intelligence work. U.S. Ambassador John Burke, who served in the CIA with Dwyer in Thailand, was an Embassy official described by Philip Agee as working for the CIA since 1963. 200 A Reagan appointee to the CIA, he is still employed by the agency, usually on State Department assignments. Burke tried to stop Ryan's investigation. 201 Also at the Embassy was Chief Consular officer Richard McCoy, described as "close to Jones," who worked for military intelligence and was "on loan" from the Defense Department at the time of the massacre. 202

According to a standard source, "The U.S. embassy in Georgetown housed the Georgetown CIA station. It now appears that the majority and perhaps all of the embassy officials were CIA officers operating under State Department covers... "203 Dan Webber, who was sent to the site of the massacre the day after, was also named as CIA. 204 Not only did the State Department conceal all reports of violations at Jonestown from Congressman Leo Ryan, but also the Embassy regularly provided Jones with copies of all congressional inquiries under the Freedom of Information Act. 205

Ryan had challenged the Agency's overseas operations before, as a member of the House Committee responsible for oversight on intelligence. He was an author of the controversial Hughes-Ryan Amendment that would have required CIA disclosure in advance to the congressional committees of all planned covert operations. The Amendment was defeated shortly after his death. 206

American intelligence agencies have a sordid history of cooperative relations with Nazi war criminals and international fascism. 207 In light of this, consider the curious ties of the family members of the top lieutenants to Jim Jones. The Layton family is one example. Dr. Laurence Layton was Chief of Chemical and Biological Warfare Research at Dugway Proving Grounds in Utah, for many years, and later worked as Director of Missile and Satellite Development at the Navy Propellant Division, Indian Head Maryland. 208 His wife, Lisa, had come from a rich German family. Her father, Hugo had represented I.G. Farben 209 as a stockbroker. Her stories about hiding her Jewish past from her children for most of her life, and her parents' escape from a train heading for a Nazi concentration camp seem shallow, as do Dr. Layton's Quaker religious beliefs. The same family sent money to Jonestown regularly. 210 Their daughter, Debbie, met and married George Philip Blakey in an exclusive private school in England. Blakey's parents have extensive stock holdings in Solvay drugs, a division of the Nazi cartel I.G. Farben. 211 He also contributed financially. 212

Terri Buford's father Admiral Charles T. Buford, worked with Navy Intelligence. 213 In addition, Blakey was reportedly running mercenaries from Jonestown to CIA-backed UNITA forces in Angola. 214 Maria Katsaris' father was a minister with the Greek Orthodox Church, a common conduit of CIA funding's, and Maris claimed she had proof he was CIA. She was shot in the head, and her death was ruled a suicide, but at one point Charles Beikman was charged with killing her. 215 On their return to the United States, the "official" survivors were represented by attorney Joseph Blatchford who had been named prior to that time in a scandal involving CIA infiltration of the Peace Corps. 216 Almost everywhere you look at Jonestown, U.S. intelligence and fascism rear their ugly heads.

The connection of intelligence agencies to cults is nothing new. A simple but revealing example is the Unification Church, tied to both the Korean CIA (i.e., American CIA in Korea), and the international fascist network known as the World Anti-

Communist League. The Moonies hosted WACL's first international conference. 217 What distinguished Jonestown was both the level of control and the openly sinister involvement. It was imperative that they cover their tracks. 218 Maria Katsaris sent Michael Prokes, Tim Carter, and another guard out at the last minute with $500,000 cash in a suitcase, and instructions for a drop point. Her note inside suggests the funds were destined for the Soviet Union. 219 Prokes later shot himself at a San Francisco press conference, where he claimed to be an FBI informant. 220 Others reported meeting with KGB agents and plans to move to Russia. 221 This disinformation was part of a "red smear" to be used if they had to abandon the operation. The Soviet Union had no interest in the money and even less in Jonestown. The Guyanese government recovered the cash. 222

Their hidden funding may include more intelligence links. A mysterious account in Panama, totaling nearly $5 million in the name of an "Association Pro Religiosa 'do San Pedro, S.A." was located. 223 This unknown Religious Association of St. Peter was probably one of the twelve phony companies set up by Archbishop Paul Marcinkus to hide the illegal investments of Vatican funds through the scandal-ridden Banco Ambrosiano. 224 A few days after the story broke about the accounts, the President of Panama, and most of the government resigned, Roberto Calvi of Banco Ambrosiano was murdered, and the Jonestown account disappeared from public scrutiny and court record. 225 The direct orders to cover up the cause of death came from the top levels of the American government. Zbigniew Brzezinski delegated to Robert Pastor, and he in turn ordered Lt. Col. Gordon Sumner to strip the bodies of identity. 226 Pastor is now Deputy Director of the CIA. 227 One can only wonder how many others tied to the Jonestown operation were similarly promoted.

The Strange Connection to the Murder of Martin Luther King

One of the persistent problems in researching Jonestown is that it seems to lead to so many other criminal activities, each with its own complex history and cast of characters. Perhaps the most disturbing of these is the connection that appears repeatedly between the characters in the Jonestown story and the key people involved in the murder and investigating of Martin Luther King. The first clue to this link appeared in the personal histories of the members of the Ryan investigation team who were so selectively and deliberately killed at Port Kaituma. Don Harris, a veteran NBC reporter, had been the only network newsman on the scene to cover Martin Luther King's activity in Memphis at the time of King's assassination. He had interviewed key witnesses at the site. His coverage of the urban riots that followed won him an Emmy award. 228 Gregory Robinson, a "fearless" journalist from the San Francisco Examiner, had photographed the same riots in Washington, D.C. When Justice approached him for copies of the films Department officials, he threw the negatives into the Potomac River. 229

The role of Mark Lane, who served as attorney for Jim Jones, is even more clearly intertwined. 230 Lane had co-authored a book with Dick Gregory, claiming FBI complicity in the King murder. 231 He was hired as the attorney for James Earl Ray, accused assassin, when Ray testified before the House Select Committee on Assassinations about King. 232 Prior to this testimony, Ray was involved in an unusual escape plot at Brushy Mountain State Prison. 233 'The prisoner who had helped engineer the escape plot was later inexplicably offered an early parole by members of the Tennessee Governor's office. These officials, and Governor Blanton himself, were to come under close public scrutiny and face legal charges in regard to bribes taken to arrange illegal early pardons for prisoners. 234

One of the people living at Jonestown was ex-FBI agent Wesley Swearington, who at least publicly condemned the COINTELPRO operations and other abuses, based on stolen classified documents, at the Jonestown site. Lane had reportedly met with him there at least a year before the massacre. Terri Buford said the documents were passed on to Charles Garry. Lane used information from Swearingen in his thesis on the FBI and King's murder. Swearingen later served as a key witness in suits against the Justice Department brought by the Socialist Workers Party. 235 When Larry Flint, the flamboyant publisher of Hustler magazine, offered a $1 million reward leading to the capture and conviction of the John F. Kennedy killers, the long distance number listed to collect information and leads was being answered by Mark Lane and Wesley Swearingen. 236

With help from officials in Tennessee, Governor Blanton's office, Lane managed to get legal custody of a woman who had been incarcerated in the Tennessee state psychiatric system for nearly eight years. 237 This woman, Grace Walden Stephens, had been a witness in the King murder. 238 She was living at the time in Memphis in a rooming house across from the hotel when Martin Luther King was shot. 239 The official version of events had Ray located in the common bathroom of the rooming house, and claimed he used a rifle to murder King from that window. 240 Grace Stephens did, indeed, see a man run from the bathroom, past her door and down to the street below. 241 A rifle, later linked circumstantially to James Earl Ray, was found inside a bundle at the base of the rooming house stairs, and identified as the murder weapon. 242 But Grace, who saw the man clearly, refused to identify him as Ray when shown photographs by the FBI. 243 Her testimony was never introduced at the trial. The FBI relied, instead, on the word of her common law husband, Charles Stephens, who was drunk and unconscious at the time of the incident. 244 Her persistence in saying that it was not James Earl Ray was used at her mental competency hearings as evidence against her, and she disappeared into the psychiatric system. 245

Grace Walden Stephens took up residence in Memphis with Lane, her custodian, and Terri Buford, a key Temple member who had returned to the U.S. before the killings to live with Lane. 246 While arranging for her to testify before the Select Committee on Ray's behalf, Lane and Buford were plotting another fate for Grace Stephens. Notes from Buford to Jones, found in the aftermath of the killings, discussed arrangements with Lane to move Grace Stephens to Jonestown. 247 The problem that remained was lack of a passport, but Buford suggested either getting a passport on the black market, or using the passport of former Temple member Maxine Swaney. 248 Swaney, dead for nearly 2-1/2 years since her departure from the Ukiah camp, was in no position to argue and Jones apparently kept her passport with him. 249 Whether Grace ever arrived at Jonestown is unclear.

Lane was also forced to leave Ray in the midst of testimony to the Select Committee when he got word that Ryan was planning to visit. Lane had attempted to discourage the trip earlier in a vaguely threatening letter. 250 Now he rushed to be sure he arrived with the group. 251 At the scene, he failed to warn Ryan and others, knowing that the sandwiches and other food might be drugged, but refrained from eating it 'himself. 252 Later, claiming that he and Charles Garry would write the official history of the "revolutionary suicide," Lane was allowed to leave the pieces of underwear to mark their way back to Georgetown. 253 If true, it seems an unlikely method if they were in any fear of pursuit. They had heard gunfire and screams back at the camp. 254 Lane was reportedly well aware of the forced drugging and suicide drills at Jonestown before Ryan arrived. 255

Another important figure in the murder of Martin Luther King was his mother, Alberta. A few weeks after the first public announcement by Coretta Scott King that she believed her husband's murder was part of a conspiracy, Mrs. Alberta King was brutally shot to death in Atlanta, while attending church services. 256 Anyone who had seen the physical wounds suffered by King might have been an adverse witness to the official version, since the wound angles did not match the ballistic direction of a shot· from the rooming house. 257 Her death also closely coincided with the reopening of the Tennessee state court review of Ray's conviction based on a guilty plea, required by a 6th Circuit decision. 258 The judge in that case reportedly refused to allow witnesses from beyond a 100-mile radius from the courtroom. 259

The man convicted of shooting King's mother was Marcus Wayne Chenault. His emotional affect following the murder was unusual. Grinning, he asked if he had hit anyone. 260 He had reportedly, been dropped off at the church, by people he knew in Ohio. 261 While at Ohio State University, he was part of a group known as "the Troop," run by a Black minister and gun collector who used the name Rabbi Emmanuel Israel. This man, described in the press as a "mentor" for Chenault, left the area immediately after the shooting. 262 In the same period, Rabbi Hill traveled from Ohio to Guyana and set up Hilltown, using similar aliases, and preaching the same message of a "black Hebrew elite." 263 Chenault confided to SCLC leaders that he was one of many killers who were working to assassinate a long list of Black leadership. The names he said were on this list coincided with similar "death lists" distributed by the KKK, and linked to the COINTELPRO operations in the 60's. 264 The real backgrounds and identities of Marcus Wayne Chenault and Rabbi Hill may never be discovered, but one thing is certain, Martin Luther King would never had countenanced the preaching's of Jim Jones, had he lived to hear them. 265

Aftermath

In the face of such horror, it may seem little compensation to know that a part of the truth has been unearthed. But for the families and some of the survivors, the truth, however painful, is the only path to being relieved of the burden of their doubts. It's hard to believe that President Carter was calling on us at the time not to "overreact." The idea that a large community of Black people would not only stand by and be poisoned at the suggestion of Jim Jones, but would allow their children to be murdered first, is a monstrous lie, and a racist insult. 266 We now know that the most direct description of Jonestown is that it was a Black genocide plan. One Temple director, Joyce Shaw described the Jonestown massacre as, "some kind of horrible government experiments, or some sort of sick racial thing, a plan like that of the Germans to exterminate Blacks." 267 If we refuse to look further into this nightmarish event, there will be more Jonestown's to come. They will move from Guyana to our own back yard.

The cast of characters is neither dead nor inactive. Key members of the armed guard were ordered to be on board the Temple Ship, Cudjoe at the hour of the massacre they were on a supply run to Trinidad. George Phillip Blakey phoned his father-in-law, Dr. Lawrence Layton, from Panama after the event. 268 At least ten members of the Temple remained on the boat, and set up a new community in Trinidad while Nigel Slinger, a Grenada businessman and insurance broker for Jonestown, repaired the 400-ton shipping vessel. Then Charles Touchette, Paul McCann, Stephan Jones, and George Blakey set up an "open house" in Grenada with the others. McCann spoke about starting a shipping company to "finance the continued work of the original Temple." 269

That "work" may have included the mysterious operations of the mental hospital in Grenada that eluded government security by promising free medical care. 270 The hospital as

operated by Sir Geoffrey Bourne, Chancellor of the St. George's
University Medical School, also staffed by his son Dr. Peter
Bourne. 271 His son's history includes work with psychological
experiments and US AID in Vietnam, the methadone clinics in
the U.S., and a drug scandal in the Carter White House. 272 The
mental hospital was the only structure bombed during the U.S.
invasion of Grenada in 1983: This was part of a plan to put Sir
Eric Gairy back in power. 273 Were additional experiments
going on at the site? 274

In addition, the killers of Leo Ryan and others at Port Kaituma
were never accounted for fully. The Guyanese courts, and the
U.S. system mishandled the trial of Larry Layton as well. 275
No adequate evidentiary hearings have occurred either at the
trial or in state and congressional reviews. The Jonestown
killer's trained assassins and mercenaries are not on trial. They
might be working in Africa or Central America. Their
participation in Jonestown can be used as an "explanation" for
their involvement in later murders here, such as the case of the
attack on school children in Los Angeles. 276 They should be
named and located.

The money behind Jonestown was never fully examined or
recovered. The court receivership only collected a fraction; the
bulk went to pay back military operations and burial costs.
Families of the dead were awarded only minimal amounts. 277
Some filed suit, unsuccessfully, to learn more about the
circumstances of the deaths, and who was responsible. Joe
Holsinger, Leo Ryan's close friend and assistant, studied the
case for two years and reached the same unnerving
conclusions these people were murdered, there was evidence
of a mass mind control experiment, and the top levels of
civilian and military intelligence were involved. 278 He worked
with Ryan's family members to prove the corruption and
injustice, but they could barely afford the immense court costs
and case preparation. Their suit, as well as a similar one
brought by ex-members and families of the victims, had to be
dropped for lack of funds. 279

The international operations of World Vision and the related evangelical groups continue unabashed. World Vision official John W. Hinckley, Sr. was on his way to a Guatemalan water project run by the organization on the day his son shot at president Reagan. 280 A mysterious "double" of Hinckley, Jr., a man named Richardson, followed Hinckley's path from Colorado to Connecticut, and even wrote love letters to Jody Foster. Richardson was a follower of Carl McIntyre's International Council of Christian Churches, and attended their Bible School in Florida. He was arrested shortly after the assassination attempt in New York's Port Authority with a weapon, and claimed he intended to kill Reagan. 281 Another World Vision employee, Mark David Chapman, worked at their Haitian refugee camp in Ft. Chaffee, Arkansas. He was later to gain infamy as the assassin of John Lennon in New York City. 282 'World Vision works with refugees worldwide. At the Honduran border, they are present in camps used by American CIA to recruit mercenaries against Nicaragua. They were at Sabra and Satilla, Camps in Lebanon where fascist Phalange massacred the Palestinians. 283 Their representatives in the Cuban refugee camps on the east coast included members of the Bay of Pigs operation, CIA financed mercenaries from Omega 7 and Alpha 66. 284 Are they being used as a worldwide cover for the recruitment and training of these killers? They are, as mentioned earlier, working to repopulate Jonestown with Laotians who served as mercenaries for our CIA. 285 Silence in the face of these murders is the worst possible response. The telling sign above the Jonestown dead read, "Those who do not remember the past are condemned to repeat it'. 286 The genocide will come home to America. How many spent time studying the rash of child murders in Atlanta's Black community or asked the necessary questions about the discrepancies in the conviction of Wayne Williams? 287 Would we recognize a planned genocide if it occurred under similar subterfuge?

Leo Ryan's daughter, Shannon, lives among the disciples of another cult today, at the new city of Rajneeshpuram in Arizona. She was quoted in the press, during the recent controversy over a nationwide recruiting drive to bring urban homeless people to the commune, saying she did not believe it could end like Jonestown, since the leader would not ask them to commit suicide. "If he did ask me, I would do it," she said. 288 Homeless recruits who had left since then are suing in court because of suspicious and unnecessary injections given them by the commune's doctor, and a liquid they were served daily in unmarked jars that many believe was not simply "beer." One man in the suit claims he was drugged and disoriented for days after his first injection. 289

The ultimate victims of mind control at Jonestown are the American people. If we fail to look beyond the constructed images given us by the television and the press, then our consciousness is manipulated, just as well as the Jonestown victims' was. Facing nuclear annihilation may see the current militarism of the Reagan policies, and military training itself, as the real "mass suicide cult." If the discrepancy between the truth of Jonestown and the official version can be so great, what other lies have we been told about major events? 290

History is precious. In a democracy, knowledge must be accessible for informed consent to function. Hiding or distorting history behind "national security" leaves the public as the final enemy of the government. Democratic process cannot operate on "need to know." Otherwise, we live in the 1984 envisioned by Orwell's projections, and we must heed his warning that those who control the past control the future. 291

The real tragedy of Jonestown is not only that it occurred, but that so few chose to ask themselves why or how, so few sought to find out the facts behind the bizarre tale used to explain away the death of more than 900 people, and that so many will continue to be blind to the grim reality of our intelligence agencies. In the long run, the truth will come out. Only our complicity in the deception continues to dishonor the dead.

REFERENCES

1. *Hold Hands and Die!* John Maguire (Dale Books, 1978), p. 235 (Story of the Century); *Raven*, Tim Reiterman (Dutton, 1982) p. 575 (citing poll result).

2. The standard version first appeared in two "instant books," so instant (12/10/78) they seemed to have been written before the event! *The Suicide Cult*, Kilduff & Javers (Bantam Books, 1978); *Guyana Massacre*, Charles Krause (Berkeley Pub. 1978) Other standard research works on the topic include: *White Night*, John Peer Nugent (Wade, 1979); Raven, op cit., and *Hold Hands and Die*, op cit.; *The Cult That Died*, George Klineman (Putnam 1980); *The Children of Jonestown*, Kenneth Wooden (McGraw-Hill, 1981); *The Strongest Poison*, Mark Lane (Hawthorn Books, 1980); *Our Father Who Art In Hell*, James Reston (Times Books, 1981); *Journey to Nowhere*, Shiva Naipaul (Simon & Schuster. 1981); *The Assassination of Representative Leo J. Ryan & The Jonestown, Guyana Tragedy*, Report, House Committee on Foreign Affairs (GPO, May 15, 1979). Personal accounts by members of People's Temple and survivors of Jonestown: *Six Years With God*, Jeannie Mills (A&W Publ., 1979); *People's Temple, People's Tomb*, Phil Kerns (Logos, Int., 1979); *Deceived*, Mel White (Spire Books, 1979); *The Broken God*, Bonnie Theilmann (David Cook, 1979); *Awake in a Nightmare*, Feinsod (Norton, 1981); *In My Father's House*, Yee & Layton (Holt, Rinehart & Winston, 1981).

3. "The People's Temple," William Pfaff, New Yorker, 12/18/78; Hold Hands, p. 241-7 (cults) and Journey to Nowhere p. 294 (period); *The Family*, Ed Sanders (Avon Press. 1974) (Charlie Manson); *Snapping*, Flo Conway (brainwashing); *Ecstasy & Holiness*, Frank Musgrove (Indiana Univ. Press. 1974). *In case you missed the decade and what happened: The Sixties* (Rolling Stone Press. 1977); *The Sixties Papers*, Judith & Stew Alben (Praeger, 1984); *By Any Means Necessary: Outlaw Manifestoes 1965-70*, P. Stansill (Penguin, 1971); *Protest & Discontent*, Bernard Crick (Penguin 1970); *Fire in the Streets*, Milton Viorst (Random House, 1982); *Blacklisted News: Secret Histories from Chicago to 1984* (Yipster Times, 1984); *The Making of a Counter-Culture*, Theodor Roszak (Doubleday, 1969)

4. "Inside People's Temple." Marshall Kilduff. New West, 8/1/77; Hold Hands p.100

5. "Rev Jones Became West Coast Power Washington Post (WP) 11/20/79 Hold Hands p.130 and Journey to Nowhere p. 47.

6. "Rev. Jones Accused of Coercion" New York Times (NYT), 4/12/79; NYT, 11/27/78 (warning letter to Ryan, 6/78)

7. Assassination of Leo J. Ryan, op cit., pp. 1-3; "Ryan to Visit," Kilduff, San Francisco Chronicle (SFC) 11/8/78.

8. "A Hell of a Story: The Selling of a Massacre," Wash. Jr. Rev., Jan-Feb, 1979. Standard details recounted in books cited above at FN 2. Children of Jonestown p. 201 (mass grave) NYT, 12/19 and 12/20/78 and 1/10/79 (28 cremated) also 1/25 and 5/25/79 (bodies cremated in mass grave, 248)

9. Raven, p. 576 (Layton charges); WP 11/19/84 (Ryan medal).

10. Hold Hands, p. 216

11. Helter Skelter, Vincent Bugliosi (Norton, 1974).

12. Hold Hands, pp. 215-16.

13. New York Post, 11/21/78 (headline); WP, 11/21/78, San Francisco Examiner (SFE), 11/22/78, Guyana Daily Mirror, 11/23/78, NYT, 11/22/78 (flee to jungle); NYT, 11/21-23/78 (estimated 4-500 missing); White Night, pp. 224-226 and NYT, 11/23/78 (U.S. search with loudspeakers).

14. Boston Globe, 11/21/78, Baltimore Sun, 11/21/78, NYT, 11/20/78 (est. 11-1200); White Night, p. 228 (Jones says 1,200) Guyanese Daily Mirror 11/23/78 (1,000)

15. WP, 11/21/78 (passports); White Night, p. 230 (809 visa applications), and Hold Hands, p. 146 (800 on busses to Florida); Children of Jonestown, p. 202, and NYT, 11/26/78 (children, 260 dead at site, 276 at Dover.

16. 'White Night p 223 NIT, 11/21/78 (408, Guyanese "pick way" to count), 11/22/78 (409, U.S. Army teams), 11/23/78 (400, Maj. Helming, U.S.), 11/24/78 (409, still)

17. White Night p. 231 and Hold Hands, pp. 226-34. NYT, 11/25/78 (775, P. Reid, Guyana), 11/26/78 (over 900, U.S. 'Final' 910 AF or 914, Reuters); 11/29/78 (900, Lloyd Barker, Guyana), 12/11/78 (911 U.S. Air Force), 12/4/78 (911, Dover AFB, Del)

18. Guyana Daily Mirror, 11/23/85

19. White Night, pp. 229-30 (can't count); NYT, 11/25/78 (State Dept. Business, "rough"), 11/25/78 (American official disagrees, says Guyanese count "film"); Children of Jonestown, p. 196 (poking).

20. White Night p. 229 (pavilion story), 230 ("mounds of people," Maj. Hickman); SFE 11/25/78 (Adults covered children) NYT, 11/25/78 ('Layered" Ridley, Guyana, but U.S. soldier "only one layer")

21. Baltimore Sun, 11/21/78 (82 children, 163 women, 138 men first count).

22. Photographs appear in most of the standard reference works, see fn. 2. Also, good pictures in the following: "Jonestown: the Survivors' Story," NYT Magazine, 11/18/79; "Death in the Jungle," 12/4/78 in time and "Cult of Death," 12/4/78 in Newsweek; "Cult Massacre," 11/27/78 and "Cult of Death," 12/4/78 in Time; "Cult of Madness," 12/4/78 and "Bloody Trail Behind Jonestown," 12/25/78 in MacLean's; "In the Valley of the Shadow of Death," Tim Cahill, Rolling Stone, 1/25/79; "Questions Linger about Guyana," Sidney Jones, Oakland Times, 12/9/78; "Cult Defectors Suspect U.S. of Cover-up," Los Angeles Times, 12/18/78.

23. White Night p. 229 (quoting State Dept. Bushnell), and Hold Hands, p. 233 (doubts); NYT, 11/23/78 (U.S. searching, Carter); 11/24/78 ("in vain"), 11/29/78 ("none"), and 12/1/78 (30-40 in Venezuela).

24. WP, 11/21/78 ("Cult Head Leads 408 to Death"); NYT, 11/20/22/78 (searching, pick up Lane

& Garry) *White Night*, p. 239 (Burnham sends in "his boys").

25. *White Night* p. 224 (over 300 U.S. troops, 11/20); Guyana Daily Mirror, 11/23/78 (325 U.S. troops); *Hold Hands*, p. 200 (200 for cleanup) and NYT, 11/23/78 (239 to evacuate). What was the function of nearly 100 additional U.S. forces? "Jocks in the Jungle" London Sunday Times, 11/78 (British Black Watch troops).

26. Photographs see FN 22. *Strongest Poison* p 194 (Lou Gurvich "dragged and laid out")

27. "Mystery Shrouds Jonestown Affair, "Guyanese Daily Mirror 11/23/78; NYT, 11/24 and 29/78 (missing in jungle disappear Guyanese say "none" Barker)

28. SFE, 11/12/78 (headline), also WP, 11/21/78 or NIT, 11/28/78.

29. *Children of Jonestown*, p. 193; NYT, 12/14/78 (Mootoo testifies to coroner's jury), 2/18/79

(Chicago Med. Examiner Robert Stein promised help, none came).

30. *A Guide to Pathological Evidence for Lawyers and Police Officers*, F. Jaffe (Carswell Press, 1983); *Poisons, Properties, Chemical Identification, Symptoms and Emergency Treatment*, V. Brooks (Van Nostrand, 1958). ·

31. Photographs see fn. 22. "Questions Linger", Oakland Times. 12/9/78.

32. "Coroner Says 700 Who Died in Cult were Slain" Miami Herald 12/23/78 NYT 12/121/78 (injections, upper arm), 11/17/78 (700 were murdered), 12/18/78 (Mootoo shocks American Academy of Forensic Scientists meeting).

33. *White Night*, pp. 230-1 (shot); WP, 11/29/78 (shot), Guyana Daily Mirror, 11/23/78 ("bullets in bodies," Ridley); NIT, 11/21/78 ("no guns/struggle," Lloyd Barker), 11/20/78 ("no violence," Ridley); NYT, 11/18,19,21/78 (Jim Jones, Annie Moore, Maria Katsaris shot in head); WP, 11/21/78 ("forced to die by guards"), also Washington Star, 11/25/78 (forced).

34. *Children of Jonestown*, p. 191 and WP, 11/21/78 (unknown if Jones shot himself); *Strongest Poison*, p. 194 (Gurvich, no nitrate test on hands) *Hold Hands*, p. 260 (gun far from body) Miami Herald 12/17/78 (Mootoo suspects murdered) NYT 11/26/78 (drug O.D shot after U.S. Major Groom) 12/17/78 (Guyanese and U.S. pathologists autopsy), 12/10178 (ballistics tests) 12/20,21/78 (illegal cremation) 12/23/78 (not suicide, Mag. Bacchus, Guyana Coroner's Jury)

35. *Raven*, p. 576 and Miami Herald, 12/17/78 (grand jury decision); *Strongest Poison*, p. 194 (Gurvich, evidence of shooting, over 600 bodies); NYT, 12/13/78 (grand jury set up), 12/14,15,17/78 (Mootoo testimony, tour of site), 12/23/78 (conclusion, "persons unknown," Katsaris, Moore suicides).

36. *Hold Hands*, cover photo, and see FN 22.

37. *White Night* p. 231 (Schuler quote), *Children of Jonestown*, p. 197 (unaware); *Strongest Poison*, pp. 182-89 (autopsy problems); NYT, 11/26/78 and 12/5/78 (no autopsies, reluctant), 11/26/78 (Mootoo's work unknown).

38. *Hold Hands*, p. 260, and see fn. 17, 28, 33 or Lloyd Barker; "Cult Defectors Suspect Cover up," LAT, 12/18/78; "Jonestown & the CIA, Daily World, 6/23/81; NYT, 12/3,8/78 (Lloyd Barker collusion), 12/78, 24/78 (Deputy Prime Minister Reid's role), 12/25/78 (U.S. attempts to discredit coroner's jury).

39. Hold Hands, p. 229; SFE, 11/22/78 ($1 million), or see NYT, 12/8/78 ($2.5 million at site); WP, 11/28/78 (cash, wallets, gold); NIT, 12/12/78 (visit to site by Burnham 's party official).

40. Journey to Nowhere, p. 58, 117 (Ptolemy Reid cover-up), see also FN 38; Daily World, 10/23/80 (Cheddi Jagan interview); Guyana Daily Mirror, 11/28/78 (1/23/79); NYT, 11/23/89 ("Templegate"); NYT, 11/20,25/78 (Ridley body counts, 408 to 708), and see FN 33; NYT, 11/26, 12/6,11/24/78 and 2/11, 5/16/79 (Guyana's collusion) and 12/3/78 (Burnham).

41. 'White Night p 225 (C-131s) NYT 11/24/78 (equipment lists)

42. 'White Night p 228 (identity strip) and Children of Jonestown, p. 196 (medical tags); Hold Hands, p. 59 (tags visible in photo)

43. Hold Hands, p. 200 and White Night, p. 224 (Vietnam "looked like Ton San Nhut"); White Night, p. 224 (planes carried 557 caskets)

44. Hold Hands, pp. 200-1 (182 arrive last day); White Night, pp. 226, 231 (Maj. Hickman, "six days," first bodies arrive Dover 11/28); NYT, 11/24, 26/78 (airlift details).

45. Hold Hands, p. 204; White Night, pp. 228-31 (description, "These were the worst").

46. Hold Hands, p. 201 (182 last day, 17 identified); White Night, p. 226 (Dover site), 227 (174 identified by Guyanese). 231(183 in 82 caskets); NIT 11/30/78 (Dover, map), 11/21/78 (50 U.S. experts sent), 12/1/78 (46 identified)

47. Hold Hands, p. 204 (Jones cremated), and see FN 8.

48. Hold Hands, p. 203 (families not permitted to see remains), and personal interviews; Baltimore Sun, 12/28/78 (only 259 claimed by families); NYT, 12/22/78, 1/8,24/79, 2/17/78, 3/31/79, 4/18/79 (Dover body counts 675 to 547) and 4/26.

49. Strongest Poison, pp. 182-9; NYT, 12/21/78, and 1/10/79 (New Jersey says cremation illegal, censures six doctors); NYT, 11/30/79 (Delaware legal problems).

50. "Medical Examiners Find Failings by Government on Cult Bodies," NYT, 12/3/78; Rescue Mission Report, Joint Chiefs of Staff, Special Operations Review (GPO, 1980); Delta Force, Charles Beckwith (Harcourt Brace & Jovanovich, 1983)

51. White Night, pp. 228-9 (no autopsies, death certificates in Guyana); NYT, 12/12/78 (Dr. Sturmer, National Assoc. of Med. Examiners); NYT, l 2/3/78 (other medical examiners complain, "legally dubious method"); NYT, 12/16/78 (Sturmer again), 12/4/78 (embalmed) and FN 8 (cremations).

52. Hold Hands, p. 203 and American Funeral Director, Jan. 1979; NYT, 12/1, 2/78 (FBI fingerprint 911, or 700, and identify 255).

53. Children of Jonestown, p. 197; Hold Hands, p. 204; Strongest Poison, pp. 182-89; NYT, 12/3,18/79 (quotes), 12/13,16,17,19/78 (autopsies, complaints), 12/25/78 ("few facts"), and FN 37 (Mootoo's work unknown)

54. Raven, p. 527; Hold Hands, pp 32 (photo), 53-4, and WP, 11/21/78 (diagram); NYT, 11/21/78 (Illus.).

55. White Night p. 197, Raven, p. 533, Strongest Poison, p. 131; Children of Jonestown, pp. 168 70; NYT, 2/20/79 (not guilty plea).

57. White Night p. 197, Raven, p. 525 ff (ambush described); Hold Hands, p. 256 (Layton's "dumb stare"), and LAT, 11/28/79 (Layton as "robot"); Journey to Nowhere, pp. 96-98 (Beikman in court "staring"); NYT, 12/15/78 (Layton insanity defense), 12/21/78 (Layton "responsible").

58. 'White Night p.197

59. WP, 11/21/78 (Laytons' role, Jones' quote); Boston Globe, "Killers Hunted," 11/21/78; SFE, 11/22/78 (7 involved); NYT, 11/20/78 and 12/18/78 (lists of dead), 11/21/78 and 12/21/78 (Kice named, Joe Wilson gave Ryan gun at ambush), 11/29/78 and 12/9/78 (claim all dead, 8 warrants dropped), 12/21/78 (survivors scared to fly with "others"), 11/22 and 12/20/78 (Stephan Jones, Tim Carter, Michael Prokes arrested or charged with murders), 11/22, 25/78 and 12/15,17/78 (Cobb, Rhodes, Moore, Clayton, named survivors), 12/6/78 (3 escape to Caracas & Miami before massacre). Who killed Ryan? 11/22/78 (FBI invest. "Conspiracy") 12/28/78 (Tim Jones takes 5th amendment on Ryan shooting).

60. Raven, p. 573 (elite squad), Hold Hands, p.145 Newsweek, 12/4/78; Daily World, 6/23/81 (Holsinger).

61. "Grim Report" Kilduff, SFC, 6/15/78 (guards, abuse); Newsweek, 12/4/78 (different food, treatment); LAT, 11/28/78 (Debbie Layton Blakey, "upper middle-class whites")

62. White Night, p.139 Raven, p. 403 (Cudjoe); and Raven, p. 241 (obeyed orders).

63. Chicago Defender, cited in Black Panther News, 12/30/78 (UNITA recruits for Africa); "Ryan Murder Suspect Resembles Robot," Hall, LAT, 11/26/78 (programmed), NYT, 11/30/78 (survivors had special privileges)

64. Hold Hands, p. 150; Strongest Poison, p. 85 (% women); "Questions Linger," Oakland Times, 12/9/78 (% Blacks); NYT, 11/20/78, 12/18/78 (death lists).

65. WP, 12/9/78 (FBI claims killers among dead), see FN 13,23 (missing people); LAT, 11/25/78 (Stanley Clayton, survivor, "hundreds were slain," "forced to die"); NYT, 12/6/78 (3 escape), 12/4/78 (Pan Am won't fly without armed guard), 1/29/74, ("cheers" heard), 12/23/78 ("persons unknown").

66. Assassination of Leo J. Ryan, p. 35, Raven, pp. 572-3, Hold Hands, p. 254 ("hit squad"); White Night, p. 224 (rumors at site), Journey to Nowhere, p. 148 ("basketball team"); LAT, 12/18/78, NYT, 12/1,4/18/78 (fears in U.S.), NYT, 12/4/78 (SF police guard Temple, "at a loss"), 12/23/78 (radio orders to kill relatives, Jonestown to San Francisco day of massacre, FBI).

67. Raven (Prokes & Tim Carter), see FN 59, and NYT, 12/12/78 (Caner arrested with pistols).

68. Hold Hands, p. 30.

69. NYT, 11/22, 23/78 (rumors, "master plan," Lane), 11/29 and 12/1/78 (FBI says "serious," Secret Service investigates), 12/11, 23/78 (Buford testifies).

70. AP, May 19, 1979 (wrongly attributed to Cong. staff investigator George Berdes).

71. "Suicide Carnage," Baltimore Sun, 11121178 ("write the story"); Hold Hands, pp. 127, 221 (Lane, Garry lawyers for People's Temple); NYT, 11/23/78 (Garry once called Jonestown "paradise," says Jones "lost reason"); NYT, 11/21/78 (picked up in jungle by Guyanese troops).

72. Raven, p. 572 (survivors); Guyana Daily Mirror, 11/23/78 (32 captured by Guyanese); NYT, 11/30, 12/3,7,30/78 (reports of returning groups, totaling 30, more remain).

73. Raven, p. 575; "Fateful Prophecy is Fulfilled," Newsweek, 3/10/80; "Mills Family Murders:

Could it be Jim Jones' Last Revenge?" People 3/17/78.

74. Hold Hands, pp. 130-31, 254 (link of Jones to Moscone and Milk); The Mayor of Castro Street, Randy Shilts (St. Martin's, 1982); NYT, 1/17, 2/19, 4/24, 5/18, 5/22, 7/4/79 (Dan White arrest, trial, conviction, sentence); NYT, 5/22/79 (gay riot in response), 5/22/79 (White biography); NYT, 11/27 (murder) 12/6 ("no link"), 12/18/78 (illegal votes for Moscone); "The Milk/Moscone Case

Reviewed," Paul Krassner, Nation, 1/14/84.

75. No note provided in original text.

76. Los Angeles Herald, 2/12/84.

77. Hold Hands, pp. 61,68 (KKK, Jones's racism). NYT, 11/26/78 (biography)

78. Hold Hands, pp. 62-3.

79. Personal interviews, Richmond, Indiana, 1981. Raven p. 26 (Jones' boyhood); Hidden Terrors, A.J. Langguth (Pantheon 1978) (Mitrione)

80. Hold Hands, pp. 63-4 (calling as minister), 66,70 (ordained as minister); NYT, 11/22, 29/79, 3/13/79 (Disciples of Christ)

81. Hold Hands, pp. 62, 64.

82. Hold Hands, pp. 66, 166 (monkey business); White Night, pp. 9-10 (Indiana U. link).

83. Hold Hands, p. 65 (faith healer); Hidden Terrors, pp. 17, 41 (chief of police).

84. Hold Hands, pp. 68, 102 (cure cancer); 75, 76, 103 (chicken livers); Six Years, p. 86 ff (photos).

85. No note supplied in original text.

86. Suicide Cult, pp. 181-2.

87. White Night, p. 236 Journey to Nowhere, pp. 95, 98 (Burnham's people defend him), NYT, 11/21 (murders), 11/26, 12/1,5,14/78 (charges and trials), 12/19/78 and 2/3/79 (Stephan Jones "confesses" and "retracts"), 11/28/78 (charged with Katsaris).

88. Hidden Terrors, p. 42; Who's Who in the CIA, Julius Mader (E. Berlin, 1968).

89. Suicide Cult, p. 21; WP, 11/22/78.

90. Hold Hands, p. 65; NYT, 3/25/79 (also recruiting black families in Cuba, 1960).

91. "Jones' Mysterious Brazil Stay" San Jose Mercury, 11/78

92. San Jose Mercury, 11/78; "Penthouse Interview: Stephan Jones," Penthouse, 4/79.

93. Hidden Terrors, p. 249; (Mitrione in Brazil '62-'67), and 63, 117

94. Ibid pp. 139-40 (reference to Who's Who in CIA); NYT, 6/11, 29/79 (Uruguay).

95. See it!

96. Journey 10 Nowhere, p. 247; Hold Hands, p. 171 (paid "pile of money," "$5,000 to have sex with Ambassador's wife" - cover story for payoff); Suicide Cult, p. 42 (money to travel around U.S. on return).

97. "Bishop's Report Names CIA," WP, 2/16/85; "Private Groups... Millions Raised," WP, 12/10/84; "Americares Foundation - Central America Gets Private Aid," WP, 2/27/85 (Knights of Malta, CIA's Casey, Brzezinski, Haig, funnel donations for "medicine" through Sterling Drugs, linked to l. G. Farben.)

98. Journey to Nowhere, p. 251.

99. "Guyana Tragedy Points to a Need for Better Care and Protection of Guardianship Children," Comptroller General Report (GPO, 1980); NYT, 1/25/79 (150 "foster children" in Ukiah), 2/14/79 (Mendocino agency says "none placed"), 2/17/79 (Sen. Cranston says 17 Ukiah children among dead).

100. "World Vision, Go Home" L. Lee, Christian Century 5/16/79 "In the Spirit of Jimmy Jones," J. Fogany Akwesasne Notes Winter 1982; NYT, 2/26, 4/4, 11/16/75 and 12/25/79 (W.V. Cambodia) 4/2-5/75 and 6/30/79 (Vietnam work)

101. Journey to Nowhere, p. 220; "Jim Jones a Republican," LAT, 12/17/78 (John Birch); Daily World, 6/23/81 (Holsinger comments), and NIT, 11/24/78 ("helpful" reputation).

102. "Jim Jones was a Republican for 6 Years," LAT, 12/17/78 Hold Hands, p. 70 (Jones held 15% vote Mendocino County).

103. Hold Hands, p. 93.

104. Hold Hands, p. 84; NYT, 11/21/78 (Tim Stoen joins, legal advisor).

105. Hold Hands, p. 95 (Debbie Layton Blakey); In My Father's House (Layton's stories); Strongest Poison (Terry Buford), NYT, 12/4/78 (Layton family, 6 join).

106. Six Years, p. 86 ff (photos); NYT, 11/22-24/78 (biography), 11/29/78 (college $)

107. Strongest Poison, p. 85; Philadelphia Inquirer, 11/19/78.

108. Hold Hands, p. 138 (family joins); "Cult Got Assets from Layton," LAT, 11/26/78; "Family Tragedy," NYT, 12/4/78 (aristocratic).

109. Washington Post, 1/22/78 (27,000 acres leased, 1974) Daily World, 6/23/81 ($600,000).

110. In My Father's House, pp. 18-19.

111. Hold Hands, pp. 94, 127-8; NYT, 12/16-17/79 (Swiss bank accounts).

112. Hold Hands, p. 96 Baltimore Sun, 11/21/78; NYT, 11/21/78 (list), 12/5/78 (Stoen close to D.A. Hunter, later investigated Temple).

113. "Statement by Joe Holsinger" 5/23/80 citing Strongest Poison (Chapter 5) (Jones as "patriotic American"); LAT, 12/1/78; NYT, 12/1/78 (Reagan says Jones "close to Democrats")

114. Hold Hands, pp. 73-75, 79, 176.

115. Hold Hands, pp. 182-3 Journey to Nowhere, pp. 223-4, WP, 11/22/78 (Housing Commission); "DA Accuses Deputy Stoen," SFE, 11/21/79; WP, 11/20/78; Baltimore Sun, 11/22/78 (election and voter fraud); NYT, 12/18, 20/78 (illegal Moscone votes)

116. Journey to Nowhere, p. 279 (welfare appointments); NYT, 12/18/79 (half of dead on Calif. Welfare sometime 10% active, 51 frauds)

117. Hold Hands, p. 132 (Angela Davis), 213 and NYT, 11/23/78 (Roslyn Carter), NYT, 11/21/78 (list), also WP, 11/20/78 and Baltimore Sun, 11/21/78.

118. Age of Surveillance, Frank Donner (Random House, 1980); Spying on Americans, Ethan Theoharis (Temple University Press, 1978; "Garden Plot and SWAT: U.S. Police as New Action Army," Counterspy, Winter. 1976.

119. Secret Agenda, Jim Hogan (Random House, 1984), pp. 99, 102; Final Report, Senate Select Committee on Presidential Campaign Activities (GPO, 1974), pp. 3-7 and Hearings, Vol. 3, pp. 1319-37 and Vol. 4, pp. 1453-64 (describes Houston plan); The Whole Truth: The Watergate Conspiracy, Sam Ervin (Random House, 1980); "A New Watergate Revelation: The White House Death Squads," Jonathan Marshall, Inquiry, 3/5/79.

120. COINTELPRO, Nelson Blackstock (Vintage, 1976); The FBI and Martin Luther King: From SOLO to Memphis, David Garrow (Norton, 1981); Assassination of Malcolm X, George Breiterman (Pathfinder Press, 1976); also see on King harassment: Nation, 6/17/78, Newsweek, 9/28/81, and NYT, 3/17/75. Also browse NYT, 11/19-23/75 and 12/3-24/75.

121. "Remembering Ed Meese: From the Free Speech Movement to Operation Garden Plot," Johan Carlisle, S.F. Bay Guardian, 4/4/84; "Officer Ed Meese," Jeff Stein, New Republic, 10/7/81; "Ed Meese," Rebel, 12/13/84, Alex Dubro; "Bringing the War Home," Ron Ridenhour, New Times, l l/28/75.

122. "Garden Plot & SWAT" Counterspy Winter 1976

123. "Why Civil Libertarians are Leery of Ed Meese," Oakland Tribune, 2/13/84.

124. "Jim Jones: The Seduction of San Francisco," J. Kasindorf, New West, 12/18/78; "Churchmen Hunt Clues on Cult's Lure for Blacks," H. Soles, Christianity Today, 3/23/79; "An Interpretation of People's Temple and Jim Jones," Journal Interdenom. Theol. Ctr., fall 1979; "Cuname, Curare & Cool Aid: The Politics that Spawned and Nurtured Jonestown," George Jackson (self-published, 1984).

125. Hold Hands, p. 87.

126. Hold Hands, pp. 88, 182-3.

127. Hold Hands, pp. 84, 100-1; "Jones Linked to Extortion," LAT, 11/25/78; NYT, 12/3/78.

128. Hold Hands, pp. 96, 172, 210-11.

129. Seven Mysterious Deaths" Kathy Hunter, Ukiah Press-Democrat.

130. LAT, 11/25/78; NYT, 11/21/78 (Jones threatens to kill defectors).

131. Journey to Nowhere, pp. 49-50, 67, 102.

132. Assassination of Leo J. Ryan, p. 316 (Debbie Layton affidavit); LAT, 11/18/78; NYT, 11/20; 12/5/78 (White Nights).

133. Hold Hands, pp. 71-2, 180; NYT, 11/21,28/78 and 12/7/78 (abuse complaints, ignored).

134. "Inside People's Temple," Kilduff, New West, 8/1/77; "Jim Jones: The Making of a Madman," Phil Tracy, New West, 12/18/78; LAT, 12/8/78. 135. Hold Hands, pp. 16, 100, 136-7; "Scared

Too Long," SFE, 11/13/77 (Houston death); NYT, 11/21/78

136. Hold Hands, p. 127, 133.

137. Hold Hands, p. 136 (against advice); NYT, 11/21/78 (Speiers makes out will).

138. Personal interviews with Joe Holsinger, Ryan's aide, 1980; NYT, 11/21/78 12/16/78 (panic).

139. Hold Hands, pp. 87-8, 100.

140. White Night, p. 226; Hold Hands, p. 232, SFC, 11/23/78 ("doubles").

141. The Second Oswald, Popkin (Berkeley, 1968).

142. See FN 34.

143. White Nights, p. 227 (autopsy, identification); Hold Hands, p. 262 (photo); "New Mystery: Is Jones Dead?" NY Daily News, 11/23/78

144. NYT, 11/24/78 (fingerprints).

145. Hold Hands, pp. 77, 83 In My Father's House, pp 115-6.

146. "Jungle Geopolitics in Guyana: How a Communist Utopia that Ended in a Massacre Came to be Sited," American Journal of Economics & Sociology, 4/81.

147. Guyana Massacre (photo of Garry at Temple).

148. SFE, 1/9/79. Also see my "Jonestown Banks" piece.

149. Journey to Nowhere, p. 126.

150. "James G. McDonald: High Commissioner for Refugees, 1933-35" Werner Lib. Bull. #43-44; "Refugee Immigration: Truman Directive," Prologue, spring 1981; Caribbean Review, fall, 1981.

151. Journey to Nowhere pp. 117-18 (interior development); "Guyana's National Service Program," Journal of Administration Overseas, 1/76; Caribbean Review, Fall, 1981, 1982.

152. "Mineral Resources Map," Area Handbook for Guyana, State Department (GPO, 1969); White Night, p. 238 (Burnham); Hold Hands, p. 149.

153. 'White Night p 238 (Burnham on importing labor, "exploit the exploitable")

154. Hold Hands, p. 144 (Embassy visits since 1973); "Consulate Officers: Babysitters," NYT, 11/29/78 and NYT, 12/6,11,24/78 (Guyana denies links), but see 5/16/79 (House Report charges collusion), and 12/5/78 5/4,16/79 (House report critical of role of U.S. Embassy)

155. Hold Hands, p. 146.

156. "Brother Forced To Go To Jonestown," LAT, 11/27/78 (kill whole family threat); Personal interview with Guyanese present, 1980 (bound and gagged)

157. Journey to Nowhere, p. 107 (guards, "state within a state"); Hold Hands, p. 127 (coercion by armed guards, Yolanda Crawford), personal interview with Guyanese living within 5 miles of site, 1981.

158. Journey to Nowhere, pp. 73-4 (adoption, 7 Guyanese children among dead); Guyana Daily Mirror, 11/23/78.

159. Hold Hands, p. 39 (Gerry Parks), 156 (Blakey), "Life in Jonestown," Newsweek, 12/4/78 "Jonestown," Michael Novak, AEI Reprint #94, 3/79 (work and food).

160. Holsinger Statement, 5/23/80, NYT, 11/23/78 ("preoccupied with").

161. Hold Hands, pp. 50-51 (Tim Bogue), 157-63, 170-1 (public rape); "People's Temple in Guyana is a Prison," Santa Rosa Press Democrat, 4/12/78; Newsweek, 12/4/78 (special treatment);

SFC, 6/15/78; Baltimore Sun, 11/21/78; NYT, 11/20/78 (slaves; torture), 12/4/78 (denials)

162. No entry supplied in original manuscript.

163. Trading with the Enemy, Charles Higham (Dell, 1983), p. 23 (Schacht role in war); NYT, 10/11/79 (Auschwitz plan).

164. Miami Herald, 3/27/79 (set up accounts); LAT, 11/18/79, and see my "Jonestown Bank"); NYT, 11/21,23,28,29/78; 12/2,3,8,16, 20/78 (millions described in various places); NYT, 1/13/79 (IRS says back taxes would be millions), 12/3/78 ($2 million real estate)

165. LAT, 1/5/78; SFC, 1/9/79, and see my "Jonestown Banks" again; NYT, 8/3/79 (puts Panama and Venezuela accounts at $15 million plus), NYT, 1/24/79 (receivership), 12/19/78 and 2/11; 10/11/79 (U.S. and Guyanese government and relatives claim it)

166. In My Father's House, pp. 18, 19.

167. Assassination, pp. 775-6, (199 SSA beneficiaries at site), Hold Hands, pp. 78, 139; NYT, 11/22/78 (200 gt $40,000/month), and 2/14/79 (Senate investigation). If the averages check is $200 a month, how to 199 people equal $65,000?

168. NYT, 11/21/78 and 12/10/78 (guns on site don't match cartridges); NYT, 12/3/78 (smuggling operations)

169. Area Handbook, op cit., 'see FN 152.

170. Operation Mind Control, Walter Bowart (Dell, 1978); The Search/or the Manchurian Candidate, John Marks (Times Books, 1978); "Project MK-ULTRA: CIA Program of Research in Behavior Modification," Senate Select Committee on Intelligence, Hearings, 8/3/77 (GPO, 1977); WP, "MK-ULTRA" (series), summer/fall 1977; NYT, 1/30/79 (overview of MK-ULTRA."

171. Individual Rights and the Federal Role in Behavior Modification, Senate Subcommittee on Constitutional Rights (GPO, 1974); NYT, 1/25/79 (children), 2/7, 1/79 (blacks), Philadelphia Inquirer, 11/26/79 (prison)

172. The Mind Manipulators, Scheflin & Opton (Grosset & Dunlap, 1978); The Mind Stealers: Psychosurgery and Mind Control, S. Chavkin (Houghton-Mifflin, 1978); "Proposal for the Center for Reduction of Life-Threatening Behavior," J. West, 9/1/78; Correspondence, Dr. J. Stubblebine, Calif. Director of Health to Dr. Louis J. West, 1/22/73 (reprinted in Individual Rights, above); "Nike Nonsense: Army Offers Unused Nike Bases to UCLA Violence Center," Madness Network News, 2/19/74; Mind Stealers, p. 91

(Drs. Mark, Ervin), and NYT, 2/7,10/79 (electrodes); LAT, 11/26/78 (Dr. West writes "psycho-autopsy" of Jonestown.)

173. NYT, 11,28,78 ("criminal rehab program at Jonestown), and 1/25/79 (children); see also FN 21, 59, 64 (race, sex, age composition of dead).

174. Raven, p. 347. Holdinger Statement 5,23/80; NYT, 11/ 23/78 (medical records)

175. Control of Candy Jones, Donald Bain (Playboy Press, 1979); "The CIA's Electric Kool Aid Acid Test," Tad Szulc, Psychology Today, 11/77. See also FN 170, 172 (books)

176. Physical Control of the Mind: Toward a Psychocivilized Society, Jose M. Delgado (Harper & Row, 1969) Psychotechnology: Electronic Control of Mind & Behavior, Robert L. Schwitzgebel (Holt, Rinehart & Winston, 1972)

177. Hold Hands, p. 17; Children of Jonestown, p. 16 (population of Georgetown, drugs); "Jones Community Found Stocked with Drugs to Control the Mind," NYT, 12/29/78

178. Children of Jonestown, p.16 NYT, 12/29/78 ("used to control").

179. Children of Jonestown, p. 16 (Thorazine); NYT, 12/29/78 (drugs found); Daily World, 6/23/81 (Holsinger).

180. Hold Hands, p. 12.

181. Hold Hands, p. 190-3 (brainwash methods); Daily World, 6/23/81 (Holsinger).

182. Hold Hands, p. 257 (Luckhoo, lawyer for Temple); White Night, pp. 257-8 (Burnham "conversion"), Sir Lionel, Fred Archer (Gift Publications, 1980) (Luckhoo biography); NYT, 12/5/79 (Luckhoo has gotten 299 murder acquittals)

183. "In the Spirit of Jimmy Jones," Akwesasne Notes, Winter, 1982.

184. "Full Gospel Businessmen Dine with Kings" LA Herald, 1/29/85 "Annual White House Prayer Breakfast" National Public Radio, 2/1/85 (mysterious fellowship)

185. "Hundreds Were Slain Survivor Says," LAT, 11/25/78 NYT, 12/6/78 (suicide plans); NYT, 11/21/78 and 12/10/78 (secrecy, panic, reaction to press coming)

186. Journey to Nowhere, pp. 56-7, 141; NYT, 11/23/78 (Freed calls Jones "Devil").

187. Newsweek, 12/4/79; WP, 11/19/78 and ff; NYT, 11/20; 12/3/78, 10/11/79; Time, 12/4/78; "Nightmare in Jonestown" (maps).

188. Journey to Nowhere, pp. 63-4; "Hill Rules Cult with Iron Fist," Cleveland Plain Dealer, 12/4/78; NYT, 12/4,5/78.

189. Daily World, 6/23/81, 10/23/80 (Holsinger and Cheddi Jagan); "Hill Rules," CPD, 12/4/78 (Hill admits); NYT, 12/19/78 (guns missing at site); Personal interview with Jagan, 1981 (guns, shoes).

190. "Hill Rules," CPD, 12/4/78; CBS, "60 Minutes," 11/18/80 (Hill interviewed)

191. "West German Concentration Camp in Chile," Conrad Edge, Counterspy, 12/78

192. Death in Washington, Don Freed (Lawrence Hill, 1980) (Townley Welch); Aftermath, Lasislas

Farago (Avon Press, 1974) (Bormann, Mengele); NYT, 11/7/84 (Pisagua camp)

193. Six Years, p. 122.

194. The Politics of Heroin in Southeast Asia, Alfred McCoy (Harper & Row, 1974); "Jonestown Resettlement Plan," SF E, 8/18/80.

195. Correspondence, EPICA, 4/2/80 (Dominica plan); NYT, 4/11, 5/6, 6/12/79 (complicated intermesh of Sam Brown, Director of Peace Corps who invented Jamaica Plan, Dr. Peter Bourne and his lover Mary King, appointed Deputy Director of Action programs, the scandal of White House Drug Abuse advisor Bourne writing fake prescriptions for Carter aide Ellen Metesky, later Peace Corps director herself, and the resignation of the first Black Peace Corps administrator, Dr. Carolyn Payton (formerly Caribbean Desk there) over disagreements with Brown on the Jamaican plans); "The Jamaican Experiment," Atlantic Monthly, 9/83 (Reagan's current plans).

196. American Labor & U.S. Foreign Policy, Ron Radosh, p. 393 (cites other sources); Journey to Nowhere, p. 21 (Burnham, CIA role, "right wing"); White Night, ($1 million destabilization plan); "How the CIA Got Rid of Jagan," Neal Sheehy, London Sunday Times, 2/23/67.

197. White Night, p. 257; "CIA Agent Witnessed Jonestown Mass Suicide," San Mateo Times, 12/14/79.

198. White Night, p. 256; Who's Who in the CIA, Julius Mader (E. Berlin, 1968); Dirty Work: CIA in Europe, Lou Wolff (Lyle Stuart, 1978); Raven, p. 590, note 66 (for Dwyer's non-denial)

199. Hold Hands, p. 29, 53; Raven, p. 534; Holsinger Statement, 5/23/80 (quote); "Don't Be Afraid to Die," Newsweek, 3/26/79; NYT, 3/15/79 (transcripts censor it); NYT, 11/19/79 (Dwyer at ambush); NYT, 12/9/78 (curious "discovery,' delay).

200. Daily World, 6/23/81 (Holsinger); NYT, 11/25/78 (biography).

201. "Ryan's Ready," and "People's Temple," Reiterman, SFE, 11/17/78; "Angry Meeting in Guyana," Javers, SFC, 11/17/78

202. Assassination of Leo J. Ryan, p. 9 (quote); Daily World, 6/23/81; NYT, 12/5,6,13/78 (role);

12/1/78 (cover-up with Blakey), 12/8/78 (biography)

203. Information Services Company, 7/80 (quote); Daily World, 6/23/81 ("sensitive Caribbean listening post," citing White Night).

204. Daily World, 6/23/81 (Holsinger).

205. "Performance of a Department of State and American Embassy in Guyana in the People's Temple Case," Dept. of State (GPO, 1979); Daily World, 6/23/78 (Holsinger blames McCoy); Assassination of Leo Ryan, pp. 699-704 (role); NYT, 11/30/78, 12/5/78, 5/4, 16/79 (Embassy criticisms); NYT, 11/20-22/78 (gave Ryan no warning); 12/2,4-6/78 (hostile to Ryan, sent FOIA to Jones)

206. Personal interview with Holsinger, 1980.

207. CIA: A Bibliography, R. Goehlert (Vance, 1980); Gehlen: Spy of the Century, Edward Spiro (Random House, 1971); The Pledge Betrayed, Tom Bower (Doubleday, 1982); The Belarus Secret, John Loftus (Knopf, 1982); Klaus Barbie: Butcher of Lyons, Tom Bower (Pantheon, 1984); Quiet Neighbors, Allan Ryan (Harcourt, Brace, Jovanovich, 1984); The Fourth Reich, Magnus Linklater (Hodder & Stroughton, 1984); Nazi Legacy, Magnus Linklater (Holt, Rinehart & Winston, 1985); Secrets of the SS, Glenn Infield (Stein & Day, 1982); Skorzeny: Hitler's Commando, Glenn Infield (St. Martin's, 1981); "The Nazi Connection to the John F. Kennedy Assassination," Mae Brussell, Rebel 1982.

208. In My Father's House, (Dugway chapter); "Family Tragedy," NYT, 12/4/1978; Holsinger Statement, 5/23/80 'Who's Who (Marquis, 1980) (Dr. Layton)

209. In My Father's House, pp. 18,19; The Crime and Punishment of I.G. Farben, Joseph Borkin (Free Press, 1978); The Sanctity of I.G. Farben's Spy Nests, Howard Armbruster (self-published, 1956); Treason's Peace, Howard Armbruster (1947); Trading with the Enemy, op cit., FN 163.

210. "Family Tragedy: Hitler's Germany to Jones Cult," Lindsey, NYT, 12/4/78.

211: NYT, 12/4/78 (met in England), see FN 209 (Farben link); "Solvay ET Cie Reorganizes U.S. Interests," Houston Post, 11/29/74.

212. Holsinger Statement, 5/23/80.

213. Philadelphia Inquirer, 11/22/78.

214. White Night, p. 256 (cites report), see fn. 63.

215. White Night, p. 252 (minister); Baltimore Sun, 11/21/78 (Maria says CIA).

216. Assassination of Leo Ryan, p. 777 (lawyer role), see FN 195 also, NYT 12/4/78.

217. 'Public Eye Vol 1, #1, 1975 Proceedings, First Conference, WACL, 9125-9167 (Taipei, R.O.C, 1967)

218. "Jones Disciple Goes to Court Tuesday," Santa Cruz Sentinel, 6/19/81 (CIA link alleged at Layton trial)

219. White Night, pp. 210-11 (note), SFE, 2/8/79 ($to USSR), NYT, 11/28/78 (suitcase); NYT, 11/28, 12/123/78 (details on her strange "suicide-murder"), NYT, 12/18/78 (letter), and 11/28, 12/18/78 (Prokes & Carter identified).

220. Nation, 3/26/79; "Jones Aide Dies After Shooting Himself," Baltimore Sun, 3/15/79, 12/8/78

($2.5 million), NYT, 3/14/78 and Strongest Poison (FBI link)

221. Hold Hands, p. 165 (move to USSR), SFC, 1/21/79 (details of rumor), NYT, 11/27,28/78,

12/10/78, 1/1/79 (more details, quotes, tapes)

222. White Night p. 229 (Guyana recovers $); NYT, 12/8 ($2.5 mil); NYT, 11/18, 12/19/78 (Soviets, $39,000, refusal), and see NYT, 11/28; 12/3, 10, 18-20/78; and 1/1,2,9/79 (for all the smarmy details)

223. SFE, 1/9/79, and my "Jonestown Banks."

224. God's Banker, DiFonzi (Calvi), NYT, 6/31/82 (Panama story); NYT. 12/5/78 (Lane and Buford knew names on accounts), and see "Jonestown Banks" (disappears).

225. Time, 7/26/82.

226. Children of Jonestown, pp. 196-7 (orders from above).

227. "Close Look at Carter's Radical Fringe," Human Events, 11/11/78 (right wing view); Migration & Development in the Caribbean, Robert Pastor (Westview Press, 1985)

228. Hold Hands, p. 256; NYT, 11/21/78 (biography); also Strongest Poison (interviews).

229. 'White Night p. 224 ("fearless"), NYT, 11/21/78 (biography)

230. "The Case Against Mark Lane," Brill, Esquire, 2/13/79; "Mark Lane: The Left's Leading Hearse Chaser," Katz, Mother Jones, 8/79; "People's Temple Colony Harassed," SFE, 10/4/78 (Lane charges CIA attack); NYT, 11/30/78 (Anthony Lewis critique); 12/5,7,16,29/78 (rumors and denials that Lane and Buford drained Swiss bank accounts) 214/79 (contradictory remarks), 2/4, 4/4, 9/2/79 (more charges, fake identity. theft), see Strongest Poison for comparison.

231. Code Name Zorro, Lane & Gregory (Prentice Hall, 1977)

232. Hold Hands, p. 222; NIT, 6/14/78 (Lane as Ray's attorney); Investigation of the Assassination of Martin Luther King, Jr., House Select Committee on Assassinations (HSCA), Hearings, Vol 1-9 (GPO 1979) NYT 8/8,16/78 (Lane's view of HSCA, conspiracy against him), and Strongest Poison.

233. "Ray's Breakout," Time, 6/23/77

234. "Tennessee Clemency Selling Scheme," Corrections, 6/79; "A Federal-State Confrontation," National law Journal, 5/11/81

235. NYT, 1/6, 20/79 (Swearingen, documents), see also 1/16-18,27/79 Swearingen); Code Name Zorro, op cit.; NYT, 11/20/79 (Swearingen, Chicago FBI to 1971) "Investigating the FBI," Policy Review, #18, fall, 1981;

David Martin "Breitel Report: New Light on FBI Use of Informants," First Principles, 10/80; "Prying Informants Files Loose from the Hands of Attorney General-SWP v. Atty. General of U.S.," Howard Law Journal, Vol. 22, #4, 1979

236. Personal call, 1978.

237. Strongest Poison, p. 402.

238. Code Name Zorro, pp. 165, 204-5.

239. Ibid, p. 165.

240. Ibid, Let the Trumpet Sound: life of Martin Luther King, Oates (Mentor, 1982), and p 473.

241. Code Name Zorro

242. Ibid, pp. 161-4; Let the Trumpet Sound, p. 476.

243. Code Name Zorro, pp. 165-70.

244. Ibid, pp. 165-8, 205.

245. Ibid, pp. 168-70.

246. NYT, 12/22/78; 1/1/79 (Buford at Lane's home); Strongest Poison, p. 402 (unconvincing denial), and see p.1114 ("our house in Memphis").

247. "Memo Discusses Smuggling Witness to Guyana," Horrock, NYT, 12/8/78; Strongest Poison,

p. 144 (testimony to HSCA)

248. "Memo Discussing Smuggling," op. cit., FN 247

249. "Seven Mysterious Deaths," op cit., FN 129

250. Hold Hands, pp. 18, 223; Assassination of

Leo Ryan, pp. 3, 52-3 (text); Journey to Nowhere, p.163 (Lane quote); NYT, 12/8/78 (discouraging Ryan)

251. Hold Hands, p. 222; "Ryan's Ready," Reiterman, SFE, 11/17/78.

252. Hold Hands, pp. 212-3, 223 (sandwiches); NYT, 12/8/78; 1/12/79 (no warning)

253. Hold Hands, pp. 43, 44; Strongest Poison, p. 175 (underwear); WP, 11/21/78

254. WP, 11/21/78.

255. Hold Hands, pp. 212-3, 222, citing Anthony Lewis in NYT.

256. No note is given in the original manuscript.

257. Let the Trumpet Sound, p. 470 (brother, A.D. King with MLK day of death); NYT, 7/1/74 ("accidental drowning" death of A.D. King); Trumpet, pp. 472-3 (wound described), also Robert Cutler analysis, Grassy Knoll Gazette, 1983; NYT, 10/25/74 (Dr. Herbert MacDonnell, "no way" from window), 8/18/78 (Dr. Michael Baden to HSCA, "shot from below").

258. NYT, 2/14/74 (Ray gets rehearing); NIT, 7/1/74 (Alberta King murdered 6/30/74); "Ray's Day in Court," Newsweek, 11/4/74 NYT, 10/8/74 (Ray v Rose reheard); "Did James Earl Ray Slay the Dreamer Alone?" Writer's Digest, 9/74.

259. NYT, 10/30/74, "Tennessee Effort to Block Testimony Overturned."

260. "Another King Killed," NYT Magazine, 6/8/74; "Third King Tragedy, "Time, 7/15/74; "Murder in a Church," Nation, 6/20174; NYT, 6/30; 7/19,12/74 (Chenault biog., trial); "That Certain Smile," Newsweek, 6/15/74; NYT, 7/1, 10/74 (psychiatric exam); NYT, 9/13/74 (blows kisses, points finger "like a gun" at judge, prosecutor)

261. NYT, 7/1-5/74 (Ohio "visitors" in Atlanta, Dayton link to ministers, legal fees paid anonymously, FBI suspicious, Justice says "no conspiracy").

262. Dayton Journal Herald, 7 /2/74 ff; NYT, 7/9/74 ("The Troop" - Steven Holinan, Walter Brooks, Ronald & Robert Scott, Ramona Catlin, Almeda Water, Harvey Cox, Jr., Marcus Wayne Chenault); NYT, 7/4,8/74 (biography of Rev. Hannah Emmanuel Israel, or Rabbi Israel, AKA Rabbi Albert Emmanuel Washington, personal interview, Journal Herald reporters, 1974.

263. Journey to Nowhere, pp. 63-4; "Hill Rules," CPD, 12/4/78, FN 188 (Hill); NYT, 12/4/74 ("Black Hebrew" Chenault)

264. NYT, 7/1,3,7,8/74 (Chenault tells Abernathy of Troop plan "to kill all Black civil rights leaders," "religious mission partly accomplished," and death list found in Chenault apartment: Jesse Jackson, Hosea, Cecil Williams, Martin Luther King, Sr., Ralph Abernathy, Rev. Washington (a cousin), and Fr. Divine (!), already deceased.

265. Let the Trumpet Sound, op cit., FN 240.

266. "Psyching Out the Cult's Collective Mania," Drs. Delgado & J West, LAT, 11/26/78; "The Appeal of the Death Trip," Robert J. Lifton, NYT Magazine, 1/7/79; NYT, 1122/78, Robert Lifton ("explains"), 12/1/78 (Carter quote); 12/3/78 ("never know," Reston); 12/5/78 (Billy Graham, "Satan")

267. "Jonestown & the CIA: Black Genocide Operation," Jonestown Research Project, 1981; "The Expendable People," Committee on Racial Justice Reporter, spring 1979; LAT, 12/18/78

268. Raven, p. 403; White Night, p. 39; In My Father's House, p. 320, see "Jonestown Banks."

269. Raven, p. 578 (ship in Caribbean); "Jonestown Banks," p. 4, (citing McCann quote on KGO, San Francisco); NYT, 11/23/78 ("continue Temple work").

270. Personal interview, relative of Grenadian family, 1984.

271. "Medical Students Were in No Danger," Peter G. Bourne, Oakland Tribune, 11/8/83

272. "Nomination of Director of Drug Abuse Policy Office," Hearings, 5/13/77 (GPO, 1977); "Pipe Dreams," P. Anderson, Washington Post Magazine, 2/14/80; NYT, 4/26/79 (White House Drug Scandal, U.N. post), see FN. 195.

273. SFC, 12/10/84 (Gairy plan), see FN 147 (Gairy/Jones link); "Blue Christmas Coming Up," Air Force Magazine, 1/84 (precision bombing).

274. "Bombed Grenada Hospital Gets Bedding," WP, 9/27/84 (US AID, $1.2 million rebuild plan)

275. Hold Hands, p. 257 (Luckhoo approached to defend); Raven, p. 576 (Layton trial); Raven, p. 571 (claims Ryan's killers dead, names Kice, Wilson, Breidenbach, Touchette; what of others?), see FN 59, 65.

276. NYT, 12/5/78 (Ryan's mother wanted full investigation) 'see FN 63; NYT, 12/8,14,15, 21/78; 11/4/79 (S.F. Grand Jury, delays, stonewalling, Stoen/Hunter).

277. White Night, p. 232; Raven, p. 576 ($12 mil. hidden in accounts, airlift cots); "Eerie Shoes: Missing Money," Time, 11/18/78; "Assets Liquidated," Christian Century, 10/21/81; "Payoff for a Massacre," Maclean, 9/6/72; NYT, 11/21,23,28,29; 12/3, 21/78 (estimates of wealth), NIT, 11/25/78 and 5/19/79 (cost of airlift, $2 to $4.4 mil.); NYT, 12/3,5,7,14/78 (Pentagon, Charles Garry, Justice Department, families claim it), 12/19/78

and 1/3, 24/79 and 2/11/79 (State Department, IRS, Guyanese, court receiver claim it).

278. Hold Hands, p. 134; Raven, p. 590, note 66; Daily World, 6/23/81 (Holsinger suit); Personal interview with Holsinger, 1982 (suspects military intelligence).

279. NYT, 1/23/79 (Ryan's children sue Temple for $1 million); Raven, p. 579; Personal interview with Holsinger, 1983; NYT, 10/11/79 (695 claims for "wrongful death," total $1.78 billion).

280. Philadelphia Inquirer, 4/1/81, "Hinckley Profile," Sid Bernstein, WNET, NY, 1981; Breaking Points, Jack & Jo Ann Hinckley (Chosen Books, 1985)

281. "Who Shot RR," Lenny Lapon, Continuing Inquiry, 5/22/81; "The Day the President Was Shot," Investigative Reporter, 1/82.

282. Lennon, What Happened? Beckley (Sunshine Pubs. 1981); "John Lennon's Killer, the Nowhere Man," C. Unger, New York, 6/22/81

283. World Vision Magazine, 1983; "Final Report of Israeli Commission of Inquiry," Journal Palestinian Studies Spring, 1983; "Kahn Commission," Midstream, 6-7/83; Guardian, 11/17/81

284. "Terrorism in Miami: Suppressing Free Speech," Counterspy, 3-5/84; Guardian, 11/17/81.

285. SFE, 12/18/80, op cit., FN 194.

286. Hold Hands, pp. 40, 165, 187 (photo).

287. Journey to Nowhere, pp. 234-5, Hold Hands, pp. 211-2 (FBI predict more); The Evidence of Things Not Seen, James Baldwin (Holt, Rinehart & Winston, 1985) (Wayne Williams, Atlanta child murders).

288. "Jonestown Massacre Recalled," WP, 11/19/84; 10/10/84 (homeless controversy); "Political Storm Swirls Around Newcomers," NYT, 11/3/84; WP, 10/4/84 (quote)

289. "Oregon City an Experiment in Medical Care," L. Busch, Amer. Med. News, 10/26/84; Eugene, Oregon Register-Guard, 11/6/84 (injections)

290. Politics of Lying, David Wise (Random House, 1973); see Aries Research catalog in epilog of this article for many sources.

291. 1984, George Orwell (New American Library, 1961) (The book was originally entitled 1948, not 1984.)

MAE IS ALIVE IN OUR HEARTS

John wrote this reflection on the death of his great
mentor Mae Brussell, in the World Watchers
International Magazine's Fall 1989 issue.

Mae Brussell, one of the foremost researchers, writers, and
broadcast journalists in the field of political assassinations,
covert operations and cover-ups, died of cancer on October 3,
1988.

For those who listened to Mae's weekly radio show, WORLD
WATCHERS, she provided a tremendous legacy of information
and analysis of the forces moving the world toward open
fascism and World War III.

For those who knew Mae as a fellow researcher, she serves as
an inspiration, and as a model of courage in the face of a
system based on secrecy and control. Her groundbreaking
research serves as an indispensable guide for future work.

For those who knew Mae personally, her warmth, love, and
sense of humor will hold their memory forever, as will her
indefatigable energy, her determination, her abiding concern,
her sense of justice and fairness, and her many talents in
making life more livable.

Following unsuccessful surgery and chemotherapy, Mae decided to move to a convalescent home. While there, Mae arranged to have her materials set up at the new research center. "The bastards thought they could stop me," she said, "but they have another thing coming."

Mae lives on in those who knew her. Her energy has passed on to all of us, and her task as well. Every time fellow researchers come across another connection in this work, we long to call Mae up and hear her laugh about it. She has gotten inside our heads and hearts and, in there, Mae is forever alive.

THE SPOOK ACROSS THE STREET

Among the many strange circumstances surrounding Mae's death, one of the most striking concerned a house across from her home on Via Crotalo, a house constructed after she had moved in. While her books and articles were packed each day to set up the Center, cars and trucks drove in and out of this neighbor's place. There was much pounding, conversation and noise, day and night. Either additional building, or perhaps dismantling was going on.

Shortly before her illness, Mae mentioned the house on one of her tapes (WWI #835, Side 2):

"And a woman came to me, she called me; she was doing indexing for Peter Dale Scott in the Bay area, the writer and researcher. And around 1975, she came to me and asked me if she could help me do the work and index my material, and be a researcher. And I really am pretty cautious about people coming to the house. She said she'd come down on a Sunday and meet me. I met her in San Francisco, her first name is Julie. Her last initials are Mc____.

"She came to my house, and instead of showing up alone, she arrived with two men and one had a camera on his neck. And I

344

said, 'What the heck is going on here?' And she said, 'Well this fellow (the one with the camera), he wants to stay with you. He's interested in the research.' So he's keeping me company. But the other one, she was going to drive down to Point Lobos to do some skin diving, do diving off of Point Lobos. And before I could turn around, he drove away with this man, and left me alone with this other one in my living room. And I sensed something was drastically wrong. They just turned around, got in the car, and drove away. And left this character sitting in the living room.

"And I couldn't do anything with him. I didn't want to leave the room, and I didn't want to discuss the research. And I wouldn't let him leave the room. I just sat in the living room, and he sat staring at me, and I stared at him. And I was fuming at what she had done, and so anyway, she came back. Luckily, left one down at the beach, and came back. I was screaming and yelling at her, 'Why have you done this? And I was simply furious and she took him away, and they drove away.

"And a couple of years later...2 or 3 years later, she called and told me that she felt very badly she had brought him there. That he was the person who had done the killing at the Stanford Campus of the Perlov girl, and she should have never brought him to my house. And that in return for doing that – she worked with people like E. Howard Hunt, who was in the CIA formally, and Mr. William Buckley (they were co-partners in the CIA) – and she felt so badly. She said, 'I just have to tell you, that there's going to be a house built across the street from you, and it's going to be an A-frame.' And she described the architecture. She said 'I wouldn't tell you this, but since I brought him to your house and jeopardized your life, I will tell you this house is going to be here.' And she described it. And about two, three months later the bulldozer came, and there were two homes across the street; and a driveway was cut in-between them, and a house went up there.

"And there's more to this story. A person moved in, she'd

moved out from Texas. The purpose of that house was to keep track or to tape record what was going on in my house. And so when the house was all built, I went up there just to introduce myself, and on the mantle in the living room was this huge, big tape recorder. Sort of like that TV movie, or the movie you've seen, there's one about cassettes, and tape recording neighbors close-by. *The Anderson Tapes*, I believe it was. And I just freaked out when I saw it, and I left my name and said hello. The woman was not home; her parents were out here, they're from Texas. And I had nothing to do with her. And the rest of the story, someday I'll tell you about it. I'll leave it at that point.

"But the reason I bring it up was then, a few years later, in 1981, there was a murder at Stanford campus again. Arlis Perry was murdered. And this was the same campus The first murder, the Perlov girl, was a few years earlier. And 1973, this was quite a few years later, 1981. And I got some calls that the same people were involved. Not the young people, there was a big age span, but some of the people involved in the murder of Arlis Perry in 1974, who was killed on Stanford campus, were the organization people behind the Perlov murder at Stanford campus. That guy had been at my house who had done that murder; and was told that they were connected by higher-ups, at a higher level. And that there were connections between the two Stanford campuses and the two murders.

"And then, all of a sudden articles came out linking Son of Sam to the Stanford murders, which made it a little closer to the one that had been to my home a few years earlier..."

On October 3, 1988, the day Mae died, the following article appeared in the *Monterey Peninsula Herald* (page 23) titled "Sunday Morning Fire Guts House in Carmel Valley":

"An estimated $200,000 damage was done to a Carmel Valley house in a fire Sunday morning that started in the garage..."

"The fire, reported at about 7:30a.m., virtually gutted the house at 25615 Via Crotalo, according to a spokesman for the Mid-Carmel Valley Fire Department, who said that 'very little was salvaged.'

"Identity of the occupants of the house was withheld. It was not immediately known whether the house was a rental or owner-occupied.

"The occupants were inside the house when the fire started in the garage, which is attached to the house, but they were able to get out unharmed, the fire department spokesman said...'Cause of fire is under investigation.'"

SUSPICIOUS DEATH

None of us can ignore the very real possibility that Mae was murdered, that the cancer was induced or aggravated in her body. She always asked those questions about others who died.

We know that cancer was studied by the Nazi scientists for use as a weapon, as early as the 1930's. We know that one of the key Nazi experts in viral cancer was Kurt Blome, a man our government later consulted in its own work on chemical and biological weaponry. We know that the National Cancer Institute is located at Ft. Dietrick, Maryland, formerly the site for much of this genocidal research.

We also know that certain cancers can be induced by ingestion or injection, and that uterine cancer (which was her diagnosis) is a viral form of the disease. We know that over twenty witnesses and characters in the John F. Kennedy assassination case died of cancer in periods under six weeks.

We know that Mae's oncologist at Stanford said that Mae's cancer was spreading faster than he had ever seen before in an older person. Mae was diagnosed, and the operation was performed to remove the tumor in June. She was admitted to the convalescent home in early September and she died in less than a month.

We know that she was exposing George Bush, and deeper layers of covert operations and control in the Contragate scandal. She had helped former White House aide Barbara Honegger expose the "October Surprise" operation of George Bush in 1980, a secret deal with Iran to hold American hostages until after the election of Ronald Reagan and Bush, in exchange of weapons.

Mae's life was seriously threatened by a phone caller, following regular broadcasting of her WORLD WATCHER shows on Los Angeles radio station KPFK. People broke in to her home, leaving a note behind with a piece of a jigsaw puzzle attached. Mae took the show off the air, and distributed weekly tapes to subscribers until her illness made that impossible.

None of these pieces alone, or even combined, prove the case for murder. We have no "smoking gun" evidence to show that the cancer was not "natural" (if any cancer can be said to be that). Mae's diet and lifestyle were not likely to have led to cancer, but other causes cannot be ruled out.

We owe Mae further investigation into the causes of her death, but more than that we owe her the continuation of her incredible work against the anti-democratic forces that hold sway in our world.

Mae knew these forces have names, they have histories, and they can be exposed. The seed of her 25 years of work has been planted firmly, and it is growing in each "Brussell Sprout" that comes forward to continue the search for truth.

THE HIDDEN HISTORY CENTER

The Hidden History Center is a Gateway for Truth ~ a source for facts our schools are not teaching, secrets our government is hiding, and information we are blinded from seeing by our culture. The Center is based on the vision of our founder, John Judge, whose scholarship, integrity and dedication to the Truth were unrelenting. The Center is a project of the Museum of Hidden History, a 501(c)(3) non-profit.

SAY SOMETHING REAL PRESS LLC

Say Something Real Press is dedicated to the premise of publishing works to better our world. In addition to *Judge for Yourself,* we have also published *The Revolution Will Include Cookies* by Dr. Faith Harper. There will be more to come.

Printed in Great Britain
by Amazon